Lecture Notes in Computer Science 6540

Commenced Publication in 1973
Founding and Former Series Editors:
Gerhard Goos, Juris Hartmanis, and Jan van

Hiroshi Sako   Katrin Y. Franke
Shuji Saitoh (Eds.)

Computational Forensics

4th International Workshop, IWCF 2010
Tokyo, Japan, November 11-12, 2010
Revised Selected Papers

 Springer

Volume Editors

Hiroshi Sako
R & D Headquarters, Hitachi Ltd.
1-6-1 Marunouchi, Chiyoda-ku, Tokyo 100-8220, Japan
E-mail: hiroshi.sako.ug@hitachi.com

Katrin Y. Franke
Gjøvik University College, 2802 Gjøvik, Norway
E-mail: kyfranke@ieee.org

Shuji Saitoh
National Research Institute of Police Science
6-3-1 Kashiwanoha, Kashiwa, Chiba 277-0882, Japan
E-mail: saitohs@nrips.go.jp

ISSN 0302-9743   e-ISSN 1611-3349
ISBN 978-3-642-19375-0   e-ISBN 978-3-642-19376-7
DOI 10.1007/978-3-642-19376-7
Springer Heidelberg Dordrecht London New York

Library of Congress Control Number: 2011921310

CR Subject Classification (1998): I.5, I.2.10, I.4, I.7.5, I.2.7

LNCS Sublibrary: SL 6 – Image Processing, Computer Vision, Pattern Recognition, and Graphics

Typesetting: Camera-ready by author, data conversion by Scientific Publishing Services, Chennai, India

Printed on acid-free paper

Springer is part of Springer Science+Business Media (www.springer.com)

Preface

This *Lecture Notes in Computer Science* (LNCS) volume contains the papers presented at the International Workshop on Computational Forensics (IWCF 2010), held in Tokyo, Japan during November 11–12, 2010. The workshop took place in conjunction with the 16th Annual Scientific Meeting of the Japanese Association of Forensic Science.

IWCF 2010 was the fourth workshop in the series. Previous workshops were held in The Hague, The Netherlands (2009), Washington D.C., USA (2008), and Manchester, UK (2007). Once again, IWCF 2010 attempted to bring together academics and industrialists, theoreticians and practitioners from numerous related disciplines involved in computational forensics, and to provide a platform for interactions between them. The preliminary call for papers was issued in September 2009. Submitted manuscripts, received from 10 countries, were peer-reviewed by members of the Program Committee. Of these, 16 papers were accepted for oral presentation. These papers cover a wide range of computational forensics related to authentication, document, face, footwear, fingerprints, multi-media, and evaluation tools.

We were honored to have two renowned researchers as IAPR keynote speakers. We would like to express our appreciation to Mario Köppen (Network Design and Research Centre, Kyushu Institute of Technology, Japan) and Minoru Sakairi (Central Research Laboratory, Hitachi Ltd., Japan). Their papers are also included in this volume.

We would like to thank the members of the Program Committee for their invaluable assistance in reviewing the contributions. It is only with their help and comments that a workshop such as IWCF can be successful. We thank the International Association for Pattern Recognition (IAPR), TC-6, for sponsoring IWCF 2010. We also wish to thank the Japanese Association of Forensic Science and Hitachi Ltd. for significant effort to achieve the joint workshop and important financial support. Special thanks are due to the members of the local Organizing Committee, Takashi Watanabe, Yoshinori Akao, and Yoko Seki, for their indispensable contributions to the proceedings preparation, the website management, and the local arrangements.

November 2010

Hiroshi Sako
Katrin Franke
Shuji Saitoh

Organization

Workshop Co-chairs

Hiroshi Sako   Hitachi Ltd., Japan
Katrin Franke   Gjøvik University College, Norway
Shuji Saitoh   National Research Institute of Police Science, Japan

Program Committee

André Årnes   Oracle Norge AS, Norway
Lashon B. Booker   The MITRE Corporation, USA
Thomas Breuel   DFKI & Technical University of Kaiserslautern, Germany
Joseph Campbell   Massachusetts Institute of Technology, USA
Óscar Cordón   European Centre for Soft Computing, Spain
Patrick De Smet   FOD Justitie, Belgium
Andrzej Drygajlo   Swiss Federal Institute of Technology, Switzerland
Cinthia Freitas   Pontifical Catholic University of Parana, Brazil
Simson Garfinkel   Naval Postgraduate School in Monterey, USA
Zeno Geradts   Netherlands Forensic Institute, The Netherlands
Peter Gill   University of Strathclyde, UK
Lawrence Hornak   West Virginia University, USA
Anil K. Jain   Michigan State University, USA
Chew Lim Tan   National University of Singapore, Singapore
Didier Meuwly   Netherlands Forensic Institute, The Netherlands
Slobodan Petrović   Gjøvik University College, Norway
Olivier Ribaux   Université de Lausanne, Switzerland
Sargur N. Srihari   University at Buffalo, USA
Dirk Vandermeulen   Katholieke Universiteit Leuven, Belgium
Cor J. Veenman   University of Amsterdam, The Netherlands
Marcel Worring   University of Amsterdam, The Netherlands
Charles Berger   Netherlands Forensic Institute, The Netherlands
Christopher J. Solomon   University of Kent, UK
Brent Ostrum   Canada Border Services Agency, Canada

Local Organization

Yoko Seki   National Research Institute of Police Science, Japan
Yoshinori Akao   National Research Institute of Police Science, Japan
Takashi Watanabe   Hitachi Ltd., Japan

Sponsoring Institutions

Table of Contents

Gestalt Aspects of Security Patterns

Mario Köppen

Kyushu Institute of Technology,
680-4 Kawazu, Iizuka, Fukuoka 820-8502, Japan

Abstract. In this contribution, we discuss specific aspects of patterns appearing in a humanized context (as for example in computational security or forensics) and that are not well reflected in a pure feature-classification framework. Gestalt laws are considered as a more appropriate way to approach these aspects, but then, we would merely focus on an empiricial description of matter, where models are needed that might even guide to engineering procedures. For the provision of such procedures, pure image processing based approaches, despite half a century of research, seemingly did not much progress. A recently emerging new family of neural network architectures, based on the model of neural group processing, on the contrary, shows even in its mostly still premature state (from engineering point of view) already a much stronger relevance to the modeling of Gestalt aspects.

Keywords: Gestalt, pattern, neural group processing.

1   Introduction

Pattern processing is a central aspect of data evaluation in many scientific disciplines, including computational security and forensics. Some of the related tasks in these fields are more or less completely based on pattern evaluation. Just take biometrics as an example, and the evaluation of patterns captured from human fingerprints, iris, face, handwriting probes, hand veins etc. But also the familiarity aspect of a pattern can play an important role. In document security, we find the majority of official document backgrounds equipped with a common Guilloche pattern. Moreover, patterns can be employed to detect digital watermarks, to recognize spam e-mail, or to break cryptographic schemes. In a similar sense we find computational forensic in a large scale based on the evaluation of patterns. Nearly all forensic evidence more or less directly refers to patterns: impression patterns like fingerprints or shoe prints, trace evidence, biological or toxicological evidence, as well as digital forensics.

This is a remarkable situation, as there is no clear concept of a pattern. The most accepted description is that of a pattern as type of theme of recurring events or objects, repeating in a predictable manner [1]. This is not very precise. And even worse: any attempt to capture the main idea behind the concept of a pattern refers to an inherent irregularity and its distorted characteristics. Then, how can pattern evaluation be objective, as this has to be seen as a central demand e.g. in forensic casework and its legal implications?

H. Sako, K. Franke, and S. Saitoh (Eds.): IWCF 2010, LNCS 6540, pp. 1–12, 2011.
© Springer-Verlag Berlin Heidelberg 2011

Over the past fifty years, many techniques have been developed to process patterns in an at least statistical reliable and thus "objective" sense. The most common processing framework is the feature classification approach, starting with an acquired image of the object that manifests itself as pattern. Following an image pre-processing stage, features are extracted that maps local pixel information taken at various image locations into a fixed-dimensional Euclidian space. Then it is assumed that pattern with the same characteristic (like being from the fingerprint of the same person) demonstrate an increased similarity in that feature space, for example by being close together in the sense of a metric. Another class of methods called classifiers then is able to capture that characteristic and to transform the numerical values into symbols. The processing might be followed by a global evaluation, for example in image segmentation. This approach has become so common that the research has been more or less restricted to the refinement of the components of the framework, by providing new feature computation methods, learning methods for classifiers, improved pre-processing like noise reduction, and image segmentation methods. Less focus has been given on the development of alternative frameworks.

However, there is some reason to doubt the universality of the feature-processing framework, especially if the human interaction is taken into account (inevitably in the security or forensic processing context). The discussion of such aspects, and some potential ways towards an alternative approach to pattern processing will be the main focus of this contribution.

2   Example Pattern Problems

For now, we can consider two examples of security pattern processing to demonstrate the points that were discussed before. Figure 1 shows the yellow channel of a scanned part of a security document that has been equipped with a watermark. The visible dot pattern was embedded into the yellow channel of the original print document in order to represent additional information, and has been encoded as a sequence of bits (where a dot stands for bit 1, and no-dot for bit 0).

The goal of processing, of course, is to re-read the embedded bit sequence. For the feature classification approach, it is a kind of problem, as the 0-bit refers to a featureless position, sharing that featureless characteristic with any other non-dot region in the image. The only indication of a non-dot position comes from the regularity of the dot positions, which are positioned in a grid. The whole task is also made more complicated by the irregular appearance of the dots, and noisy parts that can resemble dot patterns.

There is no problem to envisage other image processing approaches, for example a Hough transform based evidence accumulation technique. But the point to note here is the obvious "Prägnanz" of the problem. This term refers to the fact that the human perception of a visual scene prefers the composition from simpler forms to complex forms. So the grid perception happens in concordance with the perception of grid positions, as the grid is a more simpler, more "prägnant" shape than a random arrangement of points. But in feature classification, the

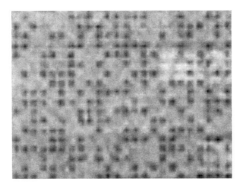

Fig. 1. Prägnanz of a pattern

grid perception would have to start from the perception of grid positions that compromise a grid, but for perceiving grid positions, it would need a grid before. And last but not least: this is just a human perception issue. An algorithm focussing on grid perceptions would also be able to handle more complex shapes in a similar way, while they might be not noticeable for the human eye anymore due to increased pattern complexity.

Another problem can be observed in Fig. 2.

NDR   N DR   NDR

Fig. 2. Different attention for modifications of a simple logo

Here we have a similar effect with respect to modification of a simple logo. The logo is composed of a partially open ring of small yellow circles, and the characters "NDR" in the central part. The logo on the left underwent two simple changes. In the middle figure, the character "D" was offset a few pixels. This change of the logo is immediately visible. The right sub-figure is more subtle: here, the number of small yellow circles in the ring was increased. It takes more careful observation of the logo to see this change. But in the latter case, many more pixels have been changed in the image than in the former case, while the perceived difference between the images is much larger. As a consequence, (perceived) image similarity does not seem to be function of a metric distance between the two images (like the number of changed pixels). It seems that higher-level structures interfere with the similarity perception. This is provoking the natural question: why and how does this happen? To which features of the images can such effects be related?

Handling such questions has some relevance in many potential application fields. The one considered here is the digital watermarking of logo images, but failures in forensic data evaluation due to be "misguided" by such structural interplay of image components is another point. In the following, we want to provide an empirical evaluation of the situation.

3   Gestalt Principles in Pattern Processing

Before continuing, we will introduce the main concept (maybe the only one so far) that was introduced a long time ago, and able to give at least an empirical description of the situation. This is the concept of Gestalt.

This concept was established in the 19th century, and beginning of 20th century, by Max Wertheimer, Kurt Koffka, Wolfgang Köhler and others, by way of so-called Gestalt psychology (see [2] for a recently republished edition). At this time, it could be considered a theory of brain and mind, focussing on a form-generating capability of the senses, and of the higher level cognition, and thus allowing for holistic perception to infiltrate the lower level processing. The so-called *Gestalt laws* then became most prominent for the visual sense (with a main contribution here of Gaetano Kanisza and his book "Organization in Vision" [6]).

The about 20 Gestalt laws give an empirical description of a number of visual phenomenons, and they are called "Law of Proximity" (we tend to group nearby objects in our visual perception, as for example at the moment of the reading of these lines of texts, where we perceive words based on the proximity of character images), "Law of Similarity", "Law of Good Continuation" etc.

Coming back to the second example in the foregoing section, we have investigated the issue by some experiments. See [7] for a more detailed description and evaluation.

Figure 3 shows a number of geometric measures on the logo image. We wanted to explore the visibility of changes for each of these measures, and were conducting an experiment where the subjects were shown a sequence of logos, each for one second, and with blank screens in between. In the sequence of logos, either a randomly picked measure was modified by a random degree, or with some chance the unmodified logo was shown. So the subject could not anticipate a change, and also could not compare the logo images directly. The subject then could reply to each logo that it was changed, not changed, or being undecided.

As a result, it came out that even a few pixel changes for some parameters were more or less immediately noted by the majority of subjects (for example $xdeg$ and $ydeg$ describing an offset of a single yellow circle from its regular ring position), while others (like Sx and Sy describing an offset of all three characters "NDR" together from its original position in the positive direction, $cnum$, i.e. the number of circles, or $gaparc$, i.e. the opening angle of the ring) were hardly perceived.

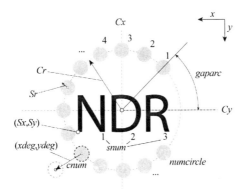

Fig. 3. Definition of the measures used for the experiments

Without going into details of the results here, it was noted that at least the grouping feature could give an explanation for the separation of geometric measures in the two classes "change easily perceived" and "change not easily perceived" and that this criterion refers to the grouping Gestalt law: geometric measures not affecting the group of three characters "NDR", and geometric measures not affecting the ring-wise arranged group of yellow circles were not easily perceived. But there was one exception regarding the second group of circles: also changes in the parameters C_r and S_r, describing size and radius of the ring of circles, were rather easily perceived by the subjects.

We can conclude two things from this experiment: at first, the perception of image similarity is influenced by the perception of groups. And second, that the groups have features too.

We may go even further by analyzing the situation shown in Fig. 4, demonstrating the interplay between various Gestalt laws.

Sub-figure (a) shows a circle that is perceived as being in front of the character string "ABCDEF". The point of interest here is that the circle, while obviously partially covering the characters "C" and "E" (and likewise a hidden "D", but this is a kind of inferencing from the scene that is not of interest here) is perceived as being in front of the character "A" as well. By itself, this is a remarkable fact, since there is no directly evaluable evidence in the image that directly relates the segment comprising the character "A" to the circle. Gestalt theory explains this by the perceptual grouping of the character string. Since the circle is covering a part of the perceptual group, it is also in front of the group as a whole and of any of its members. Both, the group relation and the foreground-background relation are perceived at the same time, and also at the same time linked together in the inference given above ("the circle is before the A"). By pure will only, we are not able to see something different.

The other sub-figures show variations of this theme, and thus also some dependencies of the phenomenon from the constituting parts of the figure.

To conclude on this brief introduction to Gestalt: it should be noted that Gestalt theory just describes phenomenons, it does not seek any explanation

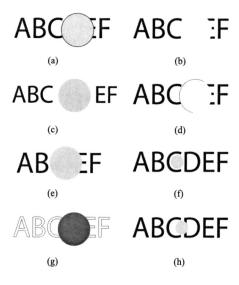

Fig. 4. Foreground-background separation of perceptual groups (from [9])

or provision of an explanatory neural mechanism. The main paradigm of form-generating capabilities of the senses is assumed to be true. We also cannot know in advance that Gestalt is a primary phenomenon of vision - a theory focussing on a "side-effect" of visual processing (e.g. for compression of visual input stimuli) can be valid as well. We just have to note that nevertheless, Gestalt laws are heavily employed in an urbanized environment, like for the arrangement of objects in rooms, the design of buildings, organization of infrastructures like airport buildings etc. Gestalt laws can be characterized as apparent in the visual perception (and not as a modification of the visual perception), they do interact with seemingly different priorities, but also there are cases where Gestalt laws are not present (see [6] for a number of examples).

4   Methodological Approaches to Gestalt

4.1   Image Processing Approaches

Recently, a survey on Gestalt related contributions from image processing and pattern recognition was presented [9]. A relevant number of contributions, having the term "Gestalt" either in the title or the abstract, were retrieved from several scientific collections. Here is the summary of the main findings (see the survey itself for relevant references).

Methodology. Due to the interest of providing a computer-based evaluation of images, it is no wonder that nearly all papers are either presenting algorithms or (often hierarchical) frameworks to incorporate Gestalt laws in the computational processing flow. A smaller number also considers the relevance of computational models for the biological modeling of Gestalt perception.

Few papers focus on the real-world application of such algorithms, models or frameworks. In general, all considered works neglect the interplay between Gestalt laws in the same scene. A remarkable large number of contributions makes reference to probabilistic concepts.

Referenced Gestalt laws. Among the various stated Gestalt laws, nearly all reference is going to perceptual grouping and (more behind in number) good continuation. Only in a few cases, other Gestalt laws are also considered (like symmetry and closure).

Studied image structure. The extraction and completion of boundaries and edges in images seems to gain highest interest for applying Gestalt laws. A smaller number of works is focussing on segmentation approaches, and from the references some overlap can also be seen. Here, Gestalt laws are mainly seen as a source of inspiration for interesting and new algorithms.

Visual concepts. Only in a few cases, the presentation is accompanied by a concept of visual processing. Notable works here are focussing on visual primitives and salient features or salient boundaries. Both, the meaning of primitive and the meaning of salient remain more or less self-evident and unspecified. Incorporating (or one can also say forcing) the Gestalt laws into the standard feature classification approach of pattern recognition has been done in a few works as well.

Semantics. We find few explicit reference to the question of semantics (in the sense of a visual grammar), the bridging of the semantic gap between primary data and content, and if Gestalt laws can be of help here. Obviously, there is a kind of semantic in the effects of Gestalt law. As indicated by fig. 4, the inferencing of "A" being behind the circle is a semantically one, as we can use the relation between abstract concepts for its formulation.

4.2   Neural Models

The sub-discipline of artificial intelligence called "neural networks" might give another approach to the explanation of Gestalt laws. It comes out that here we can find much more progress than for the image processing and pattern recognition part. This is related to some recent shift in the underlying paradigms of neural networks.

In the revival of the neural network research in the late 1980's, the focus was mostly on the organization of neurons into interacting layers. Most processing of the neurons could also be seen as a graphical representation of a computation, and the task of a neural network architecture was to adjust its computation to some application-derived function (including the estimation of probability density functions). These neural models did not much refer to the "real" neural network, i.e. the organization of cells in the brain, and were focussing on technical procedures and "learning algorithm inspriations." The brain itself was seen as still rather inaccessible system due to high parallelization of internal processing that cannot be achieved by today's computing facilities, by the dichotomy of local versus global processing, or by the so-called "semantic gap" that cannot be bridged by purely numeric processing. Other more optimistic approaches referred to the purely feed-forward processing of the brain, or the processing at different time-scales that could allow for the priming of local processing by results of processing at other parts of the brain. The latter concept culminated in the concept of neural darwinism, where evolutionary processes within the brain processing were taken into account (sometimes also called "instant evolution").

However, recent research results have changed the situation slowly. Today, there is no doubt that cognitive processing mostly takes place in the neocortex. For human and mammals, the neocortex is organized into six layers, with a similar neuron type and connection pattern for each layer. The neocortex is also organized into columns, where groups of neurons are working together in a related fashion. This principle gave raise to a new family of neural networks that might be called here neural group processing. Interestingly, these models attempt to do both: explaining the basic functionality of the brain and cognition, and providing a technical model for data processing as well. While being still a rather young discipline, these models already promise much, including approaches to the understanding of Gestalt laws. Here, we do not want to speak from a perspective of the neuro-research, but briefly consider two of these models.

In 2004, Jeff Hawkings, together with Sandra Blakeslee, published the book "On Intelligence" [3]. While not mainly being a textbook, it was discussing several paradigms related to an understanding of the function of the brain. One paradigm was to relate intelligence to prediction (and not to behavior as the more common concept these days). By prediction, the reference was not to, say, tomorrow's weather forecast, but to prediction as a continuously ongoing process of brain processing. The predictions are established based on memory patterns, and lead to a continuous updating of memory and anew predicting of outer world interactions. The other paradigm was called Mountcastle principle. Mountcastle was quoted like [10]: there is only one principle for the function of the neocortex. This means that there will be no specific processing for various senses, and that even the motoric processing is based on the same functionality of the neocortex. Another paradigm is that each sensory input is spatio-temporal.

Following these paradigms, Hawkings proposed the so-called Hierarchical-Temporal Memory model (HTM) of a neural group processing framework. In this model, groups of neurons are organized into a hierarchy. Each group ("column") performs basically the same task: it memorizes sequences of input patterns and assigns labels to them. Then, columns in the next higher level of the hierarchy receive sequences of these labels, memorize them and assign labels as well. Based on such a concept, higher columns in the hierarchy can prime lower columns by completion of missing labels; and they can even trigger substitution of real data.

The specific implementation of the HTM model is ongoing research, but independently, phenomenons like Gestalt already become accessible in such a framework. A corresponding demonstration can be already found in the book "On Intelligence."

The other neural group processing model that should be mentioned here is the Cogency Confabulation model of Robert Hecht-Nielsen [5], which was introduced around the year 2000. In this model, a set of neurons is divided into groups, and each group contains a number of sub-groups of neurons, each represent a "symbol." Then, neurons are randomly linked as in a "conventional" neural network, and a sequence of so-called coordinated thought signals can trigger the confabulation step for a group: the symbol with the highest number of activations activates also all non-activated neurons and their outgoing connections for that symbol. The physiological base for this processing is in the evolution of abundant muscle cells, as there seems to be some similarity in the internal processing. The confabulation model also defines links between groups via the thalamus, to provide a means for the learning of this architecture.

The striking point of this model is its mathematical model, which is based on cogency maximization. In inductive logic, an argument is considered *cogent*, if it is a "good, or sound argument" for some fact. Formally, cogency is computed in the same manner as a conditional probability $p(a|e)$, i.e. the frequency of events a and e occurring together, divided by the frequency of event e. However, as conditional probability this stands for the probability of a occurring if e occurs. In cogency, it means how much a is a reason or argument for e to happen or to be true. Cogency maximization then is the process of selecting an event e for which a is the best argument or reason, that is for which $p(a|e)$ is maximal. This can be seen as a conclusion from a (the best conclusion we can do from given arguments, but not necessarily a conclusion with certainty).

Then the question arises what to do if we have more than one argument. Here, the procedure of *cogency confabulation* was introduced to model the networks internal computing. Formally it can be written as in Eq. 1 for four arguments:

$$p(abcd|e) = Cp(a|e)p(b|e)p(c|e)p(d|e) \qquad (1)$$

It has to be noted that the factor C would contain a number of factors representing pairwise, tripelwise etc. dependencies among the events, but it is an essential assumption of the cogency confabulation theory that in a humanized context (like language, cognitive learning etc.), C can be taken as a constant. That is, humans organize matter in such a way that cogency maximization can be applied in this manner: select the event e as logical conclusion from the facts a, b, c and d such that the product on the right-hand side of Eq. 1 becomes maximized. In [4] it is formulated as "*Conceptually, cogency maximization works like the duck test: if a ducksized creature quacks like a duck, walks like a duck, swims like a duck, and flies like a duck (assumed facts abcd), then we accept it as a duck... There is no logical guarantee that this creature is a duck; but maximization of cogency makes the decision that it is and moves on.*" Or in other words: the constancy of C would *allow* for reasoning by confabulation, so it is useful to learn in such a way that the confabulation becomes applicable.

On first glance this sound like a "Munchhausen effect" - and this is not so wrong. But it also reminds already on a comment made about Gestalt in the text before. Also Gestalt is established into human infrastructure in a way that allows for employing Gestalt.

Robert Hecht-Nielsen demonstrated the usefulness of this idea by using it for the creation of artificial stories. The only input was the counting of frequencies of joint word occurrences in a bulk of literature. Given a sequence of words, then the next word was found as being the one maximizing the cogency product. The resulting sequences of words than appear to be rather real sounding artificial stories.

In a recent study, this method was also applied to the evaluation of questionnaire data [8]. Here, a number of users have been questioned about their impression of video quality problems, with regard to different video content types (news, animation, sports etc.). For more details see [8]. As a result, the dataset for each user was a string of length 10 of values from the set $\{1, 2, 3, 4\}$. The purpose of using cogency confabulation here could be to explore the degree, to which the answers of a user are concluded from other answers of the same user (however, in the goal of the experiment, they should be independent).

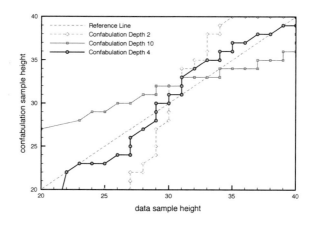

Fig. 5. Comparing the distribution of original data, and data simulated by cogency confabulation for different number of cogent facts (from [8])

After sampling the joint frequencies of same answers to different questions, this information was used to complete randomly initialized partial strings by cogency confabulation. Then, the height distribution (i.e. the sum of components) of such generated simulated data, and the original data, were compared. The result for different number of cogent facts can be seen in Fig. 5. There, the original data seem to be very good resembled when using four cogent facts. In case of using only 1 or 2 (which equals sampling from the histogram of answers only), or all 10 (which equals sampling by Bayes theorem), there is a much stronger divergence to the distribution of the original data, while for 4, it is nearly perfect (the perfect case is indicated by the dotted diagonal line).

So we can conclude, at least for this case, that the cogency confabulation is working to predict user answers from other answers of the same user (on different questions!), and also confirms the assumed constancy of the factor C in Eq. 1.

4.3   Outlook

We saw that recent brain model proposals focus on neocortical group processing of neurons. This processing has some relevance to potential explanations for
Gestalt-related phenomenons: the interplay of memory and prediction and corresponding priming; neural processing with different processing speeds of intra-
and intergroup connections; or (what is done in the cogency confabulation) *a
priori* probability maximization.

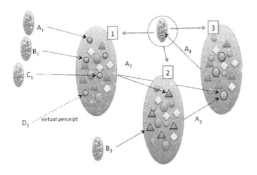

○ symbol receiving most activations (e.g. A₂)

Fig. 6. A neural model combining design principles of neural group processing models

   To give an example, consider Fig. 6. Here, the cogency confabulation network
groups are organized into a hierarchy, and, as with the HTM model, each group
forwards symbols to connected groups (but ignoring temporal aspects here).
If for example symbol A_2 receives the most activations in group 1, then the
symbol A_2 of other groups will be activated. Then, it is not possible anymore
to know which specific input activations happened in group 1. Thus, the symbol
D_1 for example, which was not activated before, could be considered a "virtual
perceipt." The following processing can assume that D_1 was true as much as it
can do this for A_1, B_1 or C_1. While this argument is rather unspecific, it resembles
the situation shown in Fig. 4 (upper-left sub-figure), where a conclusion about
foreground-background segmentation can be extended to the whole group of
characters, as well as the related assumption that the hidden character is a "D."
   This example demonstrates the rich potential of this new family of neural
network structures, coming closer to the current state of knowledge about real
brain processing at the same time.

5   Conclusions

In this contribution, we have discussed a specific aspect of patterns, their "Gestalt"
that also plays an important role in the processing of human-manipulated visual
scenes. A survey on related image processing approaches demonstrated that the
input here on the related phenomenons is rather less satisfactory. We rather found

promising approaches in recent appearance of neural network based on the neural group processing model. These models more or less directly refer to effects that are normally attributed to Gestalt. Of course, still more has to be done to make these new family of neural networks applicable to the vision processing tasks, and to come up with clearly specified processing laws for these networks. Also, the potential of their combination has to be much more explored.

References

1. Pattern - wikipedia, the free encyclopedia,
   http://en.wikipedia.org/wiki/pattern
2. Gestalt Psychology: An Introduction to New Concepts in Modern Psychology. Liveright Publishing Corporation (1992)
3. Hawkings, J., Blakeslee, S.: On Intelligence. Time Books (2004)
4. Hecht-Nielsen, R.: Cogent confabulation. Neural Networks 18(2), 111–115 (2005),
   http://www.sciencedirect.com/science/article/B6T08-4F8TK3Y-1/2/
   85d7ad6a4233d48182a0ef6c7c74e5a4
5. Hecht-Nielsen, R.: Confabulation Theory: The Mechanism of Thought. Springer, Heidelberg (2007)
6. Kanisza, G.: Organization in Vision: Essays on Gestalt Perception. Praeger Publishers, Westport CT (1979)
7. Kinoshita, Y., Köppen, M., Yoshida, K.: Perception of image similarity considering gestalt theory. In: Proc. of International Conference of Soft Computing and Human Sciences 2007, Kitakysuhu, Japan (August 2007)
8. Köppen, M., Yoshida, K.: User modeling by confabulation theory. In: Proceedings of 2008 IEEE Conference on Soft Computing in Industrial Applications (SMCia 2008), June 25-27, pp. 55–59. Muroran Institute of Technology (2008)
9. Köppen, M., Yoshida, K., Valle, P.A.: Gestalt theory in image processing: A discussion paper. In: Proceedings 2007 IEEE Three-Rivers Workshop on Soft Computing in Industrial Applications (SMCia 2007), August 1-3, VDE Verlag, Passau (2007)
10. Mountcastle, V.: An organizing principle for cerebral function: The unit module and the distributed system. In: Edelman, G., Mountcastle, V. (eds.) The Mindful Brain. MIT Press, Cambridge (1978)

Physical Security Technologies at Hitachi

Minoru Sakairi

Central Research Laboratory, Hitachi, Ltd.,
1-280 Higashi-koigakubo, Kokubunji-shi,
Tokyo 185-8601, Japan
minoru.sakairi.ef@hitachi.com

Abstract. Physical security has become one of the most important issues worldwide due to the spreading global use of explosives and illicit drugs. Under this social background, we started developing real-time monitoring technologies based on mass spectrometry for physical security applications. In these technologies, a sample gas is continuously introduced into an ion source and analyzed by a mass spectrometer. We can detect various kinds of organic compounds by analyzing the mass number of observed ions. This technology has been applied to monitor polychlorinated biphenyls and to detect explosives, illicit drugs and chemical weapons. In addition, we developed a small mass spectrometer that can detect human breath. This simple method is useful for preventing drunk driving by installing its device just behind a steering wheel.

Keywords: real-time monitoring mass spectrometry, physical security, explosive detection, illicit drug detection, chemical weapon detection, PCB monitoring, drunk driving prevention.

1 Introduction

Many safety-related issues these days have become the focus of worldwide public concern and scientific research. For example, the environmental impact of incinerators has been under public scrutiny since the 1990s. Another important issue worldwide is physical security due to the spreading global use of explosives and illicit drugs. Under this social background as shown in Fig. 1, we started developing real-time monitoring techniques based on mass spectrometry, which we call real-time monitoring mass spectrometry, for physical security applications.

In these methods, a sample gas is continuously introduced into our developed atmospheric pressure chemical ionization (APCI) ion source and the ions produced from the samples are transferred to a mass analyzing region through a differential pumping region to obtain mass spectra. In a mass spectrum, the horizontal axis represents the mass numbers of ions, while the vertical axis represents ion intensity. This information is very useful for identifying samples because specific ions of sample molecules are observed. The APCI ion source can achieve long-term stable measurements by drastically

H. Sako, K. Franke, and S. Saitoh (Eds.): IWCF 2010, LNCS 6540, pp. 13–30, 2011.

reducing contamination of the discharge electrode for ionization with organic compounds. In addition, a compact mass spectrometer based on ion trap technology was originally developed to detect explosives, illicit drugs, and other such compounds by efficiently ionizing them and mass-analyzing the produced ions. The ion trap mass spectrometer (ITMS) used here basically consists of two endcap electrodes, a ring electrode, and an electron multiplier, and a mass spectrometry/mass spectrometry (MS/MS) technique can be used by colliding sample ions with helium buffer gas in an ion trap region, followed by dissociation of the sample ions. This collision-induced dissociation (CID) method is very useful for producing rich structural information of sample ions and for reducing chemical noises. We can detect with high sensitivity various kinds of organic compounds by analyzing the mass number of observed ions or combinations of ions with different mass numbers [1-11].

The real-time monitoring mass spectrometer can be applied in various fields. One example is polychlorinated biphenyl (PCB) monitoring at PCB treatment facilities [3][4][6][7][9]. Continuous monitoring is necessary for these facilities in Japan because citizens living nearby fear the possible threat of a leakage of untreated PCBs. A PCB monitoring system is therefore used at all PCB treatment facilities.

Another application field is the detection of explosives and illicit drugs at customs checkpoints [1][3][4][5][8][10]. In this field, both X-ray and trace detection technologies are used to detect explosives and illicit drugs, as shown in Fig. 2. Trace detection is a means of detecting explosive molecules adhering to baggage touched by someone who has handled explosives. The baggage is swabbed with a special wipe, and the wipe is inserted into a detector. The Transportation Security Administration (TSA), part of the US Department of Homeland Security, says "Explosive trace detection technology is a critical tool in our ability to stay ahead of evolving threats to aviation technology" [12]. This is one of the reasons we have focused on developing a trace detection system based on real-time monitoring mass spectrometry. In the US, a trace detection device based on an ion mobility method has been used in public spaces. In this method, sample ions produced by a beta ray are drifted under atmospheric pressure by electric fields and detected with an electrometer. The principle of this method is that the drift time of ions depends on the mass number of the ions. No vacuum pump is needed, which results in miniaturization of the device. Compared to this device, higher resolution and higher sensitivity can be expected in the real-time monitoring mass spectrometer because ions are precisely mass-analyzed under vacuum and detected by a highly sensitive electron multiplier although vacuum pumps are necessary.

In addition, we recently discovered that water clusters in expired gas can be easily separated into positively and negatively charged clusters by applying an electric field. Therefore, we can easily detect these charged water clusters in a person's breath when the person blows between parallel electrodes comprising a counter electrode, to which a voltage is applied, and a detection electrode connected to a picoammeter [13][14]. From the view point of roughly mass-analyzing ion currents, this is classified as real-time monitoring mass spectrometry, although no ionization source is used for the breath detection and high resolution of the ions cannot be expected. The advantages of this method are as follows: it can be used under atmospheric pressure, which means no vacuum pumps are necessary, and the sensor used is very compact and easily coupled with a small alcohol sensor. The resultant device can be used for preventing drunk driving by installing its device just behind a steering wheel.

In this paper, Hitachi technological developments based on real-time mass spectrometry that are designed to strengthen physical security are described.

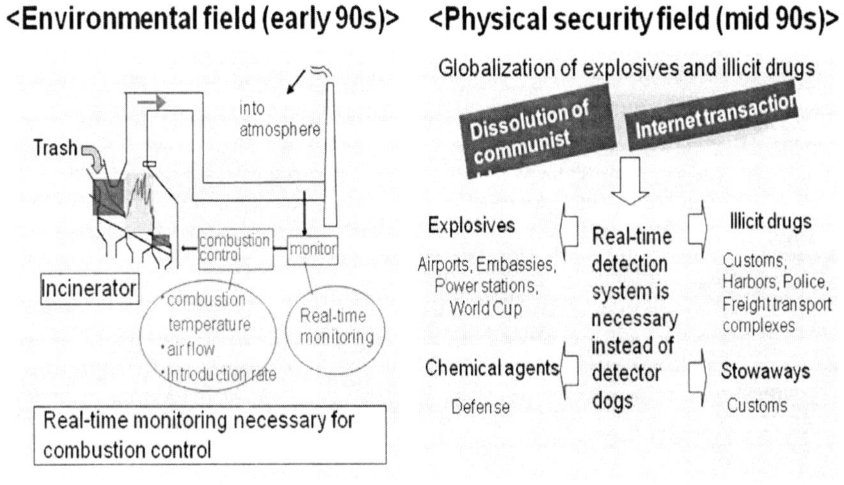

\<Environmental field (early 90s)\>   \<Physical security field (mid 90s)\>

Globalization of explosives and illicit drugs

Dissolution of communist

Internet transaction

Trash

into atmosphere

Incinerator

combustion control

monitor

combustion temperature
· air flow
· Introduction rate

Real-time monitoring

Real-time monitoring necessary for combustion control

Explosives

Airports, Embassies, Power stations, World Cup

Chemical agents

Defense

Real-time detection system is necessary instead of detector dogs

Illicit drugs

Customs, Harbors, Police, Freight transport complexes

Stowaways

Customs

Fig. 1. Social background in 1990s leading to real-time monitoring technology

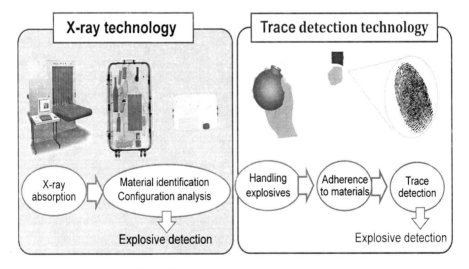

X-ray technology

X-ray absorption

Material identification
Configuration analysis

Explosive detection

Trace detection technology

Handling explosives

Adherence to materials

Trace detection

Explosive detection

Fig. 2. X-ray and trace detection technology

2 Real-Time Monitoring Mass Spectrometry

2.1 Real-Time Monitoring Mass Spectrometry for Highly Sensitive Detection of Organic Compounds

Our compact mass spectrometer is used to detect molecules of explosives, illicit drugs and chemical weapons by ionizing the molecules and then mass-analyzing the produced ions. The principle of trace detection based on mass spectrometry is illustrated in Fig. 3. In this case, our APCI method by a corona discharge using a needle electrode is used as the ionization method. The produced ions are then introduced into a mass-analyzing region through a differential pumping region. The mass-analyzing region is evacuated with a turbo-molecular pump. As a mass analyzer, we use our ITMS, in which two endcap electrodes and a ring electrode are used as an ion trapping region and the ions trapped are selectively detected based on their mass numbers by using a radio frequency electric field. As a result, mass spectra (horizontal axis: mass numbers of observed ions, vertical axis: signal intensity) are obtained, and we can detect explosives, illicit drugs and so on by analyzing the mass number of the observed ions or combinations of ions with different mass numbers. In addition, the CID method is used to produce rich structural information of the sample ions and to reduce chemical noises. This is called mass spectrometry/mass spectrometry (MS/MS) technology. The ions trapped in the ITMS are dissociated due to numerous collisions between the ions and helium buffer gas [3][4][7][9]. A photograph of one of the products (DS-1000) using the ITMS coupled with the APCI ion source is shown in Fig. 4.

Cross-sectional views of (a) a conventional APCI ion source and (b) our developed APCI ion source are shown in Fig. 5. In the conventional ion source, sample gas flows directly into the corona discharge region using a needle electrode. High negative voltage (about -3kV) is applied to the needle electrode to produce a negative corona discharge at the tip of the electrode. Ion molecular reactions occur between sample molecules and reactant ions produced by the negative corona discharge. These ions are transferred to the sampling aperture of a differential pumping region by the gas flow and an electric field produced between the needle electrode and the aperture electrode. Then, the sample ions are introduced into a mass-analyzing region under vacuum. In the new APCI ion source shown in Fig. 5(b), sample gas flows into a second chamber region then into the first corona discharge region. The negative ions are extracted in the direction opposite to the gas flow by the electric field in the first corona discharge region. Then, ions are introduced into the mass-analyzing region through the second chamber region and the sampling aperture. An electric field is also applied to the second chamber region for focusing ions. We call this method the atmospheric pressure chemical ionization method with counter-flow introduction (APCI-CFI). This is because the directions of the sample gas flow and extracted ions are opposite to each other in the first corona discharge region.

The negative ionization process of sample molecules (M) is expressed as follows in the conventional APCI ion source.

$$O_2 + e^- \rightarrow O_2^-$$
$$O_2 + N_2 \rightarrow 2NO$$
$$O_2^- + NO \rightarrow NO_3^-$$
$$O_2^- + M \rightarrow (M\text{-}H)^- + HO_2$$

Here, $(M\text{-}H)^-$ represents a negative ion with a removed proton from M. In this process, nitrogen monoxide (NO) is produced by the negative corona discharge, and NO easily reacts with O_2^- to produce NO_3^-. This reaction reduces the concentration of O_2^- and affects the ionization efficiency of the sample molecules M. However, in the new ion source, neutral NO molecules are eliminated from the ion-molecule reaction region by the gas flow. This is very effective for driving the ion-molecule reaction $(O_2^- + M \rightarrow (M\text{-}H)^- + HO_2)$ instead of the ion-molecule reaction $(O_2^- + NO \rightarrow NO_3^-)$.

The relationships between the gas flow rates and observed ion intensities of various ions $(O_2^-, CO_3^-, NO_3^-,$ and $(DCP\text{-}H)^-)$ are shown in Fig. 6. We used 2, 4-dichlorophenol (DCP) as a model compound to evaluate the new ion source because it is easily ionized by using the negative APCI-CFI ion source. The intensities of the O_2^- and 2, 4-dichlorophenol DCP ions increased with the gas flow rate, but that of NO_3^- decreased. This data supports the explanation that higher gas flow is useful for eliminating NO from the ion-molecule reaction region, and it shows the effectiveness of the APCI-CFI ion source. Typical mass spectra of DCP obtained with the conventional APCI ion source and the APCI-CFI ion source are shown in Figs. 7(a) and 7(b), respectively. The observed ion intensity of $(DCP\text{-}H)^-$ was greatly improved by using the APCI-CFI ion source. In addition to the improved efficiency in ionizing sample molecules, a stable corona discharge can be maintained for a long period of time in the APCI-CFI ion source. This is a very important feature for a monitoring system that requires long stable operation: a system without this feature cannot be called "a monitoring system." One reason a stable corona discharge cannot be maintained for a long period of time when a counter gas does not flow against the tip of a needle electrode for corona discharge is that various kinds of compounds are deposited on the tip increasing its curvature and this causing instability in the corona discharge. In such a case, fluctuation occurs in the discharge current, making the ionization unstable, and the ion intensity measured by the mass spectrometer also fluctuates.

The performance of the real-time monitoring mass spectrometer can be checked by applying it for several types of trace detection [10]. One example is shown in Fig. 8. Checking hands by using a trace detector is an important counterterrorism measure because explosive molecules such as nitro-compounds are easily adsorbed on the hands when handling explosives. The signals representing the detection of trace amounts of TNT adhering to a hand are shown in Fig. 8. When the TNT-contaminated hand was moved close to the sampling probe, a strong signal corresponding to TNT was detected on the mass chromatogram (Fig. 8(a)). Even after the hand was thoroughly washed with soap and water, the TNT signal was still detected, as shown in Fig. 8(b). The above-described results show that the detection speed, sensitivity, and selectivity of this explosive detection system are sufficient for various practical applications, such as baggage checks for airport security.

<Configuration of explosive trace detection system based on mass spectrometer and its result (mass spectrum)>

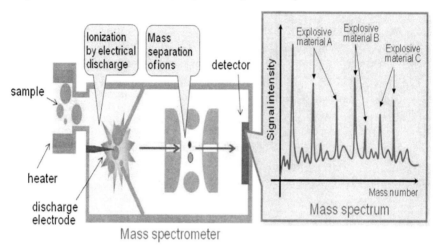

Fig. 3. Configuration of explosive trace detection system based on mass spectrometer and its result (mass spectrum)

Fig. 4. Photograph of ion trap mass spectrometer using atmospheric pressure ionization mass spectrometer (DS-1000)

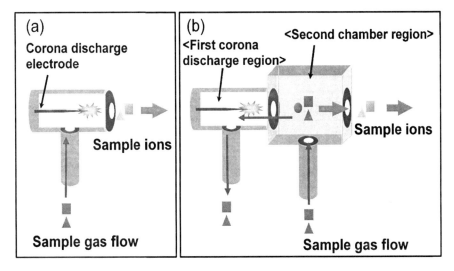

Fig. 5. Cross-sectional view of (a) conventional atmospheric pressure chemical ionization (APCI) ion source, and (b) our APCI ion source with counter-flow introduction (APCI-CFI)

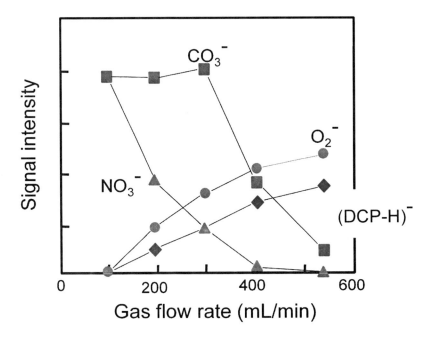

Fig. 6. Relationship between gas flow rate and observed ion intensity

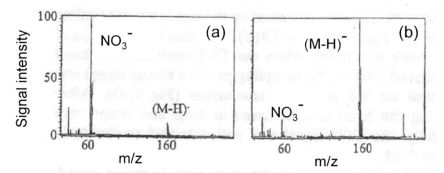

Fig. 7. Negative APCI mass spectra of 2, 4-dichlorophenol (DCP) obtained by (a) conventional ion source and (b) our developed ion source

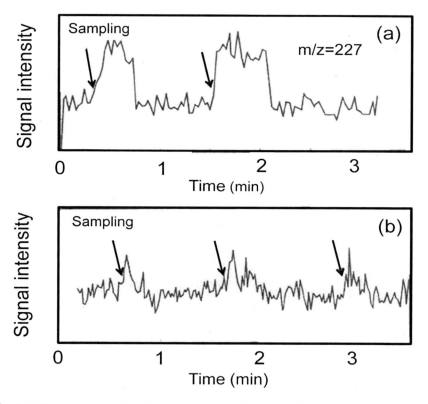

Fig. 8. TNT signal adhered to a hand: (a) after hand is wiped with wipe, and (b) after hand is washed several times with soap and water

2.2   Real-Time Monitoring Mass Spectrometry for Water Clusters in Breath

We have also investigated various safety measures against drunk driving. Recently, we have discovered that expired gas includes both positively and negatively charged water clusters and that a person's breath can be easily detected using this information [13][14].

The configuration and a photograph of our breath-alcohol sensor are shown in Figs. 9 and 10, respectively. Generally, expired gas contains water clusters that have a saturated vapor pressure of 47 mmHg and a temperature of about 37°C [15]. We recently discovered that water clusters in expired gas can be easily separated into positively and negatively charged clusters by applying an electric field. We can easily detect these charged water clusters in a person's breath when the person blows between parallel plate electrodes comprising a counter electrode, to which a voltage is applied, and a detection electrode connected to a picoammeter. Small charged water clusters are easily deflected by using an electric field to collide with the detection electrode to generate electric currents. This breath sensor is very compact and easily coupled with a small alcohol sensor (breath-alcohol sensor).

The results of serial measurements of a test subject's breath using the sensor described above are shown in Fig. 9(b). The vertical axis represents the signal intensity in the breath peak in volts, while the horizontal axis represents time in seconds. One breath peak corresponds to one breath. These results show that breath measured using our developed breath sensor distinguishes one breath from another in its measurements. During the test, the distance between the subject and breath sensor was about 8 cm. The voltage applied to the counter electrode was -500 V, with the counter and detection electrodes 10 mm apart. Negatively charged water clusters were detected using the detection electrode in this experiment, although almost the same results were obtained for positively charged water clusters.

To prove that the breath sample is of a person, not an artificial source, we have compared breath peaks obtained by our sensor with artificial peaks. Several types of artificial sources have been investigated, including an air pump coupled with a stainless water-container, which we found to be the most effective artificial source to produce peaks similar to those of a person. However, the peak width of an artificial source strongly depends on the voltage between the counter and detection electrodes, while the peak width detected by our sensor does not depend on the voltage. We consider that this is because human breath can produce finer and more uniformly sized clusters than an artificial source.

A breath sensor that measures the electric currents of charged water clusters in breath has not yet been reported, although several methods have been developed for measuring the gas flow rate and detecting chest abdomen motion [16].

The process of detecting charged water clusters can be approximately analyzed by measuring the motion of charged water clusters in the direction of the gravitational force (air resistance, buoyant force and gravitation) and at right angles to that direction (force by electric field and air resistance), as shown in Fig. 11. A comparison between measured and calculated peaks of one breath is shown in Fig. 12. The calculated peak is estimated as follows.

The motion of a charged water cluster in the direction of gravitational force is approximately given as

$$m \cdot \left(\frac{dv_g}{dt}\right) = \left(\frac{4}{3}\right) \cdot \pi \cdot r^3 \cdot \rho_p \cdot g - 6 \cdot \pi \cdot \eta \cdot r \cdot v_g - \left(\frac{4}{3}\right) \cdot \pi \cdot r^3 \cdot \rho_f \cdot g$$

where m is the mass of the charged water cluster, v_g is the velocity of the charged water cluster in the direction of gravitational force, r is the radius of the charged water cluster, ρ_p is the density of water, g is the acceleration of gravity, η is the coefficient of viscosity of air, and ρ_f is the density of air. In contrast, the motion of the charged water cluster at right angles to the gravitational force direction is described by the following equation.

$$m \cdot \left(\frac{v_r}{dt}\right) = q \cdot E - 6 \cdot \pi \cdot \eta \cdot r \cdot v_r$$

where v_r is the velocity of the charged water cluster at right angles to the gravitational force direction, q is the electric charge of the water cluster, and E is the magnitude of an electric field. If the values of v_g and v_r are positive, acceleration will become zero with time, and water clusters will attain uniform motion at constant (terminal velocity). In this case, the terminal velocities in the direction of gravitational force (v_{g0}) and at right angles to that direction (v_{r0}) are given as

$$v_{g0} = 2 \cdot r^2 \cdot \left(\rho_p - \rho_f\right) \cdot g/(9 \cdot \eta)$$

$$v_{r0} = q \cdot E/(6 \cdot \pi \cdot \eta \cdot r)$$

From these results, the times of the charged water cluster passing the detection electrode in the direction of gravitational force (t_{g0}) and reaching the detection electrode at right angles to the gravitational force direction (t_{r0}) for one position of the charged water cluster between the counter electrode and the detection electrode are described as follows.

$$t_{g0} = L_g/v_{g0}$$

$$t_{r0} = L_r/v_{r0}$$

where L_g is the distance between the position of the charged water cluster existing between the two electrodes and the bottom of the detection electrode in the direction of gravitational force, and L_r is the distance between the position of the charged water cluster between the two electrodes and the detection electrode at right angles to the gravitational force direction. If t_{g0} is larger than t_{r0}, the charged water cluster existing between the two electrodes can reach the detection electrode to generate electric currents. Therefore, a calculated peak for one breath is estimated as the probability distribution showing the frequencies of detected cluster ions occurring in certain ranges of time under the condition of $t_{r0} < t_{g0}$. Figure 12 shows the comparison between the measured peak and calculated peak estimated from charged water clusters with $0.01~\mu m \leq r \leq 0.5~\mu m$ (0.01-μm step) for $0.1~mm < L_g < 50.0~mm$ and $0.1~mm < L_r < 9.9~mm$ (0.1-mm step). The other parameters are at the values at 1atm and 25°C. The charge of the water clusters is presumed to be 1.6×10^{-19} C. It is clear that the magnitude of the measured peak width can be approximately explained by the theory described above.

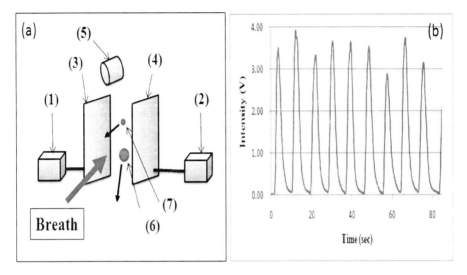

Fig. 9. (a) Configuration of breath-alcohol sensor, and (b) example of serial detection of breath. (1) Picoammeter, (2) power supply, (3) detection electrode, (4) counter electrode, (5) alcohol sensor head, (6) large charged water cluster, and (7) small charged water cluster.

Fig. 10. Photograph of breath-alcohol sensor

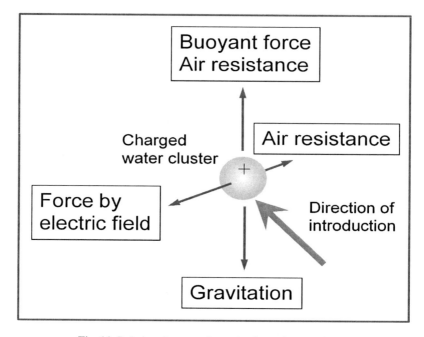

Fig. 11. Relations between forces in charged water cluster

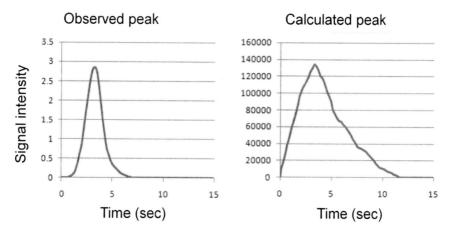

Fig. 12. Comparison between (a) measured peak and (b) calculated peak of one breath

3 Applications

3.1 Applications of Real-Time Monitoring Mass Spectrometry for Highly Sensitive Detection of Organic Compounds

The first field that the real-time monitoring mass spectrometry is applied to is PCB monitoring at PCB treatment facilities. The Japanese government has decided that systems to treat all PCBs must be in operation by 2016. Continuous monitoring is necessary for PCB treatment facilities in Japan because citizens living nearby fear the threat of untreated PCBs leaking into the atmosphere. In addition to photographs of the monitoring system, the results of monitoring PCBs in flue gas are shown in Fig. 13. In these measurements, the CID method is very effective for reducing chemical noises resulting from the various kinds of compounds contained in flue gas for precise detection of PCBs.

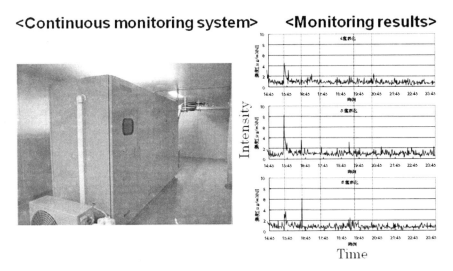

Fig. 13. PCB monitoring system, and PCB monitoring results

The second application field is detection of illicit drugs at customs checkpoints. A real-time monitoring mass spectrometry system is now used at every main customs station in Japan, and has become the main detection tool used, along with X-ray systems and detection dogs. It should be emphasized that this system has a database for many illicit drugs, and detection can be carried out using this database. MS/MS based on the ion trap method is an effective tool for identifying illicit drugs because fragment ions including structural information are easily produced by colliding illicit drug ions with helium buffer gas, which is followed by dissociation of the ions (Fig. 14). This was developed under contract research by the Ministry of Finance.

Another application is explosive trace detection. We produced a trace detection system in which traces of explosives are swabbed and entered into the system using a special wipe. The second generation of explosive trace detection is a high-throughput walkthrough portal to detect improvised explosive devices (IEDs) [17]. One of the latest threats to arise in Japan and other countries is IEDs because information can be easily found on IED synthesis using materials obtained over the Internet and because the explosive power of one of these compounds is nearly equal to that of plastic explosives. Consequently, we developed a high-throughput explosive detection system that blends in with existing equipment in public settings. This system was designed for high-throughput detection of the relatively high vapor pressure components of

<System to detect illicit drugs used by
Tokyo customs office (Narita branch)>

<Precise identification
using MS/MS technologies>

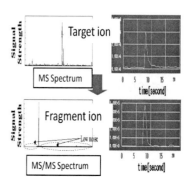

Fig. 14. Detection system for illicit drugs at Tokyo Customs Office (Narita branch) (Courtesy of Ministry of Finance)

IEDs. The configuration and a photograph of the system are shown in Fig. 15. In this system, explosive vapor is introduced into the detection section containing a mass spectrometer by using air supply and air intake sections. A good air supply and air intake section configuration is very important for maintaining a stable air flow. These sections were designed with intensive simulation of airflow. In addition, a linear ion trap mass spectrometer coupled with a new mass-selective axial ejection method is used to achieve high sensitivity due to larger ion capacity and higher trapping efficiency compared to the ITMS mentioned above [18].

<Configuration>

<Field testing at train station>

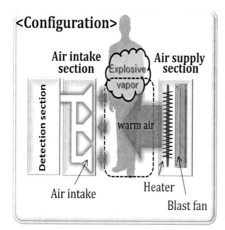

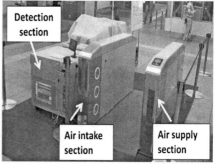

Fig. 15. Configuration of high-throughput walkthrough portal and field-testing setup at train station

Three detections of signals from improvised explosives using an overall body suction system are shown in Fig. 16. Detection results of improvised explosive components in a lab test indicate that the walkthrough portal concept worked well. The response time is about 2 s after a subject passes through the system at a walking pace of about 1 m/s.

This project was commissioned by the Ministry of Education, Culture, Sports, Science and Technology ("Science and Technology Project for a Safe and Secure Society"). The leader of this project was Dr. Yasuaki Takada of Central Research Laboratory, Hitachi, Ltd.

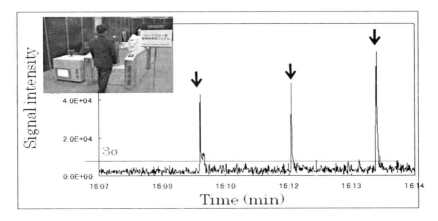

Fig. 16. Three signals showing positive detection of improvised explosives by overall body suction system

3.2   Applications of Real-Time Monitoring Mass Spectrometry for Analyzing Water Clusters

The developed breath-alcohol sensor was set just behind the steering wheel of a car mock-up, as shown in Fig. 17(a). Figure 18(a) plots the detection results obtained from the expired breath of the subject 30 minutes after drinking 200 ml of whisky and water (alcohol content: 10%) using our breath-alcohol sensor. The vertical axis represents the voltage differences observed in the breath and alcohol peaks (the difference between the top and base line in each peak) in volts, while the horizontal axis represents time in seconds. During the test, the subject was about 8 cm away from the breath-alcohol sensor. To easily distinguish between the breath peak from the breath sensor and the alcohol peak from the alcohol sensor, the output of the alcohol peak is inverted in this figure. The upper curve in the figure corresponds to the breath peak, while the lower curve corresponds to the alcohol peak. The tailing of the alcohol peak is larger than that of the breath peak, which is mainly due to the characteristics of semi-conductor alcohol sensors.

The standup position of the breath peak was almost the same as that of the alcohol peak (20.0 sec). Moreover, the difference in the peak-top position between the two peaks was much smaller (0.2 sec in this case) than the full width at half maximum value of the alcohol peak (8.4 sec). These results indicate that breath and alcohol peaks in breath containing alcohol can be simultaneously detected by using our breath-alcohol sensor. These features of our breath-alcohol sensor, shown in Fig. 18(a), are important for ensuring that the breath sample is from a person. For comparison, the result of an experiment conducted to detect background alcohol from a box of alcohol-based wet tissues is shown in Fig. 18(b). No breath peak was observed. In addition, this breath-alcohol sensor requires no contact and is easy to use, as shown in Fig. 17(b). This means that our sensor can be used for preventing drinking while driving after starting the vehicle.

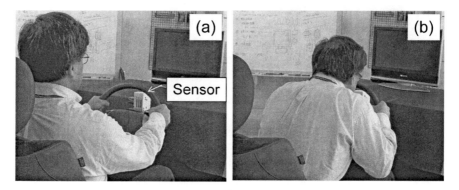

Fig. 17. (a) Breath-alcohol sensor set behind a steering wheel, and (b) test object blowing to breath-alcohol sensor

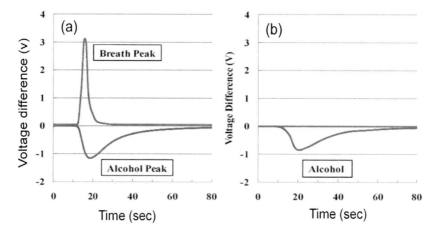

Fig. 18. (a) Simultaneous detection of breath and breath alcohol, and (b) detection of alcohol from a box of alcohol-based wet tissues

4 Conclusions

Physical security technologies based on mass spectrometry were described. Systems using these technologies have significant advantages in sensitivity and selectivity and have a very low false-positive rate compared to other methods, such as ion mobility, although they tend to be larger in size due to the use of evacuation pumps. A new APCI technique was also described. It was found to be very effective for continuous monitoring due to its stable operation.

In addition, a very compact mass spectrometer for special applications was also described. This sensor can detect breath because water clusters in breath are easily separated into positively and negatively charged clusters by an electric field. This sensor can be used to prevent drunk driving by coupling it with an alcohol sensor.

Acknowledgment

I am grateful to Dr. Yasuaki Takada, Dr. Masuyoshi Yamada, Dr. Yuichiro Hashimoto, and Mr. Hisashi Nagano (Central Research Laboratory, Hitachi, Ltd.) for their extremely helpful discussions. I am also grateful to Mr. Toru Habu, Ms. Yuriko Tsujino and Ms. Naomi Tsukada (Central Research Laboratory, Hitachi, Ltd.) for designing the sensors, supporting data acquisition and preparing materials, respectively.

References

1. Sakairi, M., Nakamura, H., Nakamura, J.: Highly Sensitive Vapor Detection of Nitro-Compounds by Atmospheric Pressure Chemical Ionization Mass Spectrometry. In: Proceedings of 6th International Symposium on Analysis and Detection of Explosives (1998)
2. Sakairi, M., Kato, Y.: Multi-atmospheric pressure ionization interface for liquid chromatography-mass spectrometry. Journal of Chromatography A 794, 391–406 (1998)
3. Sakairi, M., Hashimoto, Y., Yamada, M., Suga, M., Kojima, K.: Mass Spectrometer, Mass Spectrometry, and Monitoring System (Filed September 18, 2000). Patent No.: US 6,686,592 B1, Date of Patent: February 3 (2004)
4. Sakairi, M., Hashimoto, Y., Yamada, M., Suga, M., Kojima, K.: Mass Spectrometer, Mass Spectrometry, and Monitoring System (Filed September 2, 2003). Patent No.: US 6,838,664 B2, Date of Patent: January 4 (2005)
5. Kojima, K., Sakairi, M., Takada, Y., Nakamura, J.: Vapor Detection of TNT and RDX USING Atmospheric Pressure Chemical Ionization Mass Spectrometry with Counter-Flow Introduction (CFI). J. Mass Spectrom. Soc. Jpn. 48, 360–362 (2000)
6. Hashimoto, Y., Yamada, M., Suga, M., Kimura, K., Sakairi, M., Tanaka, S., Mizumoto, M., Sakamoto, M.: Online measurement of organic chlorides using an atmospheric-pressure chemical ionization ion-trap mass spectrometer. Bunseki Kagaku 49, 49–54 (2000)
7. Yamada, M., Sakairi, M., Hashimoto, Y., Suga, M., Takada, Y., Waki, I., Yoshii, Y., Hori, Y., Sakamoto, M.: On-line Monitoring of Dioxin Precursors in Flue Gas. Analytical Sciences 17(Supplement), i559–i562 (2001)
8. Takada, Y., Nagano, H., Suga, M., Hashimoto, Y., Yamada, M., Sakairi, M.: Detection of Military Explosives by Atmospheric Pressure Chemical Ionization Mass Spectrometry with Counter-Flow Introduction. Propellants, Explosives, Pyrotechnics 27, 224–228 (2002)

 9. Yamada, M., Waki, I., Sakairi, M., Sakamoto, M., Imai, T.: Real-time-monitored decrease of trichlorophenol as a dioxin surrogate in flue gas using iron oxide catalyst. Chemosphere 54, 1475–1480 (2004)
10. Takada, Y.: Explosives Trace Detection by Mass Spectrometry. J. Mass Spectrom. Soc. Jpn. 55, 91–94 (2007)
11. Sakairi, M., Nishimura, A., Suzuki, D.: Olfaction Presentation System Using Odor Scanner and Odor-Emitting Apparatus Coupled with Chemical Capsules of Alginic Acid Polymer. IEICE Trans. Fundamentals, E92-A, 618–629 (2009)
12. Transportation Security Administration homepage, http://www.tsa.gov/
13. Sakairi, M., Suzuki, D., Nishimura, A., Ichige, Y., Kiguchi, M.: Simultaneous detection of breath and alcohol using breath-alcohol sensor for prevention of drunk driving. IEICE Electronics Express 7, 446–472 (2010)
14. Sakairi, M., Togami, M.: Use of Water Cluster Detector for Preventing Drunk and Drowsy Driving. In: Proceedings of IEEE Sensors (2010) (in press)
15. Guyton, A.C., Hall, J.E.: Textbook of Medical Physiology (9th edn.), 503, Igaku-Shoin Ltd (Japanese edition), Tokyo (1999)
16. Yamakoshi, K., Togawa, T.: Biomedical Sensors and Instruments, pp. 103–109. Corona Publishing Co., Ltd., Tokyo (2005)
17. Takada, Y.: High-throughput walkthrough portal to detect improvised explosive devices. Safety Engineering 149, 4–8 (2008)
18. Sugiyama, M., Hasegawa, H., Hashimoto, Y.: Mass-selective axial ejection from a linear ion trap with a direct current extraction field. Rapid Communications in Mass Spectrometry 23, 2917–2922 (2009)

Exploiting Character Class Information in Forensic Writer Identification

Fernando Alonso-Fernandez, Julian Fierrez, Javier Galbally, and Javier Ortega-Garcia

Biometric Recognition Group - ATVS, Escuela Politecnica Superior
Universidad Autonoma de Madrid, Avda. Francisco Tomas y Valiente, 11
Campus de Cantoblanco, 28049 Madrid, Spain
{fernando.alonso,julian.fierrez,
javier.galbally,javier.ortega}@uam.es
http://atvs.ii.uam.es

Abstract. Questioned document examination is extensively used by forensic specialists for criminal identification. This paper presents a writer recognition system based on contour features operating in identification mode (one-to-many) and working at the level of isolated characters. Individual characters of a writer are manually segmented and labeled by an expert as pertaining to one of 62 alphanumeric classes (10 numbers and 52 letters, including lowercase and uppercase letters), being the particular setup used by the forensic laboratory participating in this work. Three different scenarios for identity modeling are proposed, making use to a different degree of the class information provided by the alphanumeric samples. Results obtained on a database of 30 writers from real forensic documents show that the character class information given by the manual analysis provides a valuable source of improvement, justifying the significant amount of time spent in manual segmentation and labeling by the forensic specialist.

1 Introduction

Analysis of handwritten documents with the aim of determining the writer is an important application area in forensic casework, with numerous cases in courts over the years that have dealt with evidence provided by these documents [1]. Handwriting is considered individual, as shown by the wide social and legal acceptance of signatures as a mean of identity validation, which is also supported by experimental studies [2]. The goal of writer recognition is to determine whether two handwritten documents, referred as to the known and the questioned document, were written by the same person or not. For this purpose, computer vision and pattern recognition techniques have been applied to this problem to support forensic experts [3,4].

The forensic scenario present some difficulties due to their particular characteristics in terms of [5]: frequently reduced number of handwriting samples, variability of writing style, pencil or type of paper, the presence of noise patterns, etc. or the unavailability of online information. As a result, this application domain still heavily relies on human-expert interaction. The use of semi-automatic recognition systems is very useful to, given a questioned handwriting sample, narrow down a list of possible candidates which are into a database of known identities, therefore making easier the subsequent confrontation for the forensic expert [5,4].

H. Sako, K. Franke, and S. Saitoh (Eds.): IWCF 2010, LNCS 6540, pp. 31–42, 2011.

Fig. 1. Connected components from a handwritten sample

In the last years, several writer recognition algorithms have been described in literature based on different group of features [7]: i) general geometric script features, like word or line spacing; ii) textural features capturing for example slant and curvature of the script; iii) placement features, i.e. writers placement preferences in the process of placing ink elements across the page; iv) micro level features measuring ink deposition characteristics; and v) character-fragment features measuring writer' preferred use of allographic elements.

A machine expert for off-line writer recognition making use of textural features based on contour information has been built in this work. It is focused on discriminating writers by capturing the distinctive visual appearance of the samples. Previous works following this direction used connected-component images or contours [8,9] using automatic segmentation. Perfect automatic segmentation of individual characters still remains an unsolved problem [5], but connected components encompassing several characters or syllables can be easily segmented, and the elements generated (see Figure 1) also capture shape details of the visual appearance of the samples used by the writer [9]. The system in this paper, however, makes use of individual characters segmented manually by a forensic expert or a trained operator which are also assigned to one of the 62 alphanumeric classes among digits "0"~"9", lowercase letters "a"~"z", and uppercase letters "A"~"Z". This is the setup used by the Spanish forensic group participating in this work. For a particular individual, the authenticated document is scanned and next, a dedicated software tool for character segmentation is used. Segmentation is done manually by a trained operator, who draw a character selection with the computer mouse and label the corresponding sample according to the 62 classes mentioned. We depict in Figure 2 (right) some examples of the manual selection of characters. In this work, we adapt the recognition method based on contour features from [9] to work with this setup. Additionally, the system is evaluated using a database created from real forensic documents (i.e. confiscated to real criminals or authenticated in the presence of a police officer), which is an important point compared with experiments of other works where the writing samples are obtained with the collaboration of volunteers under controlled conditions [10]. We evaluate in this paper three different

Fig. 2. Left: the 62 classes of alphanumeric characters used in this paper (digits "0"~"9", lowercase letters "a"~"z", and uppercase letters "A"~"Z"). Right: manual selection of individual characters with the computer mouse using a dedicated software tool. Images from [6].

scenarios for identity modeling, exploiting to a different degree the class information provided by the manual segmentation of alphanumeric samples: modeling *per individual sample*, modeling *per alphanumeric channel*, and modeling *per writer*. Results show that the class information provides a considerable improvement, justifying the writer identification approach used in our forensic system, where a significant amount of time is spent every time a new writer is included.

The system is evaluated in identification mode, in which an individual is recognized by searching the reference models of all the subjects in the database for a match (one-to-many). As a result, the system returns a ranked list of candidates. Ideally, the first ranked candidate (Top 1) should correspond with the correct identity of the individual, but one can choose to consider a longer list (e.g. Top 10) to increase the chances of finding the correct identity. Identification is a critical component in negative

Table 1. Features used in this work

	Feature	Explanation	Dimensions	Source
f1	$p(\phi)$	Contour-direction PDF	12	contours
f2	$p(\phi_1, \phi_2)$	Contour-hinge PDF	300	contours
f3h	$p(\phi_1, \phi_3)_h$	Direction co-occurrence PDF, horizontal run	144	contours
f3v	$p(\phi_1, \phi_3)_v$	Direction co-occurrence PDF, vertical run	144	contours
f5h	$p(rl)_h$	Run-length on background PDF, horizontal run	60	binary image
f5v	$p(rl)_v$	Run-length on background PDF, vertical run	60	binary image

recognition applications (or watchlists) where the aim is checking if the person is who he/she (implicitly or explicitly) denies to be, which the typical situation in forensic/criminal cases [11].

The rest of the paper is structured as follows. In Section 2 we describe the main stages of our recognition system. Section 3 describes the database, the scenarios for identity modeling and the experimental results. Finally, conclusions are drawn in Section 4.

2   System Description

The writer recognition system of this paper makes use of the contour features presented in [9], which are adapted to the particular setup of this paper. It includes three main stages: i) preprocessing of the individual characters, ii) feature extraction, and iii) feature matching. These stages are described next.

2.1   Pre-processing Stage

The writer identification method used by the forensic group participating in this work is based on manually reviewing the handwritten material, as mentioned in Section 1. After manual segmentation and labeling of alphanumeric characters from a given document, they are binarized using the Otsu algorithm [12], followed by a margin drop and a height normalization to 120 pixels, preserving the aspect ratio. Elimination of noise of the binary image is then carried out through a morphological opening plus a closing operation [13]. Next, a connected component detection, using 8-connectivity, is done. In the last step, internal and external contours of the connected components are extracted using the Moore's algorithm [13]. Beginning from a contour pixel of a connected component, which is set as the starting pixel, this algorithm seeks a pixel boundary around it following the meaning clockwise, and repeats this process until the starting pixel is reached for the same position from which it was agreed to begin the algorithm. The result is a sequence with the pixels coordinates of the boundary of the component. This vectorial representation is very effective because it allows a rapid extraction of many of the features used later.

2.2   Feature Extraction Stage

Features are calculated from two representations of the handwritten samples extracted during the preprocessing stage: the binary image without noise and the contours of the connected components. The features used in this work are summarized in Table 1, including the image representation used by each one. A handwritten sample is shaped like a texture that is described with probability distribution functions (PDFs). Probability distribution functions used here are grouped in two different categories: direction PDFs (features f1, f2, f3h, f3v) and length PDFs (features f5h, f5v). A graphical description of the extraction of these features is depicted in Figure 3. To be consistent with the work in which these features where proposed [9], we follow the same nomenclature used in it.

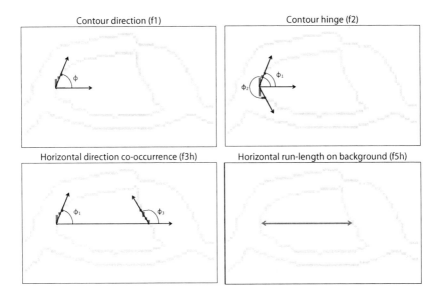

Fig. 3. Graphical description of the feature extraction: contour direction (f1), contour hinge (f2), horizontal direction co-occurrence (f3h) and horizontal run-length (f5h)

Contour-Direction PDF (f1)

This directional distribution is computed very fastly using the contour representation, with the additional advantage that the influence of the ink-trace width is eliminated. The contour-direction distribution f1 is extracted by considering the orientation of local contour fragments. A fragment is determined by two contour pixels (x_k, y_k) and $(x_{k+\epsilon}, y_{k+\epsilon})$ taken a certain distance ϵ apart. The angle that the fragment makes with the horizontal is computed using

$$\phi = \arctan(\frac{y_{k+\epsilon} - y_k}{x_{k+\epsilon} - x_k}) \qquad (1)$$

As the algorithm runs over the contour, the histogram of angles is built. This angle histogram is then normalized to a probability distribution f1 which gives the probability of finding in the handwritten sample a contour fragment oriented with each ϕ. The angle ϕ resides in the first two quadrants because, without online information, we do not

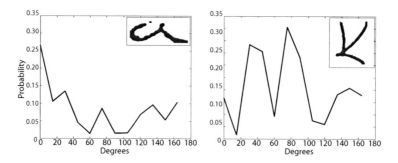

Fig. 4. Example of the countour direction feature (f1) for two different handwritten characters

know which inclination the writer signed with. The histogram is spanned in the interval $0°$-$180°$, and is divided in $n = 12$ sections (bins). Therefore, each section spans $15°$, which is a sufficiently detailed and robust description [9]. The parameter ϵ controls the length of the analyzing contour fragment, which is set to $\epsilon = 5$. These settings will be used for all of the directional features presented in this paper. An example of extraction of this feature for two handwritten characters is depicted in Figure 4.

Contour-Hinge PDF (f2)

In order to capture the curvature of the contour, as well as its orientation, the "hinge" feature f2 is used. The main idea is to consider two contour fragments attached at a common end pixel and compute the joint probability distribution of the orientations ϕ_1 and ϕ_2 of the two sides. A joint density function is obtained, which quantifies the chance of finding two "hinged" contour fragments with angles ϕ_1 and ϕ_2, respectively. It is spanned in the four quadrants ($360°$) and there are $2n$ sections for every side of the "contour-hinge", but only non-redundant combinations are considered (i.e. $\phi_2 \geq \phi_1$). For $n = 12$, the resulting contour-hinge feature vector has 300 dimensions [9].

Direction Co-occurrence PDFs (f3h, f3v)

Based on the same idea of combining oriented contour fragments, the directional co-occurrence is used. For this feature, the combination of contour-angles occurring at the ends of run-lengths on the background are used, see Figure 3. Horizontal runs along the rows of the image generate f3h and vertical runs along the columns generate f3v. They are also joint density functions, spanned in the two first quadrants, and divided into n^2 sections. These features give a measure of a roundness of the written characters and/or strokes.

Run-Length PDFs (f5h, f5v)

These features are computed from the binary image of the handwritten sample taking into consideration the pixels corresponding to the background. They capture the regions

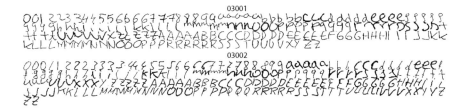

Fig. 5. Training samples of two different writers of the forensic database used in this paper

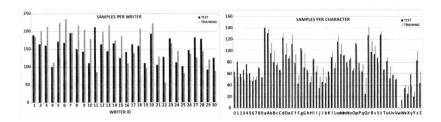

Fig. 6. Distribution of samples per writer (left) and per character (right) of the forensic database used in this paper

enclosed inside the letters and strokes and also the empty spaces between them. The probability distributions of horizontal and vertical lengths are used. These features gives the probability of finding in the handwritten sample an enclosed region with each length.

2.3 Feature Matching Stage

Each writer is represented in the system by a PDF or set of PDFs (depending on the experiment at hand, see 3). To compute the similarity between two PDFs $\mathbf{o}$ and $\boldsymbol{\mu}$ from two different writers, the χ^2 distance is used:

$$\chi^2_{\mathbf{o}\boldsymbol{\mu}} = \sum_{i=1}^{N} \frac{(o_i - \mu_i)^2}{o_i + \mu_i} \tag{2}$$

where N is the dimensionality of the vectors $\mathbf{o}$ and $\boldsymbol{\mu}$.

3 Experimental Framework

3.1 Database

To evaluate the system, we use a real forensic database from original confiscated/ authenticated documents provided by the Spanish forensic laboratory of the Dirección General de la Guardia Civil (DGGC). Alphanumeric characters of the handwritten samples are segmented and labeled by a trained operator of the DGGC. The whole database contains 9,297 character samples of real forensic cases from 30 different writers, with around 300 samples on average per writer distributed between a training and a testing data set. In Figure 5 we plot the training samples of two different writers of the database. For each writer, training and testing data are extracted from different confiscated documents, meaning that they were "acquired" at different moments. Given the nature of the database, it does not contain uniformly distributed samples of every character, nor time span between training and testing data. Figure 6 shows the distribution of samples per writer and per character of our database.

3.2   Writer Identity Modeling

Given a writer of the test set, *identification experiments* are done by outputting the N closest identities of the training set. An identification is considered successful if the correct identity is among the N outputted ones.

For a particular writer, several samples of individual characters pertaining to one of the 62 alphanumeric classes among digits "0"~"9", lowercase letters "a"~"z", and uppercase letters "A"~"Z" are available thanks to the manual segmentation and labeling. For each feature described in Section 2.2, we evaluate the following three scenarios for writer identity modeling:

1. Modeling *per individual sample* (channel dependent). For example, if a writer has x samples of the digit "0", features for each of the x samples are computed. This process is repeated with all the 62 alphanumeric channels. This modeling captures particular variations in each alphanumeric character (e.g. if the writer has different "a", "b", etc.) Due to the nature of the database, it will not be a uniform number of features among the different channels. It could also be the case that a writer many not have samples in a particular channel, in whose case no features will be extracted. For each individual sample, we find the closest identity by comparing with all the training samples pertaining to the same channel. We then compute the closest identity to each alphanumeric channel based on the majority rule: the winning identity will be the writer having the maximum number of winning samples. In case of writers having the same number of winning samples, they are subsequently ranked using the next 2 criteria, listed in descending order of weight: 1) average of winning sub-distances, and 2) minimum winning sub-distance. Finally, identification is based again on the majority rule, applied in this case to the alphanumeric channels: the winning output identity will be the writer having the maximum number of winning alphanumeric channels, the second winning identity will be the next writer, and so on. In case of writers having the same number of winning channels, we apply the same above criteria.

2. Modeling *per alphanumeric channel* (channel dependent). For example, if a writer has x samples of the digit "0", histograms of the feature are combined (added) to obtain a unique probability distribution. This process is repeated for all the 62 alphanumeric classes. This modeling averages the different variations of a given alphanumeric character. Therefore, we obtain 62 sub-distances between two writers, one per channel. We then compute the closest identity to each alphanumeric channel based on its distance. Identification is based on the majority rule: the winning output identity will be the writer having the maximum number of winning alphanumeric channels, the second winning identity will be the next writer, and so on. This

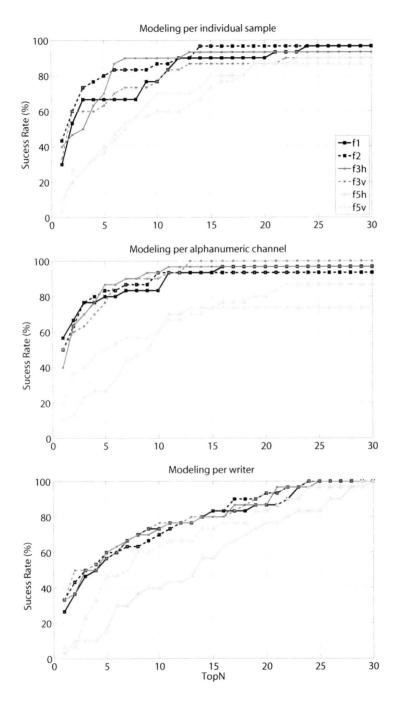

Fig. 7. Writer identification rates for the three scenarios of identity modeling considered

results in $62 \times 30 \times 30 = 55{,}800$ computed distances. In case of writers having the same number of winning channels, we apply the same above criteria.

3. Modeling *per writer* (channel independent). This case computes a unique probability distribution per writer by combining all the available samples of all the alphanumeric characters. In this case, we do not use the character class information, obtaining a unique writing identity model that averages information from the 62 channels. Only one distance between two writers is obtained, which is used for identification. This results in $30 \times 30 = 900$ computed distances.

3.3   Results

We plot in Figure 7 results of the identification experiments varying the size of the hit list from $N=1$ (Top 1) to $N=30$ (Top 30). Results are shown for the different features described in Section 2.2 and for the three identity modeling scenarios considered.

We observe that, in general, working with the class information provided by the alphanumeric channels (top and medium plot in Figure 7) results in considerable better performance with respect to using a unique single identity model that does not exploit this information (bottom plot in Figure 7). Thus, the class information given by the character segmentation and labeling carried out by the trained operator provides a considerable improvement. This justifies the writer identification approach used in our forensic system, in which a considerable amount of time is spent every time a new writer is included in the database. It can be seen in Figure 7, for example, that a success rate of 80% is already achieved with some features for a hit list size of $N=5$ or less when using channel information. However, when using a channel independent identity modeling, it is not achieved until a hit list size of $N=13$ is considered.

It is worth noting that directional features (f1, f2, f3h, f3v) work consistently better that features based on length properties (f5h, f5v). This suggests that the length of the regions enclosed inside the letters and strokes is not a good distinctive feature in the setup presented in this paper, where we are using a database of isolated alphanumeric handwritten characters. Better results are obtained in other studies making use of complete lines or pages of handwritten material [9].

Finally, by comparing the two scenarios for writer identity modeling that make use of channel information (top and medium plot in Figure 7), it can be seen that the best results are obtained when using identity models per alphanumeric channel. In this case, for a hit list size of $N=5$, all the directional features achieve a success rate of $\tilde{8}0\%$. On the other hand, when using identity models per individual sample and a hit list size of $N=5$, the success rate exhibited by the directional features are between 60% and 80%. Thus, averaging all the samples of a given channel provides more robustness than using the samples separately.

4   Conclusions and Future Work

A machine expert for off-line writer identification based on contour features has been evaluated. It encodes several directional properties of contour fragments as well as the length of the regions enclosed inside letters. The system presented in this work is based on manual review of the handwritten material, in which segmentation and labeling of characters is made using a dedicated software tool according to 62 alphanumeric classes (10 numbers and 52 letters, including lowercase and uppercase letters). This particular setup is used by the Spanish forensic group participating in this work, which has also provided us with a database of real forensic documents from 30 different writers, an important point in comparison with other works where data is obtained from collaborative writers under controlled conditions. Experiments are done in identification mode (one-to-many), which the typical situation in forensic/criminal cases.

The system of this paper is evaluated in three different scenarios for identity modeling which exploit to a different degree the class information provided by the manual segmentation of alphanumeric samples: *i*) modeling *per individual sample*, *ii*) modeling *per alphanumeric channel*, and *iii*) modeling *per writer*. The two first scenarios make use of the class information given by the manual labeling, whereas the third one is channel independent (i.e. does not use the character class information). Results show that much better performance is obtained by using channel information, justifying the considerable amount of time spent by the trained operator in the segmentation and labeling process. The best scenario is based on identity modeling *per alphanumeric channel*, meaning that averaging all the samples of a given channel provides more robustness than using the samples separately. The latter approach may work better if enough samples representative of writer' particular variations are included in the database, or for specific channels commonly used in the language of the database (as can be seen in Figure 6, characters like 'w' and 'W' are not often used in the Spanish language, while "a", "A", "r" or "t" are quite common).

A drawback found in our experiments is that a success rate of 100% is never achieved with some features and/or identity modeling scenarios. It means that there are some writers in the database whose identity are never found, and test samples from this writer are assigned as pertaining to someone else. It could be due to the majority rule used for identification, as well as the decision criteria when several writers have the same number of winning samples (see Section 3.2).

The analysis of these results with a limited database suggest that the proposed approach can be used for forensic writer identification, pointing out the advantages of manual segmentation and labeling by a trained operator. Future work includes evaluating of our system with a bigger forensic database and improving the performance by applying advanced alphanumeric channel combination methods [14]. Another source of future work is the use of advanced approaches for user-dependent selection and combination of alphanumeric channels [15,16], so that the most discriminative channels for each user are used in the fusion.

Acknowledgements

This work has been partially supported by projects Bio-Challenge (TEC2009-11186), BBfor2 (FP7 ITN-2009-238803) and "Cátedra UAM-Telefónica". Postdoctoral work of author F. A.-F. is supported by a Juan de la Cierva Fellowship from the Spanish MICINN. The authors would like to thank to the forensic "Laboratorio de Grafística" of the 'Dirección General de la Guardia Civil' for its valuable support.

References

1. Srihari, S., Huang, C., Srinivasan, H., Shah, V.: Biometric and Forensic Aspects of Digital Document Processing. In: Digital Document Processing, ch. 17, pp. 379–406. Springer, Heidelberg (2007)
2. Srihari, S.N., Cha, S.H., Arora, H., Lee, S.: Individuality of handwriting. Journal of Forensic Sciences 47(4), 856–872 (2002)
3. Plamondon, R., Srihari, S.: On-line and off-line handwriting recognition: A comprehensive survey. IEEE Trans. on Pattern Analysis and Machine Intelligence 22(1), 63–84 (2000)
4. Srihari, S., Leedham, G.: A survey of computer methods in forensic document examination. In: Proc. 11th International Graphonomics Society Conference, IGS, pp. 278–281 (November 2003)
5. Schomaker, L.: Writer identification and verification. In: Sensors, Systems and Algorithms, Advances in Biometrics. Springer, Heidelberg (2008)
6. Tapiador, M.: Análisis de las Características de Identificación Biométrica de la Escritura Manuscrita y Mecanográfica. PhD thesis, Escuela Politécnica Superior, Universidad Autónoma de Madrid (2006)
7. Schomaker, L.: Advances in writer identification and verification. In: Proc. Intl. Conference on Document Analysis and Recognition, ICDAR, vol. 2, pp. 1268–1273 (2007)
8. Schomaker, L., Bulacu, M.: Automatic writer identification using connected-component contours and edge-based features of upper-case western script. IEEE Trans. on Pattern Analysis and Machine Intelligence 26(6), 787–798 (2004)
9. Bulacu, M., Schomaker, L.: Text-independent writer identification and verification using textural and allographic features. IEEE Trans. on Pattern Analysis and Machine Inteligence 29(4), 701–717 (2007)
10. Tapiador, M., Sigüenza, J.: Writer identification method based on forensic knowledge. In: Zhang, D., Jain, A.K. (eds.) ICBA 2004. LNCS, vol. 3072, pp. 555–560. Springer, Heidelberg (2004)
11. Jain, A., Flynn, P., Ross, A. (eds.): Handbook of Biometrics. Springer, Heidelberg (2008)
12. Otsu, N.: A threshold selection method for gray-level histograms. IEEE Trans. on Systems, Man and Cybernetics 9, 62–66 (1979)
13. Gonzalez, R., Woods, R.: Digital Image Processing. Addison-Wesley, Reading (2002)
14. Jain, A., Nandakumar, K., Ross, A.: Score Normalization in Multimodal Biometric Systems. Pattern Recognition 38(12), 2270–2285 (2005)
15. Fierrez-Aguilar, J., Garcia-Romero, D., Ortega-Garcia, J., Gonzalez-Rodriguez, J.: Adapted user-dependent multimodal biometric authentication exploiting general information. Pattern Recognition Letters 26, 2628–2639 (2005)
16. Galbally, J., Fierrez, J., Freire, M.R., Ortega-Garcia, J.: Feature selection based on genetic algorithms for on-line signature verification. In: Proc. IEEE Workshop on Automatic Identification Advanced Technologies, AutoID, pp. 198–203 (2007)

Toward Forensics by Stroke Order Variation — Performance Evaluation of Stroke Correspondence Methods

Wenjie Cai[1,2], Seiichi Uchida[2], and Hiroaki Sakoe[2]

[1] O-RID Company, Japan
`caiwenjie@o-rid.com`
[2] Faculty of Information Science and Electrical Engineering,
Kyushu University, Japan
`uchida@ait.kyushu-u.ac.jp`

Abstract. We consider personal identification using stroke order variations of online handwritten character patterns, which are written on, e.g., electric tablets. To extract the stroke order variation of an input character pattern, it is necessary to establish the accurate stroke correspondence between the input pattern and the reference pattern of the same category. In this paper we compare five stroke correspondence methods: the individual correspondence decision (ICD), the cube search (CS), the bipartite weighted matching (BWM), the stable marriage (SM), and the deviation-expansion model (DE). After their brief review, they are experimentally compared quantitatively by not only their stroke correspondence accuracy but also character recognition accuracy. The experimental results showed the superiority CS and BWM over ICD, SM and DE.

1 Introduction

In this paper, we assume that the writing order of a multiple-stroke character pattern (i.e., stroke order) represents writer's individuality and thus discuss how we can determine the stroke order of an unknown input character pattern. Our target is "online" character patterns, which are acquired from electric tablets or other electric pen devices and represented as the motion trajectory of the pen-tip. Different from "image" character patterns acquired from scanners or cameras, online character patterns can convey the stroke order information and thus we can examine the effectiveness of the stroke order on forensic applications by them. Figure 1 shows three different stroke orders of a four-stroke Chinese character "king", acquired by an electric tablet. The numerals in this figure indicate the order of the four strokes.

The authors' preliminary observation on a small dataset of online character patterns indicates that stroke orders are *not* random. For example, in the case of the character "king" of Fig. 1, only those three stroke orders were found among $4! = 24$ possible orders in a dataset by 30 different writers. Another preliminary observation indicates that each writer always uses the same stroke order. For

H. Sako, K. Franke, and S. Saitoh (Eds.): IWCF 2010, LNCS 6540, pp. 43–55, 2011.

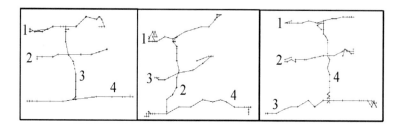

Fig. 1. Three typical stroke orders of Chinese character "king"

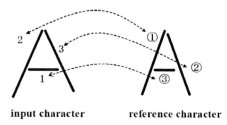

input character   reference character

Fig. 2. Stroke order determination via stroke correspondence

example, the stroke orders of "king" by the same writer were the same in the database. Thus, we can expect that the stroke order is useful for forensics.

Toward the realization of forensics systems based on the individuality of stroke order, we need some methodology to determine the stroke order of an unknown input pattern automatically and accurately. In fact, without such a methodology, it is difficult to prove that the above preliminary observations are reliable through a very large-scale experiment. In addition, it is also difficult to realize an automatic forensic system that can identify the writer based on stroke order.

The determination of the stroke order is equivalent to the determination of the *stroke correspondence* between the input character pattern and the reference character pattern with the standard stroke order. As an example, let us consider the case of Fig. 2, where the stroke correspondence between input pattern "A" and reference pattern "A" can be determined as 1 ↔ ③, 2 ↔ ①, and 3 ↔ ②. From this correspondence, we can determine that this writer writes the "A" in the order of ③ → ① → ②.

Several research groups have proposed promising stroke correspondence methods for stroke-order-free online character recognition systems. Here, we pick-up the following five methods.

- The individual correspondence decision method (ICD) by Wakahara and his colleagues [1,2].
- The cube search method (CS) by Sakoe and his colleagues [3,4].
- The method based on bipartite weighted matching (BWM) by Hsieh et al. [5].
- The method based on the stable marriage algorithm (SM) by Yokota et al. [6].
- The deviation-expansion model (DE) by Lin et al. [7].

As we will see in Section 2.1, those methods generally tackle an optimization problem where a *stroke distance* (i.e., dissimilarity of a pair of strokes) is first evaluated between each of input strokes and each of reference strokes and then the stroke correspondence with smaller stroke distances is determined between input strokes and reference strokes. A bijection (one-to-one) constraint is generally imposed on the correspondence for excluding unnatural results. The *character distance* is then calculated between the input and the reference patterns by accumulating the stroke distance between corresponding strokes. Although we generally focus the character distance in recognition application, we focus the optimized stroke correspondence in forensic application.

In this paper, we evaluate the performance of those methods, i.e., ICD, CS, BWM, SM, and DE, through a recognition task of online multiple-stroke character patterns. The result of the comparative evaluation in this paper will be valuable for selecting the stroke correspondence method for forensics. We will evaluate the methods not only at their stroke correspondence accuracy but also their recognition accuracy. Computation time will also be compared. In past researches, those methods have not been compared even on the task of online character recognition by using a common dataset (and, of course, have not been compared on any writer identification task).

In Section 2, the general problem of determining the optimal stroke correspondence is described and then the above five methods for solving the problem are reviewed. Section 3 provides the experimental results and a discussion on the above methods. In Section 4, a conclusion is presented with future work.

2   Stroke Correspondence Methods

2.1   General Problem of Determining Optimal Stroke Correspondence

We define an input pattern with N strokes as a sequence,

$$A = A_1 A_2 \ldots A_k \ldots A_N,$$

where A_k is the kth stroke and represented as a feature vector. For example, A_k is represented as a vector being comprised of a sequence of local directions and $x - y$ coordinates of the stroke. Similarly, we define the reference pattern as

$$B = B_1 B_2 \ldots B_l \ldots B_N.$$

We define $\delta(k, l) = D(A_k, B_l)$ as a *stroke distance* between input stroke A_k and reference stroke B_l. Note that the dimensionality of A_k and B_l are often different due to the difference of their stroke lengths. Thus, we cannot calculate the simple Euclidean distance between them. Instead, DP-matching distance [8] has been utilized for calculating a distance between a pair of strokes with different lengths.

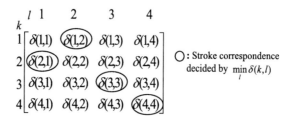

Fig. 3. Individual correspondence decision ($N = 4$)

Consider a mapping $l = l(k)$ for representing the stroke correspondence between $\boldsymbol{A}_k$ and $\boldsymbol{B}_l$. Under the mapping $l(k)$, the stroke $\boldsymbol{A}_k$ corresponds to $\boldsymbol{B}_{l(k)}$. Thus, the *character distance* between $\boldsymbol{A}$ and $\boldsymbol{B}$ is $\sum_k \delta(k, l(k))$. The mapping $l(k)$ should be bijective (one-to-one) from $\{\boldsymbol{A}_k\}$ onto $\{\boldsymbol{B}_{l(k)}\}$.

Again, the stroke correspondence $\{l(k)\}$ is equivalent to the stroke order of $\boldsymbol{A}$; the stroke order of $\boldsymbol{A}$ can be obtained as $l(1), \ldots, l(k), \ldots, l(N)$, which will minimize the criterion $\sum_k \delta(k, l(k))$. It is very important to note there are many methods to minimize the criterion $\sum_k \delta(k, l(k))$. Some of them are very efficient suboptimal methods and others are global optimization methods. Hereafter, we will compare five stroke correspondence methods.

2.2   Individual Correspondence Decision (ICD) [1,2]

In the ICD method, the stroke $\boldsymbol{B}_l$ corresponding to the stroke $\boldsymbol{A}_k$ is determined independently. First, an $N \times N$ stroke distance matrix whose element equals $\delta(k, l)$ is defined. Then, the minimum value in each row k of the matrix is searched for as shown in Fig. 3. That is, for the kth input stroke, the lth reference stroke with the minimum stroke distance from k is determined as the corresponding stroke. Consequently, the minimized character distance $D(\boldsymbol{A}, \boldsymbol{B})$ can be described as

$$D(\boldsymbol{A}, \boldsymbol{B}) = \sum_{k=1}^{N} \min_{l} \delta(k, l(k)).$$

Clearly, there is no guarantee that the resulting stroke correspondence becomes one-to-one. The time complexity of ICD is $O(N^2)$.

2.3   Cube Search (CS) [3,4]

In the CS method, an N-dimensional cube graph, shown in Fig. 4, is used for representing stroke correspondence; every path from the leftmost node to the rightmost node represents a stroke correspondence $l(1), \ldots, l(k), \ldots, l(N)$ and the graph can represent all ($N!$) possible correspondences.

Specifically, as shown in Fig. 4, the graph is comprised of 2^N nodes and each of them is indexed by an N-bit binary number; each bit position corresponds to the reference pattern stroke number l, and the bit value 1 means that this

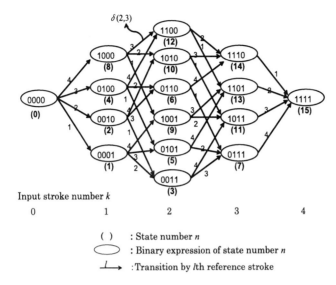

Input stroke number k

| 0 | 1 | 2 | 3 | 4 |

( )   : State number n

⬭   : Binary expression of state number n

⤳   : Transition by lth reference stroke

Fig. 4. Cube search graph $(N = 4)$

reference stroke has already been matched to some input stroke. For example, the node "1100" indicates that the first and the second input strokes corresponds to the third and the fourth reference strokes, respectively, *or*, the fourth and the third reference strokes, respectively.

Since the CS method treats the stroke correspondence problem as a sequential optimization problem from 1 to N, the two nodes linked by an edge should have only one different bit. For example, there is an edge from the node "0000" to "0100". This edge indicates that the first input stroke corresponds to the third reference stroke. Similarly, there is an edge from the node "0100" to "1100". This edge indicates that the second input stroke corresponds to the fourth reference stroke. Clearly, any path from the leftmost node "0000" to the rightmost node "1111" will satisfy this condition and represents a bijective correspondence.

Since each edge indicates that a specific input stroke corresponds a specific reference stroke, the stroke distance $\delta(k, l)$ is attached to the edge. For example, the distance $\delta(2, 4)$ will be attached to the edge from the node "0100" to "1100". Note that the same distance $\delta(2, 4)$ will also be attached to the another edge from "0001" to "1001".

Consequently, the optimal stroke correspondence problem (to find the correspondence $l(1), \ldots, l(N)$ which minimizes the criterion $\sum_k \delta(k, l(k))$) is organized as a minimum distance path problem. An efficient DP algorithm is used to search for the "globally" minimum distance path on the cube graph. The recurrence equation of DP is formulated as,

$$G(n) = \min_m \left[G(m) + \delta(k, l) \right],$$

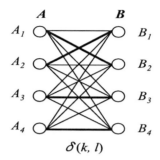

Fig. 5. A weighted bipartite graph ($N = 4$). A perfect matching is marked by thick lines.

where $G(n)$ is the minimum cumulative score to the state n and there should be the relation that the binary number n has k "1"-bits and two binary numbers m and n are different only at the l-th bit. The character distance $D(\boldsymbol{A}, \boldsymbol{B})$ is obtained as $G(n)$ at the final state $n = $"1111". The time complexity of CS is $O(N \cdot 2^{N-1})$.

Since the computational complexity of the original CS method is an exponential order of N, we need to introduce some technique to reduce it for practice (especially, for dealing with a multi-stroke character with large N). The *beam search* acceleration technique or pruning technique has been often used at a cost of global optimality. Hereafter the CS method with beam search is abbreviated as CSBS. By use of beam search we can considerably reduce the time complexity. For more details see [3,4].

2.4 Bipartite Weighted Matching (BWM) [5]

In [5], Hsieh et al. modeled the matching problem of strokes between input pattern and reference pattern as a bipartite weighted graph matching problem. Figure 5 shows an example of bipartite weighted graph for determining the stroke correspondence. The kth input stroke $\boldsymbol{A}_k$ stands for the kth left vertex, whereas the lth reference stroke $\boldsymbol{B}_l$ stands for the lth right vertex. Let stroke distance $\delta(k, l)$ be the weight of edge $(\boldsymbol{A}_k, \boldsymbol{B}_l)$. A matching in a graph is a set $\boldsymbol{M}$ of edges, no two of which share a vertex. If every vertex $\boldsymbol{A}_k \in \boldsymbol{A}$ is incident with an edge of $\boldsymbol{M}$, then the matching is perfect. Under the assumption that the stroke distances are given, the BWM problem is to find an optimal perfect matching such that the sum of the weights (i.e. stroke distances) of matching edges is minimum. Hsieh et al. [5] formulated this minimization problem by the following LP:

$$\text{minimize } \sum_{k=1}^{N} \sum_{l=1}^{N} \delta(k, l) x_{kl}$$

$$\text{subject to } \sum_{k=1}^{N} x_{kl} = 1, \forall l, \sum_{l=1}^{N} x_{kl} = 1, \forall k, x_{kl} \in \{0, 1\}.$$

Note that $x_{kl} = 1$ when $\boldsymbol{A}_k$ is matched with $\boldsymbol{B}_l$.

Table 1. Stroke distance table to the example of SM

Input stroke k	Reference stroke l			
	①	②	③	④
1	61.9	14.2⋆	13.0	86.5
2	60.5	139.3	10.3⋆	86.3
3	87.1	25.1	97.3	36.4⋆
4	158.2⋆	63.5	96.5	42.0

⋆ Mark "⋆" denotes the stroke correspondence to be determined by SM.

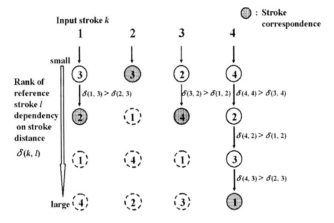

Fig. 6. Finding the correspondence between input strokes and reference strokes by SM ($N = 4$)

They applied the Hungarian method [9,10,11], the well-known primal-dual algorithm, to solve this LP problem. By applying the Hungarian method, the algorithm solves the N strokes correspondence problem in $O(N^3)$ arithmetic operations. For more details see [5].

2.5   Stable Marriage (SM) [6]

We assume that N men and N women have expressed mutual preferences (each man must say exactly how he feels about each of the N women and vice versa). The SM problem is to find a set of N marriages that respects everyone's preferences [12]. A set of marriages is called unstable if two people who are not married both prefer each other to their spouses. Yokota et al. [6] applied the SM to the stroke correspondence problem, where input strokes $\{A_k\}$ and reference strokes $\{B_l\}$ stand for men and women, respectively. A natural way to express the preferences is to have each stroke list in the order of value of stroke distance $\delta(k, l)$. Clearly, these preferences often conflict. By iteratively comparing the values of $\delta(k, l)$ of the preference lists, the process of the stable matching is to remove unstable matchings one at a time, until some stroke finds a spouse stroke which can match the stroke stably. For more details see [6,12].

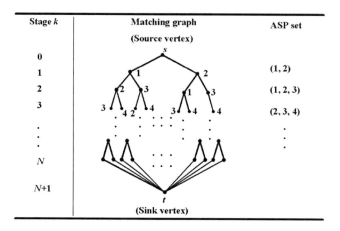

Stage k	Matching graph (Source vertex)	ASP set

Fig. 7. The matching graph characterized by stages

Figure 6 shows an example of SM with $N = 4$. Table 1 gives stroke distance table between input strokes and reference strokes. Figure 6 presents a set of preference lists of input strokes derived from Table 1, and illustrates how the input strokes find their stable spouse reference strokes. For example, when $k = 1$, the reference stroke ③ is selected as the candidate stroke and matched with the input stroke 1 firstly. Then, when $k = 2$, since $\delta(2,3) < \delta(1,3)$, the input stroke 2 will match with the reference stroke ③ and the input stroke 1 has to select the lower order reference stroke ②.

On the basis of the correspondence $l(k)$ determined by the above method, the summation of stroke distances $\delta(k, l(k))$ gives character distance $D(\boldsymbol{A}, \boldsymbol{B})$.

$$D(\boldsymbol{A}, \boldsymbol{B}) = \sum_{k=1}^{N} \delta(k, l(k)).$$

The time complexity of SM is $O(N^2)$.

2.6   Deviation-Expansion Model (DE) [7]

Lin et al. [7] proposed a general concept of stroke correspondence model, called deviation expansion (DE) model, which can deal with arbitrary stroke order deviation. What they reported, however, was almost no more than a "concept". They gave no solution algorithm except for a very limited case, where stroke position deviation is limited to the two directly adjacent positions (to the left, to the right, or no deviation). The correspondence algorithm for this limited case is briefly given below.

As shown in Fig. 7, a noncyclic directed matching graph characterized by stages (which map to the input stroke number k) is constructed by converting the DE model into the graph directly. Each vertex is labeled with reference stroke number l and means that, actually, the stroke at the lth standard stroke

Table 2. Time complexity

Methods	Time complexity
ICD [1] (Individual correspondence decision)	$O(N^2)$
CS [3,4] (Cube search)	$O(N \cdot 2^{N-1})$
CSBS [3] (CS with beam search)	Depends on pruning threshold
BWM [5] (Bipartite weighted matching)	$O(N^3)$
SM [6] (Stable marriage)	$O(N^2)$
DE [7] (Deviation-expansion model)	$O(2^N)$

position is written here instead of the stroke at the kth standard stroke position. In the above limited case, the considered stroke number l within each stage k is constrained by an adjacency stroke position (ASP) set of the kth standard stroke position. Let $MG_{A,B}$ be the matching graph constructed from input pattern A and the DE model of reference pattern B. In $MG_{A,B}$, the source vertex s and the sink vertex t are two dummy vertices, all vertices in stage N are connected to the sink vertex t. Each complete matching path in the graph is defined as the path beginning from the source vertex s to the sink vertex t.

With the $MG_{A,B}$, the best matching can be defined by the character distance function $D(A, B)$ as mentioned above, where stroke distance $\delta(k,l)$ is the cost of each vertex of $MG_{A,B}$. The minimum distance path searching is implemented by DP. Let $P(k, w)$ be the distance cumulative score of the minimum distance path from vertex w in stage k to sink t. $P(k, w)$ is calculated from stage N to stage 0 by the following recurrence equation,

$$P(k, w) = \min[P(k + 1, v) + \delta_w],$$

where δ_w denotes the stroke pair distance determined by the vertex w, and v denotes a vertex in stage $k + 1$. The result of $D(A, B)$ is obtained as $P(0, s)$. The time complexity of DE is $O(2^N)$.

2.7 Computational Complexity

Table 2 summarizes time complexities of the above five methods. We can observe that ICD, SM and BWM have the relative superiority of time complexity. On the other hand, by use of the beam search technique, the time complexity of CS can be considerably reduced. In next section, the experimental result will show that the search speed of CSBS is fast and practical as well.

Table 3. Rates of characters with perfect stroke correspondences (%)

Methods	Test patterns with correct stroke order	Test patterns with incorrect stroke order
DM	100.00	0.00
ICD	68.55	54.02
CS	98.34	95.75
CSBS	98.32	95.53
BWM	98.34	95.75
SM	83.67	73.66
DE	98.62	47.79

3   Comparative Experiment

3.1   Experimental Setup

Toward forensic applications based on stroke order, an comparative recognition experiment was conducted by using the five stroke correspondence methods. We will first observe the accuracy of the stroke correspondence by the methods. We also observe the recognition accuracy by the methods.

A total of 17,983 Chinese character patterns (882 categories, 1-20 strokes) written by 30 persons were used as the test set. Among those patterns, 14,786 patterns were written with correct stroke order and 3,197 patterns were written with incorrect stroke order. Note that we intentionally used the input and reference patterns with the correct number of strokes; that is, stroke number variations by cursive writing were not considered in this experiment. While this limits the variety of actual online character patterns, it will be good for understanding only the effect of stroke order variations.

Each stroke (A_k, B_l) was represented as a sequence of the $x - y$ coordinate feature and the (quantized) directional feature. Consequently, for a stroke A_k comprised of J points, the dimensionality of feature vector for A_k becomes $3J$. The stroke distance $\delta(k, l)$ were calculated by DP-matching and all of the methods used the same $\delta(k, l)$.

3.2   Experimental Results

Table 3 shows the accuracy of stroke correspondences. Specifically, this is the rate of characters with perfect stroke correspondences. The evaluation was done on test patterns with the correct stroke order and test patterns with incorrect stroke order, separately, for finer observation. Note that for emphasizing the importance of stroke correspondence optimization, the results of direct matching method (DM), are also listed in the table. DM establishes stroke correspondence directly by original stroke orders and thus cannot deal with stroke order variations.

Table 4 shows the experimental results showing recognition rates and computation times (on a computer with 1.7GHz CPU) for each of the five methods.

Table 4. Character recognition rates and computation times

Methods	Recognition rate(%)	Computation time per character(ms)
DM	93.38	< 0.1
ICD	96.37	0.4
CS	99.17	553.8
CSBS	99.15	43.5
BWM	99.17	6.4
SM	98.54	2.2
DE	96.59	1212.9

Note that 39ms for calculating local distances $\{\delta(k, l)\}$ were excluded from the computation times in the table because this 39ms were common for all of the methods.

3.3   Discussions

From Table 3, CS (including CSBS) and BWM are of better accuracy performances of stroke correspondence in whether correct stroke order input or incorrect stroke order input. In particular, for the incorrect stroke order test subset, in which the patterns are always accompanied with heavier handwriting distortions, CS (including CSBS) and BWM show remarkable performance superiority than the other methods.

Table 4 shows that all of the mentioned stroke correspondence search methods can give higher recognition accuracy than DM and demonstrates the significance of stroke correspondence search. From Table 4, we observe that CS (including CSBS) and BWM can obtain higher recognition accuracy, and ICD, SM, and BWM can obtain higher recognition speed. Meanwhile, although CSBS is slower than ICD, SM, and BWM, its recognition speed is also fast and practical. However, for DE, since it doesn't use any acceleration technique, its search speed is very slower than the other methods.

For the above methods, it can be summarized that:

- As two optimal stroke correspondence methods, both of CS and BWM can give the same optimal stroke correspondence and obtain the highest recognition accuracy. It may be said that the high accuracy of CS and BWM come from the fact that they are based on their well defined objective functions, and that their correspondence search ranges cover whole stroke order deviations. For CS, the global optimum solution is achieved by DP. And for BWM, the global optimum solution is achieved by Hungarian method.
- For CSBS, the little difference of experimental result between CSBS and CS is just due to the application of beam search acceleration technique in CS.
- For ICD, although it is a very simple and fast method, it can not guarantee an one-to-one stroke correspondence between input pattern and reference pattern to simulate the actual stroke order variation.

– For SM, in each iterative operation, only depending on the ranking of stroke distance in a certain preference list, or the comparison of two stroke distance values in different preference lists, the input stroke decides its matching stroke. Thereby, SM doesn't consider the global optimum problem. Local error of stroke correspondence caused by stroke distances, will influence the stroke correspondence searching of other input strokes.
– Indeed, DE can not give correct stroke correspondence results for those input patterns whose stroke order variation ranges exceed the range permit of model assumption. However, enlarging the permit of stroke order variation range of model assumption means that the DE tree will be expanded and cause increasing the time complexity sharply.

From above results, clearly, for the performance of recognition accuracy, relative superiority of CS and BWM over ICD, SM, and DE are established.

4   Conclusion

In this paper, the stroke order variation is viewed as a novel feature for forensics identification, and the stroke correspondence methods for extracting the stroke order variations are crucial. We have discussed five stroke correspondence search methods — ICD, CS, BWM, SM, and DE. Mainly in regard of recognition accuracy, the five methods have been experimentally compared on a common test set and their performances are analyzed. According to the experimental results in stroke-number-fixed mode, performance superiority of CS and BWM over ICD, SM, and DE are established.

Our future studies will focus on the following points. First, using a certain stroke correspondence method (especially CS and BWM), we must confirm the stability of the stroke order within each writer quantitatively and qualitatively through a large-scale experiment. This is a very important study for realizing forensics based on stroke order. Second, we should treat "stroke-number-free" condition, where some strokes are connected into one stroke by cursive writing. Since the stroke connection will also represent writer's individuality as well as stroke order, we must extend the stroke correspondence methods for dealing with connected strokes. Note that CS has already been extended to deal with connected stroke [3,13].

References

1. Odaka, K., Wakahara, T., Masuda, I.: Stroke Order Free On-line Handwritten Character Recognition Algorithm. IEICE Trans. Inf. & Syst. J65-D(6), 679–686 (1982) (in Japanese)
2. Wakahara, T., Murase, H., Odaka, K.: On-Line Handwriting Recognition. Proc. IEEE 80(7), 1181–1194 (1992)
3. Sakoe, H., Shin, J.: A Stroke Order Search Algorithm for Online Character Recognition. Research Reports on Information Science and Electrical Engineering of Kyushu University 2(1), 99–104 (1997) (in Japanese)

4. Cai, W., Uchida, S., Sakoe, H.: An Efficient Radical-Based Algorithm for Stroke-Order-Free Online Kanji Character Recognition. In: Proc. ICPR, vol. 2, pp. 986–989 (2006)
5. Hsieh, A.J., Fan, K.C., Fan, T.I.: Bipartite Weighted Matching for On-line Handwritten Chinese Character Recognition. Pattern Recognition 28(2), 143–151 (1995)
6. Yokota, T., et al.: An On-line Cuneiform Modeled Handwritten Japanese Character Recognition Method Free from Both the Number and Order of Character Strokes. IPSJ Journal 44(3), 980–990 (2003) (in Japanese)
7. Lin, C.K., Fan, K.C., Lee, F.T.P.: On-line Recognition by Deviation-expansion Model and Dynamic Programming Matching. Pattern Recognition 26(2), 259–268 (1993)
8. Sakoe, H., Chiba, S.: Dynamic Programming Algorithm Optimization for Spoken Word Recognition. IEEE Trans. Acoust., Speech, Signal Processing ASSP-26(1), 43–49 (1978)
9. Kuhn, H.W.: The Hungarian Method for the Assignment Problem. Naval Research Logistics Quarterly 2, 83–97 (1955)
10. Munkres, J.: Algorithms for the Assignment and Transportation Problems. J. Soc. Indust. Appl. Math. 5(1), 32–38 (1957)
11. Papadimitriou, C.H., Steiglitz, K.: Combinatorial Optimization: Algorithms and Complexity. Prentice-Hall, Englewood Cliffs (1982)
12. Sedgewick, R.: Algorithms, 2nd edn. Addison-Wesley, Reading (1988)
13. Shin, J., Sakoe, H.: Stroke Correspondence Search Method for Stroke-Order and Stroke-Number Free On-Line Character Recognition — Multilayer Cube Search —. IEICE Trans. Inf. & Syst. J82-D-II(2), 230–239 (1999) (in Japanese)

A Novel Seal Imprint Verification Method Based on Analysis of Difference Images and Symbolic Representation

Xiaoyang Wang and Youbin Chen

Room 404F, Building F, Graduate School at Shenzhen, Tsinghua University,
518055 Shenzhen, P.R.China
xiaoyang.wangs@gmail.com, chenyb@sz.tsinghua.edu.cn

Abstract. This paper proposes a novel seal imprint verification method with difference image based statistical feature extraction and symbolic representation based classification. After several image processing procedures including seal imprint extraction and seal registration with the model seal imprint, the statistical feature was extracted from difference images for the pattern classification system of seal verification. Symbolic representation method which requires only genuine samples in the learning phase was used to classify genuine and fake seal imprints. We built up a seal imprint image database for training the seal verification algorithms and testing the proposed verification system. Experiments showed that the symbolic representation method was superior to traditional SVM classifier in this task. Experiments also showed that our statistical feature was very powerful for seal verification application.

Keywords: Seal imprint verification, Analysis of difference images, Pattern classification, Symbolic representation, Seal imprint image database.

1 Introduction

In oriental countries such as China, Korea and Japan, seals instead of signatures are widely used for identifying a person, a social group or the government in different kinds of documents, e.g. bank checks, invoices, business letters, etc. Because of the high frequency of seals in daily-life documents, a lot of seal imprints have to be verified manually every day. However, manual seal verification has obvious drawbacks: (1) the verification speed is slow; (2) the accuracy is not stable. Therefore, automatic seal imprint verification is very desirable in real-life application such as the fraud detection on Chinese bank checks.

An automatic seal imprint verification system usually includes three procedures: (1) seal imprint extraction from document images; (2) seal registration between sample seal (SS) and model seal (MS); (3) seal verification to identify true or fake seals. In the seal extraction procedure, Ueda and Matsuo [1] used two histogram thresholds in HSV color space to segment seal imprint from document images. In the seal registration procedure, W. Shuang and L. Tiegen [2] proposed a two-stage registration method including rough and precise registration. In the final seal verification procedure, verification based on the difference images between SS and MS were used

H. Sako, K. Franke, and S. Saitoh (Eds.): IWCF 2010, LNCS 6540, pp. 56–67, 2011.
© Springer-Verlag Berlin Heidelberg 2011

by Q. Hu, etc. [3] and W. Gao, etc. [4]. Many other seal verification oriented method were brought out [5~11] but there still is a distance for practical use.

In this work, we propose a novel approach for seal verification in which features are extracted from difference images and seals are verified with the classifier called as symbolic data classification. This method is different and efficient compared to the previous methods [1~11]. In the feature selection stage of seal verification, our verification feature has been proved to be very effective for seal imprint verification application by experiments. And in the classifier design stage, symbolic data analysis has been extensively studied in [12,13] and proved that the clustering approaches based on symbolic data outperform conventional clustering techniques. Guru and Prakash [14] brought up the symbolic representation method for signature verification. To the best of our knowledge, no work has been published in the literature which uses symbolic representation for seal verification. We applied this method to seal verification field and received promising results.

The remainder of this paper is organized as follows: Section 2 introduces the procedure to extract the statistical feature we proposed for seal verification. Section 3 discusses the symbolic representation method for seal verification. In Section 4, the seal verification experiments along with results are presented. Finally, Section 5 follows with conclusions.

2   Feature Extraction for Seal Verification

In the feature extraction step of seal imprint verification in document images, the major processing approaches are related to image processing and machine vision fields. Fig. 1 gives an illustration of a scanned image which includes several seal imprints stamped on a Chinese bank check. Fig. 2 provides a genuine seal imprint and three types of forgeries which were all binarized. Type G Forgery means forging the seal by guessing without seeing the genuine seal; Type W Forgery means forging the seal by watching and simulating the genuine seal during the machine seal design procedure; and Type S Forgery means forging the seal by scanning the genuine seal imprint into the computer and generating the forged seal from this scanned real seal template. Sometimes we call the Type S forged seal as clone seal.

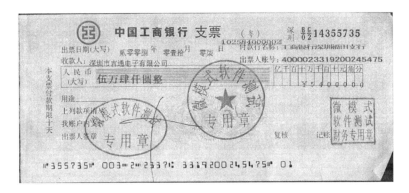

Fig. 1. Seal imprints on a bank check

Before the feature extraction step for the seal verification procedure, two pre-processing procedures are required: (1) seal extraction procedure that provides extracted seal imprints for the following procedures; (2) seal registration procedure that aligns the SS with MS geometrically with best correspondence between them. After the feature extraction step, classification into the "Genuine" or "Fake" category is required for a practical seal verification system. Thus, the workflow of a seal verification system is shown in Fig. 3.

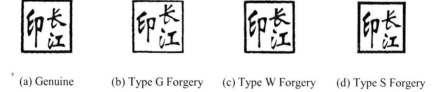

    (a) Genuine   (b) Type G Forgery   (c) Type W Forgery   (d) Type S Forgery

Fig. 2. (a) A genuine seal imprint. (b)(c)(d) Three types of forgeries.

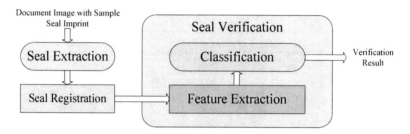

Fig. 3. The workflow of our seal verification system

2.1 Pre-processing for Feature Extraction

Pre-processing includes seal extraction and seal registration procedures. In the seal extraction, RGB color model was used to find the seal region of interest (ROI), and HSI color model was used for extraction [15]. Fig. 4 shows our seal extraction steps.

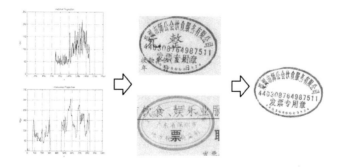

Fig. 4. Find the seal ROI and seal extraction

We proposed a seal registration method based on shape and layout characteristics [16]. All extracted seal imprints are rotated to the horizontal direction with our method. Then, best correspondence aimed translation transform was carried out between the SS and MS.

Difference images between SS and MS can be calculated after pre-processing including seal extraction and seal registration procedures.

2.2 Statistical Feature Extraction from Difference Images

We use the difference images to detect the distinction between MS and SS, and then extract statistical feature from the difference images as the fingerprint to tell whether the distinction comes from genuine SS or forgery SS. After extraction and registration steps, let's define the binary seal images of SS and MS respectively as $f(x,y) \in \{0,1\}$ and $g(x,y) \in \{0,1\}$, where "1" stands for foreground and "0" stands for background. Thus, the total difference image (TDF) can be defined using an XOR operation:

$$d(x,y) = f(x,y) \oplus g(x,y) \qquad (1)$$

In Formula (1), "$\oplus$" stands for the XOR operation, and $d(x,y)$ is the TDF to be calculated. Take the four seal images in Fig. 2 (a), (b), (c) and (d) as SS. Their TDFs with the MS are respectively shown in Fig. 5 (a), (b), (c) and (d).

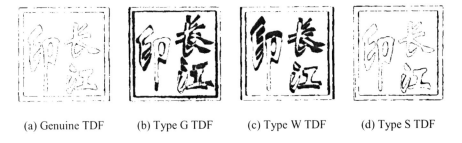

(a) Genuine TDF   (b) Type G TDF   (c) Type W TDF   (d) Type S TDF

Fig. 5. TDFs when taking genuine and three types of forgery seal imprints as the SS

To describe the distinct between the SS and MS more precisely, we further adopted the concepts of positive difference image (PDF) and negative difference image (NDF). Let the PDF and NDF be $d^+(x,y)$ and $d^-(x,y)$ respectively. Their definitions are as follows:

$$d^+(x,y) = \begin{cases} 1 & f(x,y)=1, g(x,y)=0 \\ 0 & \text{else} \end{cases} \qquad (2)$$

$$d^-(x,y) = \begin{cases} 1 & f(x,y)=0, g(x,y)=1 \\ 0 & \text{else} \end{cases} \qquad (3)$$

Where PDF stands for the pixels that exist in SS but do not exist in MS, and NDF is just the opposite. Fig. 6 shows the PDF and NDF of a genuine SS and a forgery SS with the MS respectively.

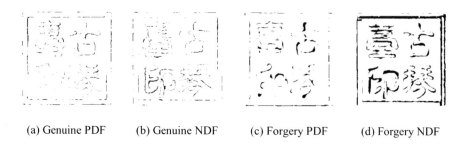

(a) Genuine PDF   (b) Genuine NDF   (c) Forgery PDF   (d) Forgery NDF

Fig. 6. PDFs and NDFs when taking genuine and three types of forgery seal imprints as the SS

The difference image between two genuine seal imprints consists of only shape patterns like dots and lines, while the difference image between the fake and genuine seal imprints consists of a lot of block shaped patterns. In this paper, we propose a novel feature to reflect the distribution rate of different shape patterns.

This statistical feature based on difference images can be extracted in following steps. Set the difference image (TDF, PDF or NDF) to be Δ. $ST()$ stands for a function that extracts the statistical feature. Thus, The extracted feature for a single difference image can be written as: $X = ST(\Delta)$.

We divide the difference image Δ into $M \times N$ equally-sized rectangle cells. Set the cell height and width to be H and W respectively. For the rectangle cell p ($p=1,2,\ldots, M \times N$), the number for pixels whose value are "1" is $Cnt(p)$. Define the local difference rate $R(p)$ as:

$$R(p) = \frac{Cnt(p)}{W \cdot H} \tag{4}$$

Fig. 7 illustrates the statistical process in cells of difference images.

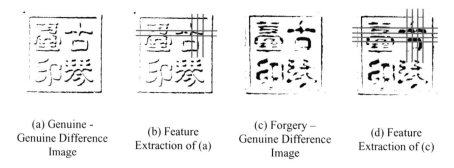

(a) Genuine - Genuine Difference Image

(b) Feature Extraction of (a)

(c) Forgery – Genuine Difference Image

(d) Feature Extraction of (c)

Fig. 7. Illustrations of statistical feature extraction in difference images

The range in which that $R(p)$ value would possibly distribute in can be quantized into D equal-scale sectors. Set the number of $R(p)$ values that locate in sector q ($q=1,2,..., D$) is $Num(q)$. Then, the normalized histogram statistics can reflect the number distribution of shape patterns in difference images. We define the normalize histogram as:

$$Hist(q) = \frac{Num(q)}{M \cdot N} \qquad (5)$$

Now, the function $X = ST(\Delta)$ for feature extraction can be written as (6).

$$X = [Hist(1), Hist(2), ..., Hist(D)]^{T} \qquad (6)$$

In the above feature extraction function, the difference image Δ can be TDF, PDF or NDF between the SS and MS. In our experiment, we combined the features extracted from both PDF and NDF. The dimension of our feature vector is $2D$.

For each SS, the above statistical feature can be extracted from the chosen difference images between that SS and the MS stored in the database. For future convenience, we set the feature vector extracted from the SS-MS difference images to be F, and set the feature dimension to be m.

3   Classification for Seal Verification

For the high performance and robustness of a seal verification system, classification methods based on learning were usually adopted. As to traditional classification methods like neural networks or SVM, two different pattern classes, C_1 and C_2, are needed for the learning task. C_1 represents the genuine seal imprint set and C_2 represents the forged seal imprint set.

On the other hand, what is unique for the seal verification problem is that: the simulated forgeries cannot be used as C_2 in the learning phase. The reasons are that: (1) simulated forgeries are not obtainable in the learning phase; (2) the using of those forgeries in learning phase can decrease the discrimination ability for new stimulated forgeries that may appear in the future,i.e. poor generalization capability. Thus, in the learning phase for the traditional classifiers like the ones mentioned above, only random forgeries that are represented by other genuine samples of different seals can be used as C_2.

The symbolic representation method provides a different solution for seal verification. There is no C_2 set in the learning phase in symbolic representation based classification. In our experiments, the symbolic representation method performs better than the SVM classifier when random forgeries were taken as C_2 set in the SVM learning phase. The experiment results are listed in Section 4.

3.1   Symbolic Representation Based Classification

In the application of seal verification, the basic principles of symbolic representation based classification are as follows [14]:

For a genuine seal S, its n genuine training samples $[S_1, S_2, ..., S_i, ..., S_n]$ are taken as SS. Extract the statistical features from the difference images between the above SSs and the MS and let the feature vectors to be $[F_1, F_2, ..., F_i, ... F_n]$ respectively.

Let $F_i=[f_{i1},f_{i2},\ldots,f_{ik},\ldots,f_{im}]$ to be the m dims feature for sample S_i. Then, the average value of the kth feature for all n genuine training samples is:

$$\mu_k = \frac{1}{n}\sum_{i=1}^{n} f_{ik} \qquad (7)$$

The standard deviation of the kth feature for all training samples is:

$$\sigma_k = \left[\frac{1}{n}\sum_{i=1}^{n}(f_{ik}-\mu_k)^2\right]^{1/2} \qquad (8)$$

Then, the interval-valued feature $[f_k^-,f_k^+]$ can be used to capture the inner variations in each kth feature in all m dims. Their definitions are as follows:

$$f_k^- = \mu_k - \alpha\sigma_k \quad f_k^+ = \mu_k + \alpha\sigma_k \qquad (9)$$

Where, α is the first control scalar for symbolic representation method.

Then, the symbolic vector for the genuine seal S is:

$$RF_S = \{[f_1^-,f_1^+][f_2^-,f_2^+],\ldots,[f_k^-,f_k^+]\ldots,[f_m^-,f_m^+]\} \qquad (10)$$

The above symbolic vector is stored in the system knowledge base as a verification representative of the seal S.

The symbolic representation method introduces an acceptance count A_c to evaluate the number of features of a test seal imprint that fall inside the corresponding interval of the symbolic vector described in (10). Let the feature vector of a test sample S_T is $F_T=[f_{T1},f_{T2},\ldots,f_{Tk},\ldots,f_{Tm}]$. The A_c is defined using a "voting strategy" as follows:

$$A_c(F_T,RF_S) = \sum_{k=1}^{m} C(f_{Tk},[f_k^-,f_k^+]) \qquad (11)$$

Where

$$C(f_{Tk},[f_k^-,f_k^+]) = \begin{cases} 1 & if\,(f_k^- \le f_{Tk} \le f_k^+), \\ 0 & otherwise. \end{cases} \qquad (12)$$

An acceptance count threshold T can be used to discriminate fake seals from genuine ones with the acceptance count defined in (11). It means that:

$$\begin{cases} if\,(A_c(F_T,RF_S)>T) & S_T \rightarrow Genuine \\ else & S_T \rightarrow Forgery \end{cases} \qquad (13)$$

3.2   Seal-Dependent Acceptance Count Threshold Design

Similar to the writer-dependent threshold for signature verification in [14], we use a seal-dependent acceptance count threshold to discriminate the fake seal imprints from the genuine ones. Learning strategy is still required to define this threshold.

From the n genuine training samples in Section 3.1, we take n_1 samples to define this threshold. Let the n_1 samples to be $[S_1, S_2, \ldots, S_j, \ldots, S_{n_1}]$. Calculate the acceptance count A_{cj} ($j=1,2,\ldots,n_1$) for the n_1 samples respectively according to (11). The average acceptance count for the n_1 samples are:

$$A_{vg} = \sum_{j=1}^{n_1} A_{cj} / n_1 \tag{14}$$

Then, the seal-dependent acceptance count threshold can be defined as:

$$T = \beta \cdot A_{vg} \tag{15}$$

Where, β is the second control scalar for symbolic representation method.

The acceptance count threshold calculated by (15) is stored in the knowledge base together with the symbolic vector calculated by (10) as the verification knowledge for seal S with the symbolic representation method.

4 Experiments

Firstly, we introduce our job for building up the seal verification data sets from self-collected seals that include both genuine seals and forgeries. Then, verification results in different control scalars are given for genuine seal imprints and different types of forgeries respectively. False acceptance rate (FAR) and false rejection rate (FRR) were used to evaluate the system performance [1]. The error trade-off curves are given according to the variations of control scalars. Finally, a comparison between the SVM with random forgery training samples and the symbolic representation method is given based on the proposed statistical feature in difference images.

4.1 The Data Set

Our seal verification data set includes totally 30 genuine seals, in which 15 seals are rectangle shaped, 10 seals are circle shaped and 5 seals are ellipse shaped. For each genuine seal, four simulated fake seals were collected respectively. Among the four fake seals for each genuine seal, one is Type G Forgery, another two are Type W Forgeries from two different manufacturers, and the rest one is Type S Forgery.

We collected totally 3249 seal imprints from the above 150 seals. Among all the seal imprints, 1344 seal imprints are genuine and the rest 1905 seal imprints are forgery ones. We made up two sets from the above seal imprints database.

1. L1 Set: This set consists of all the rectangle shaped seal imprints in the above seal imprints database.
2. L2 Set: This set consists of all shaped seal imprints in the above seal imprints database.

The two sets were used mainly for the consideration of seal registration procedure. It is relatively easier for rectangle shaped seal imprints to reach high quality registration. Thus, building up the L1 and L2 sets can help evaluate the registration accuracy for elliptical and circular seal imprints, which would better prove the performance of the whole seal verification system.

Both L1 and L2 sets are split into training and test sets. The detailed sample number in each subsets of the L1 and L2 sets are listed in Table 1 and Table 2 respectively.

Table 1. Detailed sample number in each subsets of L1 Set

L1 Set	Training	Test				
Type	Genuine	Genuine	Forgery			
			Type G	Type W	Type S	Total
Number	264	354	306	417	240	963

Table 2. Detailed sample number in each subsets of L2 Set

L2 Set	Training	Test				
Type	Genuine	Genuine	Forgery			
			Type G	Type W	Type S	Total
Number	552	792	594	831	480	1905

In the L1 and L2 sets, we selected the training and test genuine samples randomly from the seal imprints database. All forgery samples were taken as test samples.

4.2 Experiments on Control Scalars

Here, we tested the FARs and FRRs of the system respectively when the two control scalars α and β in symbolic representation method took different values. Several typical experiment results are listed in Table 3.

Table 3. Typical experiment results with different control scalars

Data Set	α	β	G-FAR[*]	W-FAR[*]	S-FAR[*]	FAR	FRR
L1	3.2	0.7	0%	0%	21.25%	5.30%	5.93%
L1	1.6	0.8	0%	0%	0%	0%	18.36%
L1	3.3	0.8	0%	0%	9.58%	2.39%	9.32%
L2	2.4	0.6	0%	0%	20.00%	5.35%	5.43%
L2	3.6	0.8	0%	1.08%	8.96%	2.73%	8.59%
L2	2.6	0.9	0%	0%	0%	0%	20.08%

[*]. G-FAR, W-FAR and S-FAR are the FARs of Type G, Type W, Type S forgeries respectively.

The experiments showed that our method can discriminate Type G and Type W forgeries. And the verification error occurred mainly in the task of discriminating Type S forgeries from the genuine seal imprints. Thus, we provide the plots of Type S Forgery FAR, total sample FAR and FRR against control scalars in Fig. 8 to show the detailed experiment results.

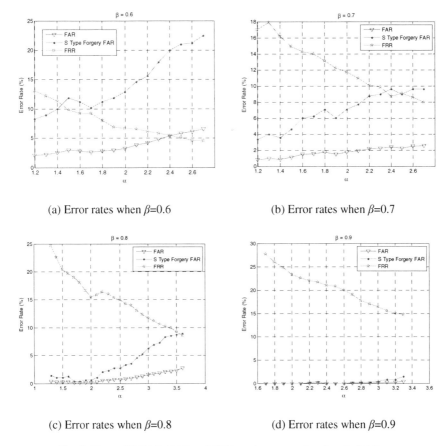

(a) Error rates when β=0.6   (b) Error rates when β=0.7

(c) Error rates when β=0.8   (d) Error rates when β=0.9

Fig. 8. Plots of S-FAR, FAR and FRR against control scalars in L2 Set

The error trade-off curves of Type S Forgery FAR against FRR, and total sample FAR against FRR are shown in Fig. 9. Usually, the equal error rate (EER) which means FRR equals FAR is used to evaluate the system performance. Here, we used the average error rate (AER) of FAR and FRR when the distance between the FAR and FRR values is minimal to be an evaluation. Define that minimal distance AER between total sample FAR and FRR to be AER_1, and the minimal distance between Type S Forgery FAR and FRR to be AER_2.

We adopted another practical evaluation: the FRR value when the total sample FAR reached zero. Define this evaluation to be FRR_0. The FRR0, AER1 and AER2 values with L1 and L2 sets are listed in Table 4.

Table 4. System Evaluations with L1 and L2 Sets

Data Set	FRR_0	AER_1	AER_2
L1 Set	18.36%	5.61%	9.45%
L2 Set	20.08%	5.39%	8.77%

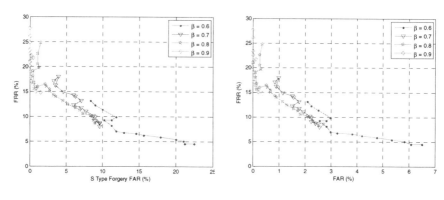

(a) Error trade-off curve of S-FAR against FRR

(b) Error trade-off curve of total sample FAR against FRR

Fig. 9. Error trade-off curves in L2 Set

4.3 Performance Comparison

Here, we give out a comparison between the proposed system using symbolic representation with the system using SVM classification. In this comparison, SVM classifier was trained using random forgeries which were actually genuine training samples for other seals. Our proposed statistical feature extracted from difference images was used for both classification methods. When extracting the feature, pre-processing procedures including seal extraction and seal registration were the same.

The control scalars of symbolic representation (SR) methods were set as: $\alpha=3.3$, $\beta=0.8$. The L1 Seal Verification Set was used for this comparison. The results are listed in Table 5.

Table 5. Comparison between SVM and SR($\alpha=3.3$, $\beta=0.8$) in L1 Set

Classifier	G-FAR	W-FAR	S-FAR	FAR	FRR
SVM	0.65%	10.55%	61.25%	20.04%	1.70%
SR	0%	0%	9.58%	2.39%	9.32%

The FRR was low in the system when choosing SVM classification. While, the SVM based system was weaker in discriminating fake seals. For practical use, the symbolic representation method is superior for seal verification applications.

5 Conclusions

In this paper, we attempted to use difference image based statistical feature and symbolic representation based classification for seal imprint verification applications. After pre-processing procedures including seal extraction and seal registration, the total, positive and negative difference images were calculated. We extracted novel statistical feature that can reflect the distribution rate of different shape patterns from the above difference images. The symbolic representation method was adopted in our proposed method for classification.

We built up a seal imprint image database for training the seal verification algorithms and testing the proposed verification system. Our experiments showed that the symbolic representation method was superior to traditional SVM classifier in this task. And tests also showed that our statistical feature was very powerful for seal verification application.

References

1. Ueda, K., Matsuo, K.: Automatic seal imprint verification system for bank check processing. In: Proc. 3rd Int. Conf. Inf. Tech. & Applications, vol. 1, pp. 768–771 (2005)
2. Wang, S., Liu, T.: Research on registration algorithm for check seal verification. In: Proc. SPIE, Vol. 6833, 68330Y (2007)
3. Hu, Q., Yang, J., Zhang, Q., Liu, K., Shen, X.: An automatic seal imprint verification approach. Pattern Recognition 28(8), 1251–1266 (1995)
4. Gao, W., Dong, S., Chen, X.: A System for Automatic Chinese Seal Imprint Verification. In: ICDAR 1995, vol. 2, pp. 660–664 (1995)
5. Matsuura, T., Yamazaki, K.: Seal imprint verification with rotation invariance. In: The 2004 IEEE Asia-Pacific Conference on Circuits and Systems, pp. 597–600 (2004)
6. Ueda, K.: Automatic seal imprint verification system with imprint quality assessment function and its performance evaluation. IEICE Trans. Inf. & Syst. E77-D(8), 885–894 (1994)
7. Horiuchi, T.: Automatic seal verification by evaluating positive cost. In: Proc. 6th Int. Conf. Document Analysis and Recognition, pp. 572–576 (2001)
8. Fan, T.J., Tsai, W.H.: Automatic Chinese seal identification. Comput. Vision Graphics & Image Process. 25(33), 311–330 (1984)
9. Lee, S., Kim, J.H.: Unconstrained seal imprint verification using attributed stroke graph matching. Pattern Recognition 22(6), 653–664 (1989)
10. Chen, Y.S.: Automatic identification for a Chinese seal image. Pattern Recognition 29(11), 1807–1820 (1996)
11. Ueda, K., Mutoh, T., Matsuo, K.: Automatic verification system for seal imprints on Japanese bankchecks. In: ICPR 1998, vol. 1, pp. 629–632 (1998)
12. Gowda, K.C., Diay, E.: Symbolic Clustering Using New Dissimilarity Measure. Pattern Recognition 24, 567–578 (1991)
13. Guru, D.S., Bapu, K., Nagabhushan, P.: Multivalued Type Proximity Measure and Concept of Mutual Similarity Value Useful for Clustering Symbolic Patterns. Pattern Recognition Letters 15, 769–790 (2000)
14. Guru, D., Prakash, H.: Online Signature Verification and Recognition: An Approach Based on Symbolic Representation. IEEE Trans on PAMI 31(6) (2009)
15. Wang, X., Chen, Y.: Research on Seal Extraction, Registration and Verification Methods in Document Images. M.S. Dissertation, Tsinghua University (2010)
16. Wang, X., Chen, Y.: Seal Image Registration Based on Shape and Layout Characteristics. In: Proceedings of the 2nd International Congress on Image and Signal Processing, vol. 7, pp. 3440–3444 (2009)

Extraction of 3D Shape of a Tooth from Dental CT Images with Region Growing Method

Ryuichi Yanagisawa and Shinichiro Omachi

Graduate School of Engineering, Tohoku University, Japan
ryuichi@aso.ecei.tohoku.ac.jp, machi@ecei.tohoku.ac.jp

Abstract. Dental information is useful for personal identification. In this paper, a method for extracting three-dimensional shape of a tooth automatically from dental CT images is proposed. In the previous method, one of the main issue is the mis-extraction of the adjacent region caused by the similarity of feature between a tooth and its adjacent teeth or the surrounding alveolar bone. It is important to extract an accurate shape of the target tooth as an independent part from the adjacent region. In the proposed method, after denoising, the target tooth is segmented to parts such as a shaft of a tooth or a dental enamel by the mean shift clustering. Then, some segments in the certain tooth is extracted as a certain region by the region growing method. Finally, the contour of the tooth is specified by applying the active contour method, and the shape of the tooth is extracted.

Keywords: tooth shape, dental CT image, region extraction, region growing.

1   Introduction

Dental information is useful for personal identification. For example, Jain and Chen proposed a method for human identification with contours of teeth [4]. In this paper, we focus on the precise extraction of teeth and propose a method for extracting three-dimensional shape of a tooth automatically from dental CT (Computer Tomography) images is proposed. The general structure of a tooth is shown in Fig. 1. The portion buried with periodontal tissues such as gum and alveolar bone is called a root, and the portion which can be viewed is called a crown. As a method for extracting tooth shape from images, Su et al. proposed a method for extracting the crowns from a photographed mouth image [8]. However, since we focus on extracting three-dimensional whole tooth structure, we use dental CT images instead of photographed images. Fig. 2 displays dental CT images viewed from three directions.

As a previous method for extracting dental three-dimensional structure from CT images, a method that uses the active contour model had been proposed [6]. However, in this method, it is difficult to extract the ends of the root and the crown accurately. A result of shape reconstruction by the previous method is shown in Fig. 3(a), while Fig. 3(b) is a manually reconstructed one. Comparing

H. Sako, K. Franke, and S. Saitoh (Eds.): IWCF 2010, LNCS 6540, pp. 68–77, 2011.
© Springer-Verlag Berlin Heidelberg 2011

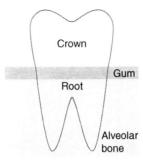

Fig. 1. Structure of a tooth

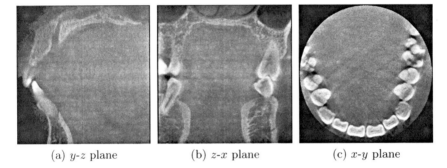

(a) y-z plane   (b) z-x plane   (c) x-y plane

Fig. 2. CT images of teeth from three directions

these images, it is obvious that the end of the root cannot be reconstructed correctly.

The proposed method is based on the region growing method [7,10]. Considering the structural information of a tooth, precise extraction of the root part and crown part is realized. In the proposed method, after denoising, the target tooth is segmented to parts such as a shaft of a tooth or a dental enamel by the mean shift clustering [1,2]. Then, some segments in the tooth are extracted as regions by the region growing method. Finally, a tooth contour is specified by applying the active contour method [5], and the shape of the tooth is extracted. Experimental results show the effectiveness of the proposed method.

2   Proposed Method

The proposed method consists of five steps.

- Contrast enhancement by the slice energy
- Smoothing by the bilateral filter
- Region division by the mean shift method
- Region extraction by the region growing method
- Segmentation of tooth region by the active contour model

Details of these steps are explained in the following subsections.

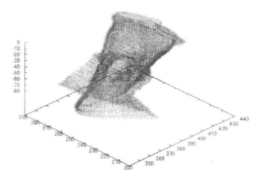

(a) Previous method [6]

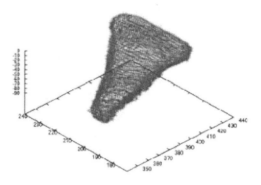

(b) Manually reconstructed

Fig. 3. Result of tooth reconstruction by the previous method

2.1 Contrast Enhancement

First, the contrast is enhanced by normalizing the brightness values based on the slice energy (SE) [3]. The slice energy is the summation of brightness values of each slice on the x-y plane defined by Eq.(1).

$$SE = \sum_{(x,y,z)\in P_z} I(x, y, z). \tag{1}$$

where $I(x, y, z)$ is the brightness value of the voxel on the coordinate (x, y, z), and P_z is the plane perpendicular to z-axis of which z-coordinate is z. Dispersion of the distribution of brightness values in a tissue is reduced by normalizing the slice energy of every slice to be the same value.

In addition, the brightness value distribution of a tooth region is emphasized by Eq.(2).

$$\hat{I}_i = \begin{cases} 0 & (I_i < I_a) \\ \dfrac{255}{255 - I_a}(I_i - I_a) & (I_i > I_a) \end{cases}, \tag{2}$$

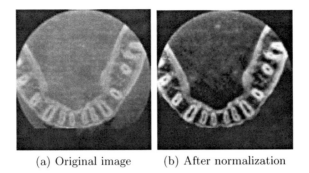

(a) Original image   (b) After normalization

Fig. 4. Normalization by the slice energy and contrast enhancement

where I_i and $\hat{I}_i$ are the brightness values before and after the adjustment, and I_a is a threshold.

2.2   Smoothing

When CT images are taken by a CT scanner, noises particular for CT images are added. To clean up these noises, the proposed method introduces the smoothing filter. In the proposed method, the bilateral filter [9] that is one of the edge-preserving smoothing filters is introduced for smoothing. This filter achieves strong smoothing between two voxels on the condition that the distance of there voxels is short or these voxels have similar brightness values. Thus it is possible to eliminate the noise with preserving difference of important characteristics between the target region and surrounding tissues. The bilateral filter is defined as:

$$\hat{I}_i = \frac{\sum_j w(i,j) I_j}{\sum_j w(i,j)}, \tag{3}$$

where

$$w(i,j) = w_x(x_i, x_j) w_d(I_i, I_j),$$

$$w_x(x_i, x_j) = \frac{1}{\sqrt{2\pi}\sigma_x} \exp\left(-\frac{\|x_i - x_j\|^2}{2\sigma_x^2}\right),$$

$$w_d(I_i, I_j) = \frac{1}{\sqrt{2\pi}\sigma_d} \exp\left(-\frac{\|I_i - I_j\|^2}{2\sigma_d^2}\right).$$

In these equations, i is the voxel that is the target of smoothing, j is one of the neighboring voxels, I and $\hat{I}$ are the brightness values before and after smoothing, x is the coordinate of the voxel, and σ_x and σ_d are the variances of Gaussian function used on the distance-based and brightness-based smoothing. By introducing this smoothing method, the noise reduction and preserving the edge information are achieved simultaneously.

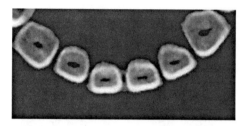

Fig. 5. Smoothing by the bilateral filter

Fig. 5 displays an image smoothed by the bilateral filter. The figure shows that an image without noise is obtained and edge information between teeth region and background is well preserved, and the bilateral filter is quite helpful for preprocessing of region extraction.

2.3 Clustering

To unify multiple voxels into the same region, clustering is carried out. In the proposed method, the mean shift method [1] is used. Given d-dimensional data points $\{x_1, ..., x_n\}$, the data density of point x can be approximated by Eq.(4) and the mean shift vector is given by Eq.(5).

$$\hat{f}(x) = \frac{1}{nh^d} \sum_{i=1}^{n} k(\|\frac{x - x_i}{h}\|^2) \tag{4}$$

$$m(x) = \frac{\sum_{i=1}^{n} x_i g(\|\frac{x - x_i}{h}\|^2)}{\sum_{i=1}^{n} g(\|\frac{x - x_i}{h}\|^2)} - x \tag{5}$$

where $k(x)$ is a function that is called kernel profile and h is the kernel width. In this study, $k(x) = \exp(-\frac{1}{2}x)$ is used. In Eq.(5), $g(x) = -k'(x)$. Here, $k'(x)$ is the differential of $k(x)$. Fig. 6 displays the result of clustering by the mean shift method.

2.4 Region Growing

Considering the characteristics of the structure of a tooth, the region growing method [7,10] is applied to the images after the clustering by the mean shift method. Fig.7 shows a simple overview of the region growing method. This method extracts some regions with the same characteristic as one connected region, by setting a seed point on the target structure and aggregating the neighboring regions under specific constraints. The target of extraction is the entire structure of a tooth including dental pulp, dentine and enamel, and it is to be extracted by setting a seed point on dental pulp and aggregating the surface of enamel. Fig.8 shows an example of the detected tooth region by the region growing method.

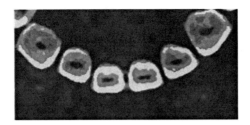

Fig. 6. Clustering by the mean shift method

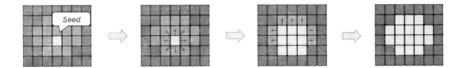

Fig. 7. Flow of the region growing

2.5   Active Contour Method

The active contour method [5] is applied to the region extracted by the region growing method. Given some control points for an initial contour, a closed curve which connects the control points is created, and an evaluation function is defined to that closed curve. A suitable contour can be obtained by changing the position of the control points and the form of the closed curve to maximize or minimize the value of the function. This function is given by Eq.(6).

$$E = E_{int}(\boldsymbol{v}) + E_{ext}(\boldsymbol{v}), \tag{6}$$

where

$$E_{int}(\boldsymbol{v}) = \int_0^1 (\alpha(s)|\boldsymbol{v}_s(s)|^2 + \beta(s)|\boldsymbol{v}_{ss}(s)|^2)ds,$$

$$E_{ext}(\boldsymbol{v}) = \int_0^1 P(\boldsymbol{v}(s))ds,$$

$$P(\boldsymbol{v}(s)) = \gamma I(\boldsymbol{v}(s)),$$

Fig. 8. Object extraction by the region growing method

Fig. 9. Segmentation by the active contour method

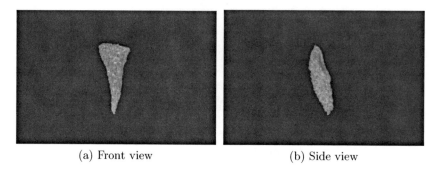

(a) Front view   (b) Side view

Fig. 10. Result

and $I(\boldsymbol{v}(s))$ is the brightness value of a voxel. Fig. 9 shows the result of segmentation of the object region from the result of the region growing method.

3   Experiment

In order to show the effectiveness of the proposed method, an experiment was carried out. The target was a lower left central incisor. We regard the portion above the seed point as the crown and the portion below the seed point as the root. Different process and parameters were used for each portion since the characteristics of these portions are quite different. The parameters used in each process are shown in Tables 1 and 2. The seed point was given manually.

Fig. 10 displays the three-dimensional structure of the tooth obtained by the proposal method. The figure shows that an appropriate reconstruction was achieved by the the proposed method by suppressing incorrect extractions of surrounding regions. Especially the root berried in the alveolar bone was clearly extracted where the previous method failed. Figs. 11 and 12 show the detailed extraction results of the region of the crown and the root that are difficult to extract by the previous method. Fig. 11 shows a slice of the crown. Since the target tooth and the adjacent tooth touch in this region, it is difficult to extract only the target region correctly. On the other hand, an appropriate region was detected by the active contour. Fig. 12 shows a slice of the root. A good result was obtained by suppressing the extension to the alveolar bone.

Table 1. Parameters for extracting crown

Process	parameter	value
Normalization	Base SE	180000
	I_a	100
Smoothing	Number of iterations	3
	Window size	1
	σ_x	40.0
	σ_d	4.0
Clustering	Window size of position	3
	Window size of brightness	8
Region growing	Window size for seed searching	5
	Range of region growing	$-3 \sim 255$
	Number of iterations for morphology	3
Active contour	Number of control points	10
	α	1.0
	β	1.5
	γ	0.2

Table 2. Parameters for extracting root

Process	parameter	value
Normalization	Base SE	180000
	I_a	100
Smoothing	Number of iterations	1
	Window size	1
	σ_x	40.0
	σ_d	4.0
Clustering	Window size of position	3
	Window size of brightness	8
Region growing	Window size for seed searching	5
	Range of region growing	$-3 \sim 255$
	Number of iterations for morphology	5

Fig. 11. Result of the end of the crown

On the other hand, the end (top part) of the crown was not correctly extracted. As shown in Fig. 13, the proposed method could not detect correct edges. This is because the variance of the brightness values is very large. Extracting the end of the crown correctly is an important future work.

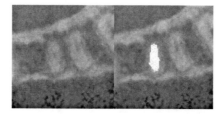

Fig. 12. Result of the end of the root

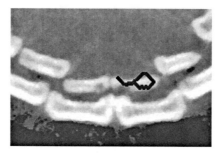

Fig. 13. Applying the active contour for the end of the crown

4   Conclusions

In this paper, a method for extracting a tooth shape from CT images is proposed. The proposed method first enhances the contrast by considering the slice energy, and the image is smoothed by the bilateral filter. Then the target tooth is segmented to parts by the mean shift clustering. Some segments in the tooth are extracted as regions by the region growing method. Finally, the contour of the tooth is detected by the active contour method.

Experimental result show that the proposed method can extract the root correctly compared to the previous method. Improving the extraction accuracy of the end of the crown is a future work. Quantitative evaluation with more teeth data is also an important future work.

Acknowledgment

The authors would like to thank Prof. Hirotomo Aso from Nihon University and Prof. Shin Kasahara from Tohoku University for their fruitful comments.

References

1. Cheng, Y.: Mean shift, mode seeking, and clustering. IEEE Transaction on Pattern Analysis and Machine Intelligence 17, 790–799 (1995)
2. Comaniciu, D.: Mean shift: a robust approach toward feature space analysis. IEEE Transaction on Pattern Analysis and Machine Intelligence 24, 603–619 (2002)

3. Grenier, T., Revol-Muller, C., Costes, N., Janier, M., Gimenez, G.: Automated seeds location for whole body NaF PET segmentation. IEEE Transaction on Nuclear Science 52, 1401–1405 (2005)
4. Jain, A.K., Chen, H.: Matching of dental X-ray images for human identification. Pattern Recognition 37, 1519–1532 (2004)
5. Kass, M., Witkin, A., Terzopilos, D.: Snakes: active contour models. International Journal of Computer Vision 1, 321–331 (1988)
6. Omachi, S., Saito, K., Aso, H., Kasahara, S., Yamada, S., Kimura, K.: Tooth shape reconstruction from CT images using spline curves. In: Proceedings of the International Conference on Wavelet Analysis and Pattern Recognition, pp. 393–396 (2007)
7. Satake, K., Yamaji, Y., Yamaguchi, S., Tanaka, H.: Liver segmentation method for 3D non-contrast abdominal CT image based on the region growing and the probabilistic atlas. Technical Report of IEICE, PRMU2008-15 (2008)
8. Su, T., Funabiki, N., Kishimoto, E.: An improvement of a tooth contour extraction method and a tooth contour database design based on WEB applications. Technical Report of IEICE, PRMU2004-168 (2005)
9. Tomasi, C., Manduchi, R.: Bilateral filtering for gray and color images. In: Proceedings of the Sixth International Conference on Computer Vision, pp. 839–846 (1998)
10. Yokoyama, K., Kitasaka, T., Mori, K., Mekada, Y., Hasegawa, J., Toriwaki, J.: Liver region extraction from 3D abdominal X-ray CT images using distribution features of abdominal organs. Journal of Computer Aided Diagnosis of Medical Images 7, 48–58 (2003)

Cancellable Face Biometrics System by Combining Independent Component Analysis Coefficients

MinYi Jeong and Andrew Beng Jin Teoh

Biometrics Engineering Research Center (BERC),
School of Electrical and Electronic Engineering
Yonsei University, Republic of Korea
{myjeong,bjteoh}@yonsei.ac.kr

Abstract. A number of biometric characteristics exist for person identity verification. Each biometric has its strengths. However, they also suffer from disadvantages, for example, in the area of privacy protection. Security and privacy issues are becoming more important in the biometrics community. To enhance security and privacy in biometrics, cancellable biometrics have been introduced. In this paper, we propose cancellable biometrics for face recognition using an appearance based approach. Initially, an ICA coefficient vector is extracted from an input face image. Some components of this vector are replaced randomly from a Gaussian distribution which reflects the original mean and variance of the components. Then, the vector, with its components replaced, has its elements scrambled randomly. A new transformed face coefficient vector is generated by choosing the minimum or maximum component of multiple (two or more) differing cases of such transformed coefficient vectors. In our experiments, we compared the performance between the cases when ICA coefficient vectors are used for verification and when the transformed coefficient vectors are used for verification. We also examine the properties of changeability and reproducibility for the proposed method.

Keywords: cancellable biometrics, face recognition, independent component analysis component.

1 Introduction

Some traditional methods for identifying persons, for example, the user's ID or PIN, can be canceled and re-issued when these are compromised [1]. However, this is not always possible with biometric data. Security and privacy issues are becoming more important in the biometrics community. To enhance security and privacy in using biometric systems, cancellable biometrics have been introduced. The idea is to replace the stored biometric data by a new one when it is compromised.

Cancellable biometrics have been proposed by Ratha et al. [2][3], and private biometrics have been proposed by Davida et al. [4]. Cancellable biometrics use transformed or distorted biometric data instead of the original biometric data for identifying a person. When a set of data is found to be compromised, it can be discarded and a new set of data can be regenerated.

H. Sako, K. Franke, and S. Saitoh (Eds.): IWCF 2010, LNCS 6540, pp. 78–87, 2011.

In generating cancellable biometrics, there are some conditions that must be met [5]. The first point is that even if the biometric features are known, the original biometrics cannot be recovered. The second, cancellable, refers to the degree of deformation for transformed data as compared to the original data or the new transformed data. The third point is that transform functions can be created indefinitely. The last is that after transformation, the recognition rate must not be much lower than the original recognition rate.

Recently, several methods have been proposed regarding cancellable biometrics [5-13]. In this paper, we propose a method for generating cancellable biometrics derived from face images. And we have tried to satisfy the conditions for producing a secure method for cancellable biometrics with the desired properties mentioned previously.

To describe the method proposed here, the organization of this paper is as follows. In Section 2, we describe the proposed method for cancellable face biometrics. In Section 3, the proposed method is evaluated with respect to performance accuracy, changeability and reproducibility. Finally, concluding remarks are presented in Section 4.

2   Cancellable Biometrics for Appearance Based Face Recognition

In this section, we give a brief explanation on appearance based face recognition using Independent Component Analysis (ICA), and describe the proposed method for cancellable face biometrics.

2.1   Independent Component Analysis

Appearance based techniques have been widely used in face recognition research. They employ feature vectors consisting of coefficients that are obtained by simply projecting facial images onto their basis images. ICA [14], [15] is an unsupervised learning rule that was derived from the principle of optimal information transfer. ICA minimizes both second-order and higher-order dependencies in the input. It keeps the assumption of linearity but abandons all the other aspects that PCA uses. The directions of the axes of this coordinate system are determined by both the second and higher order statistics of the original data. The goal is to perform a linear transform, which makes the resulting variables as statistically independent from each other as possible. There are two kinds of architectures based on ICA, architecture I and a architecture II. In this paper, we used ICA architecture I. Fig. 1 shows the facial image representations using based on ICA basis images.

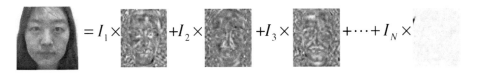

$$= I_1 \times \quad + I_2 \times \quad + I_3 \times \quad + \cdots + I_N \times$$

Fig. 1. Facial image representation using ICA

2.2 Cancellable Face Biometrics Using ICA Coefficients

The main idea of the proposed method is to generate transformed coefficient vectors by choosing the minimum or maximum component from the replaced and scrambled ICA coefficient vectors. In this paper we used ICA, but other appearance based methods can be applied in the same way. Figure 2 shows the overall block diagram of the face recognition system using the proposed method. For convenience, we will describe the method using just two ICA coefficient vectors, but this method can be applied to larger numbers of vectors.

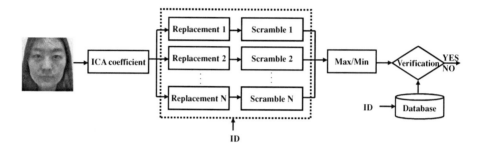

Fig. 2. Overall procedure of proposed method

Replacement. First, ICA coefficient vectors $I = [i_1, i_2, \cdots, i_N]$ were extracted from an input face image. Then, some components are replaced randomly with values selected from a Gaussian distribution with the mean and variance as the original ICA coefficient component. Replacing component values ensures that an attacker cannot recover the original information. Here, the two ICA coefficient vectors have components replaced according to different rules; these replacement functions are determined by the user ID.

Scrambling the Replaced Coefficient vector. To increase reproducibility and heighten changeability, we can apply scrambling to components of the ICA coefficients. Scrambling increases the reproducibility of cancellable biometrics, because the order of components for each ICA vector is scrambled differently.

Each coefficient vector is randomly scrambled, and the scrambling rule is determined by a user ID [8]. It is possible to define two scrambling functions $S_{ID}^{ICA}(\bullet)$ and $Z_{ID}^{ICA}(\bullet)$. $S_{ID}^{ICA}(\bullet)$ is a function for scrambling the first replaced ICA coefficient vector I_1, and $Z_{ID}^{ICA}(\bullet)$ is a function for scrambling the second normalized ICA coefficient vector I_2. The replaced and scrambled ICA coefficient vectors are given by

$$I_1^s = S_{ID}^{ICA}(I_1)$$
$$I_2^s = Z_{ID}^{ICA}(I_2)_.$$
(1)

When the transformed coefficient vector is found to be compromised, new transformed coefficient vectors can be generated by replacing the user ID or the scrambling rule associated with the user ID. In this way, many transformed face coefficient vectors can be easily generated.

Combining Replaced and Scrambled Coefficient vectors. Finally, the transformed face coefficient vector is generated by choosing the minimum or maximum components from the two differently replaced and scrambled ICA coefficient vectors as follows:

$$c_{max} = \max(I_1^s, I_2^s) = \max(S_{ID}^{ICA}(I_1),\ Z_{ID}^{ICA}(I_2))$$

$$or \tag{2}$$

$$c_{min} = \min(I_1^s, I_2^s) = \min(S_{ID}^{ICA}(I_1),\ Z_{ID}^{ICA}(I_2))$$

One of the conditions for cancellable biometrics is that transformed biometric data should not be easily converted back to the original biometric data even if an attacker knows both the transformed biometric data and the transforming method. Even if an attacker can find the transformed face coefficient vector (c_{max}, c_{min}) and the two scrambling functions ($S_{ID}^{ICA}(\bullet)$, $Z_{ID}^{ICA}(\bullet)$), it is impossible to recover the ICA coefficient vector from the transformed coefficient vector.

3   Experiments

In this section, experimental analysis is presented in three parts, relating to matching performance, changeability and reproducibility. In this paper, we examined 4 cases of the proposed method, i.e., when the number of ICA coefficient vectors (k) was changed from 5 to 2. We also examined how the recognition rate and changeability varies when the number of dimensions is changed from 300 to 10. In our experiments, the number of components to replace (r) was set at 30 percent of the dimension of the basis (n).

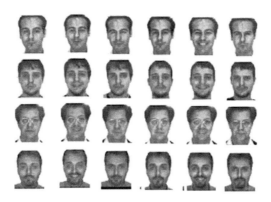

Fig. 3. Sample images from the AR database

3.1 Database

We used the AR Face database [16] to evaluate recognition performance. In our experiments, we used only 672 frontal facial images without occlusion and illumination changes, for a total of 6 different images per subject. Each image consisted of a 56 by 46 array of pixels. The number of images used for training and testing was both 336, respectively. The training set contained images for each of the 56 subjects. The images of the remaining 56 subjects were used as the test set. Figure 3 shows some sample images taken from the database.

3.2 Matching Performance

We used the Euclidian distance for a dissimilarity measurement. Within this framework, we compared the performance using conventional ICA, and the proposed method. The experimental results of the proposed method require multiple instances for each case because the scrambling function for the coefficients is a randomly

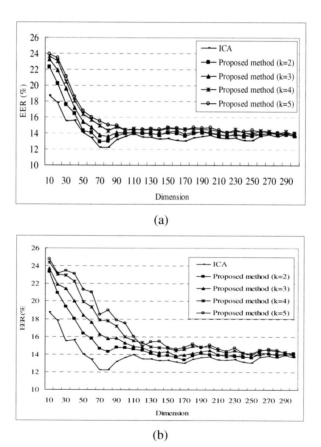

(a)

(b)

Fig. 4. Recognition performance of conventional ICA and the proposed method as dimensions vary (a) maximum, (b) minimum

changing function. Therefore we conducted a total of 100 experiments for each case, and averaged the results.

Figure 4 shows EER results when conventional ICA coefficient vector are used for verification, and when the transformed coefficient vectors are used, as the number of coefficient dimension varies. The experimental results show that EER of the proposed method does not degrade highly over using conventional ICA based methods. Also, it can be seen that matching performance becomes similar as the number of dimensions increases, regardless of how many terms are used in the combination.

3.3 Changeability

Next, experiments were carried out to examine the two types of changeability. Changeability 1 refers to the degree of dissimilarity between the original coefficients and transformed coefficients. This is measured quantitatively by finding the distribution of L_2 distances between original and transformed coefficients relative to a system threshold. Changeability 2 refers to the degree of dissimilarity between different instances of the transform of the original coefficients, e.g., using transform function 1 and transform function 2. The distributions of L_2 distances of coefficients from these transforms are then found, relative to a system threshold. The distribution due to transform of the original coefficients is called a pseudo-genuine distribution, and the portion of the pseudo-genuine distribution that lies to the right relative to the system threshold can be construed as a measure of the changeability. The more the pseudo-genuine distribution moves to the right, the greater the distance between the coefficients, showing that transformed coefficients are recognized as being different from the original coefficients. Figure 5 shows the determination of the system threshold from the genuine and imposter distributions, along with the pseudo-genuine distribution.

In our experiments, all pseudo-genuine distributions resulting from transform of the original coefficients lay to the right of the system threshold. Figure 6 shows changeability when $n = 50$, $r = 15$ (30%), and two coefficient vectors ($k = 2$) are used

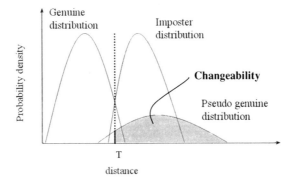

Fig. 5. Distance distributions for assessing changeability: genuine, imposter, and pseudo genuine distributions (T: system threshold) [12]

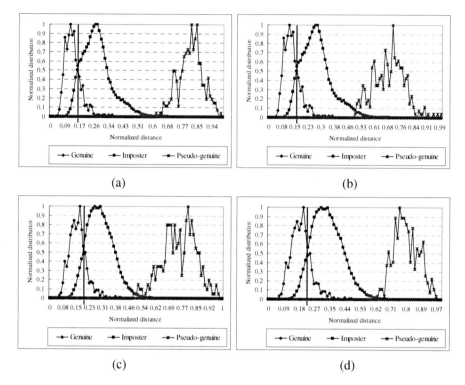

Fig. 6. Genuine and imposter distributions, and pseudo genuine distribution after applying the proposed method when n=50, r=15, and k=2 used in the combination (a) maximum, changeability 1, (b) maximum, changeability 2, (c) minimum, changeability 1, (d) minimum, changeability 2

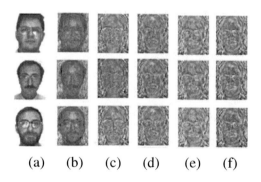

(a)   (b)   (c)   (d)   (e)   (f)

Fig. 7. Reconstructed images (a) original image, (b) conventional ICA, (c) applying proposed maximum method using two ICA vectors, (d) applying proposed maximum method using three ICA vectors, (e) applying proposed maximum method using four ICA vectors, (f) applying proposed maximum method using five ICA vectors in the combination. These results show that after transformation, coefficients derived from the same person are recognized as being different, for a single transform, or between two different transforms.

Additionally, we restored the face images using the transformed coefficients and the original ICA basis. For cancellable biometrics, the changed restoration images must differ from the original restoration image. Restoration results are as shown in figure 7 and figure 8. The restored images from the transformed coefficient were completely different from the original images. By the use of different methods (that is, different number of ICA coefficient vectors in combination) for the deformation transform, the restored images from the transformed coefficients were shown to be quite different from the original images.

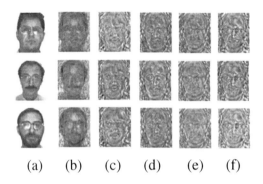

(a)   (b)   (c)   (d)   (e)   (f)

Fig. 8. Reconstructed images (a) original image, (b) conventional ICA, (c) applying proposed minimum method using two ICA vectors, (d) applying proposed minimum method using three ICA vectors, (e) applying proposed minimum method using four ICA vectors, (f) applying proposed minimum method using five ICA vectors

3.4 Reproducibility

Reproducibility was calculated by the number of values that can be replaced, and the number of cases of coefficients produced by scrambling, which is especially large. If r is chosen as the number of components to be replaced, the number of cases for an n coefficient scrambling method is $\frac{n!}{r!(n-r)!} \times n!$. Here, the number of cases is numerous because each ICA coefficient vector is differently scrambled and then combined. Further, we can use a larger number of ICA coefficient vectors k, where $k \geq 2$. In this case, the total number of cases for the proposed method is $(\frac{n!}{r!(n-r)!} \times n!)^k$, obtained by using different random scrambling. For example, if we use 50 coefficients ($n = 50$), $r = 15$ (30%) and five ICA coefficient vectors in the combination ($k = 5$), we have $(\frac{50!}{15!(50-15)!} \times 50!)^5 = 2.09 \times 10^{472}$ cases for reproducibility. Therefore, this method satisfies the property of sufficient reproducibility.

4 Conclusion

Cancellable biometrics uses transformed or distorted biometric data instead of original biometric data for identifying a person. When a set of biometric data is found to be compromised, it can be discarded and a new set can be generated. In this paper, we proposed a cancellable biometric system for face recognition using an appearance-based approach. The main idea was to replace and scramble the ICA coefficient vectors and find minimum or maximum component of the transformed vectors. From experimental results, it is shown that this method does not degrade performance much compared to that of conventional methods. Also, matching performance converges for various numbers of ICA coefficient vectors used. Therefore, a system can choose the number of ICA coefficient vectors used by considering of computation complexity and robustness to attack. After transformation, all pseudo-genuine distributions appeared on the right of the system threshold t, so that the same image after transformation was classified as an imposter element. These results show that the proposed method satisfies a good level of changeability. By scrambling the order of the coefficients in the transform function, we were able to generate numerous instances of cancellable face data. Moreover, this method is non-invertible. The proposed method is not only resolves a weak point of biometric systems, but also maintains performance accuracy.

Acknowledgment

This work was supported by the National Research Foundation of Korea (NRF) grant funded by the Korea government (MEST) through the Biometrics Engineering Research Center(BERC) at Yonsei University. (No.R112002105080020 (2010))

References

1. Pankanti, A., Bolle, R.M., Jain, A.K.: Biometrics: the future of identification. IEEE Computer 33(2), 46–49 (2000)
2. Ratha, N.K., Connell, J.H., Bolle, R.M.: Enhancing security and privacy in biometrics-based authentication systems. IBM Systems Journal 40(3) (2001)
3. Bolle, R.M., Connel, J.H., Ratha, N.K.: Biometrics Perils and Patches. Pattern Recognition 35, 2727–2738 (2002)
4. Davida, G.I., Frankel, Y., Matt, B.J.: On enabling secure applications through off-line biometric identification. In: Proc. of IEEE Symposium on Security and Privacy, September 4, pp. 148–157 (2006)
5. Jeong, M.Y., Lee, C., Kim, J., Choi, J.Y., Toh, K.A., Kim, J.: Cancelable Biometrics for Appearance based Face Recognition. In: Proc. of Biometrics Consortium Conference (September 2006)

6. Savvides, M., Vijaya Kumar, B.V.K., Khosla, P.K.: Cancelable Biometric Filters for Face Recognition. In: Proceedings of the 17th International Conference on Pattern Recognition (ICPR 2004), vol. 3, pp. 922–925 (2004)
7. Teoh, A.B.J., Ngo, D.C.L.: Cancellable biometrics featuring with tokenized random number. Pattern Recognition Letter 26(10), 1454–1460 (2005)
8. Kang, J., Nyang, D., Lee, K.: Two Factor Face Authentication Scheme with Cancelable Feature. In: Li, S.Z., Sun, Z., Tan, T., Pankanti, S., Chollet, G., Zhang, D. (eds.) IWBRS 2005. LNCS, vol. 3781, pp. 67–76. Springer, Heidelberg (2005)
9. Jeong, M.Y., Lee, C., Choi, J.Y., Kim, J.: Changeable Biometrics for PCA based Face recognition. In: IEEK Summer Conference, vol. 29(1), pp. 331–332 (2006)
10. Boult, T.: Robust Distance Measures for Face-recognition supporting revocable biometrics token. In: 7th International Conference Automatic Face and Gesture Recognition, Southampton, UK, April 10-12 (2007)
11. Jeong, M.Y., Kim, J.: A Study of Generation for Changeable Face Template. In: IEEK Summer Conference, vol. 30(1), pp. 391–392 (2007)
12. Jeong, M.Y., Lee, C., Choi, J.Y., Kim, J.: Generation of Changeable Face Template by Combining Independent Component Analysis Coefficients. Journal of IEEK 44-SP(6), 16–23 (2007)
13. Jeong, M.Y., Choi, J.Y., Kim, J.: Using Genetic Algorithms to Improve Matching Performance of Changeable biometrics from Combining PCA and ICA Methods. In: Computer Vision and Pattern Recognition (CVPR) (June 2007)
14. Bartlett, M.S., Movellan, J.R., Sejnowski, T.J.: Face Recognition by Independent Component Analysis. IEEE Trans. Neural Networks 13, 1450–1464 (2002)
15. Bae, K., Noh, S., Kim, J.: Iris Feature Extraction Using Independent Component Analysis. In: Kittler, J., Nixon, M.S. (eds.) AVBPA 2003. LNCS, vol. 2688, pp. 838–844. Springer, Heidelberg (2003)
16. Martinez, A.M., Benavente, R.: The AR Face Database. CVC Technical Report #24 (1998)

Footwear Print Retrieval System for Real Crime Scene Marks

Yi Tang, Sargur N. Srihari, Harish Kasiviswanathan, and Jason J. Corso

Center of Excellence for Document Analysis and Recognition (CEDAR)
University at Buffalo, The State University of New York
Amherst, New York 14228, U.S.A.
{yitang,srihari,harishka,jcorso}@buffalo.edu
http://www.cedar.buffalo.edu

Abstract. Footwear impression evidence has been gaining increasing importance in forensic investigation. The most challenging task for a forensic examiner is to work with highly degraded footwear marks and match them to the most similar footwear print available in the database. Retrieval process from a large database can be made significantly faster if the database footwear prints are clustered beforehand. In this paper we propose a footwear print retrieval system which uses the fundamental shapes in shoes like lines, circles and ellipses as features and retrieves the most similar print from a clustered database. Prints in the database are clustered based on outsole patterns. Each footwear print pattern is characterized by the combination of shape features and represented by an Attributed Relational Graph. Similarity between prints is computed using Footwear Print Distance. The proposed system is invariant to distortions like scale, rotation, translation and works well with the partial prints, color prints and crime scene marks.

Keywords: Footwear Impression Evidence, ARG, Footwear Print Distance, Hough transform, Content-based Image Retrieval.

1 Introduction

Footwear marks are often found in crime scenes and can serve as a clue to link two crimes. At present there is no reliable and fully automated footwear print retrieval system to assist the forensic examiners. Therefore the foot wear marks are manually matched against the local/national database to determine the brand and model of the most similar print. Existing footwear print retrieval systems works well only with clear prints but the crime scene marks are highly degraded and partial. Most of the present systems [1] fail with crime scene marks because they use features that are hard be captured from the crime scene marks.

Retrieval process can be made faster if prints in the database are grouped into clusters based on similar patterns. Clustering footwear prints is an uphill task because of the difficulty in the computation of the similarity matrix. Hence, we cluster them by retrieving the most similar prints for each of the recurring patterns in footwear prints. The proposed fully automated footwear print retrieval

H. Sako, K. Franke, and S. Saitoh (Eds.): IWCF 2010, LNCS 6540, pp. 88–100, 2011.
© Springer-Verlag Berlin Heidelberg 2011

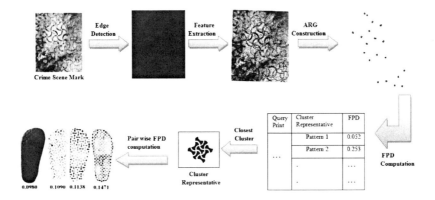

Fig. 1. System Flow Diagram of our footwear print retrieval system

system (shown in Figure1) is invariant to affine transformation of prints and avoids the computation of similarity matrix.

Most of the existing shoe print classification systems are semi-automatic [1] , such as SICAR, SoleMate etc. De Chazal (2005) et al. [2] proposed a fully automated shoe print classification system which uses power spectral density (PSD) of the print as a pattern descriptor. Zhang and Allinson (2005) [3] proposed an automated shoe print retrieval system in which 1-D Discrete Fourier Transform on the normalized edge direction histogram is used as a feature of the print. Gueham (2008) et al. [6] evaluated the performance of 'Optimum Trade-off Synthetic Discriminant Function (OTSDF)' filter and unconstrained OTSDF filter in the automatic classification of partial shoeprints. Dardi (2009) et al. [7] described a texture based retrieval system for shoeprints. Mahalanobis map is used to capture the texture and then matched using correlation coefficient. Though fully automated footwear print retrieval system exists in literature, most of them is tested only with synthetic prints and clean prints. No one has reported satisfying performance with real crime scene marks.

2   Feature Extraction

Features such as color, texture and shape [8] can be used to distinguish the images. Color features are missing in crime scene marks and texture features are hard to be captured but shape features can be easily captured. Shapes are the most durable and reliable features of the outsole that can resist various wears and are well preserved over a long period of time. Hence, we chose shape as features to classify footwear prints.

Based on visual inspection of 5034 prints, we found that 91.8% of the prints can be represented using three basic shapes: *straight line segments, circles/arcs* and *ellipses.* Based on these shapes, footwear prints can be classified into 8 types: Piecewise Lines, Only Circles/Arcs, Only Ellipses, Circles & Ellipses, Lines & Circles, Lines & Ellipses, Lines, Circles & Ellipses and Only Texture. Shapes other than circles and ellipses are approximated by piecewise lines. Combinations of these shapes is used to identify the pattern of the shoeprint. Distribution of fundamental shapes in footwear prints are shown in Table 1. Eight types of footwear prints are shown in Figure 2.

Table 1. Fundamental shapes in footwear prints

Fundamental Shapes	Number of Prints
Piecewise Lines	3397
Lines & Circles	812
Lines & Ellipses	285
Only Circles/Arcs	73
Lines, Circles & Ellipses	37
Only Ellipses	15
Circles & Ellipses	5
Only Texture	410
Total - 5034 prints	

Fig. 2. Eight types of Footwear prints: From left to right (a) Piecewise Lines. (b) Lines & Circles. (c) Lines & Ellipses (d) Only Circles/Arcs. (e) Lines, Circles & Ellipses. (f) Only Ellipses. (g) Lines, Circles & Ellipses. (h) Circles & Ellipses. (i) Only Texture.

Morphological operations (MO) such as dilation and erosion are applied to make the interior region of prints uniform and then extract the boundary using Canny edge[9] detector(ED). The result for a sample print is shown in Figure 3.

2.1   Line Detection and Circle Detection

Most footwear prints have complex geometric structures. The number of line segments in a print is 200-300 on average. Each group of collinear points forms a peak in accumulator. Detecting all the true peaks while suppressing spurious ones is difficult. In addition, short line segments are easily missed, which may be useful for discriminating similar prints. So Standard Hough Transform (SHT) [10] cannot be applied directly on footwear prints. Thus, we propose Iterative Straight-line Hough Transform (ISHT). First, connected components are labeled in the edge image. For each component, Hough transform is applied and peaks are detected. When a peak is identified and the line segments are extracted, the

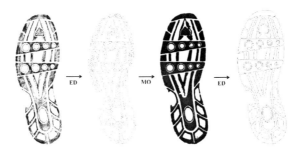

Fig. 3. Edge Detection after dilation and erosion

pixels contributing to those line segments are eliminated from the edge image, and an updated accumulator is obtained by applying SHT on the modified edge image. The algorithm is summarized in Figure 4 and results of the two algorithms on two sample prints are shown in Figure 5.

Circles and arcs are detected using SHT and validated using gradient orientation. Spatial relationship constraints are used to eliminate spurious circles.

2.2 Ellipse Detection

In a Cartesian plane, an ellipse is described by its centre (p,q), length of the semi-major axis a, length of the semi-minor axis b and the angle θ between the major axis and the x-axis. Hence the five parameters (p,q,a,b,θ) are required to uniquely describe an ellipse. These five parameters demand a five dimensional accumulator which is computationally expensive but Randomized Hough transform (RHT) [11] for ellipse detection is computationally advantageous.

In case of ellipse detection in footwear prints, RHT cannot be used directly. This is because there are around 50,000 foreground pixels in the edge image of a print of typical size 600×800 and picking three pixels from them in random will never narrow down to the right ellipse. Hence, we propose a modified RHT (MRHT) that incorporates ideas like decomposition of footwear prints into connected components, elimination of unwanted components using eccentricity, smart selection of three points based on the standard deviation of gradient orientation at each pixel and elimination of spurious ellipses by comparing the tangent of edge direction and the analytical derivative. MRHT is shown as Algorithm 2. Sample Results of the feature extraction are shown in Figure 6.

3   Attributed Relational Graph (ARG)

After feature extraction, the footwear print has been decomposed in to a set of primitives. An Attributed Relational Graph (ARG) [12], is constructed for every footwear print to obtain a structural representation of the extracted features. An ARG is a 3-tuple (V,E,A) where V is the set of nodes, E is the set of edges and A is the set of attributes. Each edge describes the spatial relationship between nodes. The attributes include node and edge attributes.

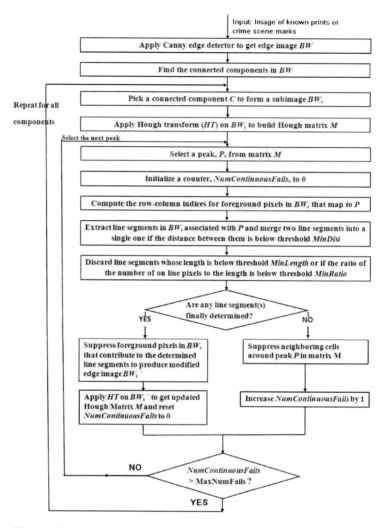

Fig. 4. Algorithm 1: Iterative Straight-line Hough Transform (ISHT)

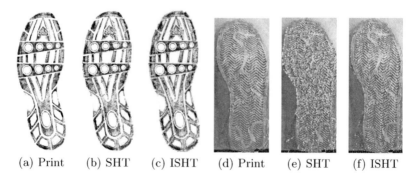

(a) Print   (b) SHT   (c) ISHT   (d) Print   (e) SHT   (f) ISHT

Fig. 5. Comparison of the results of SHT and ISHT on sample prints

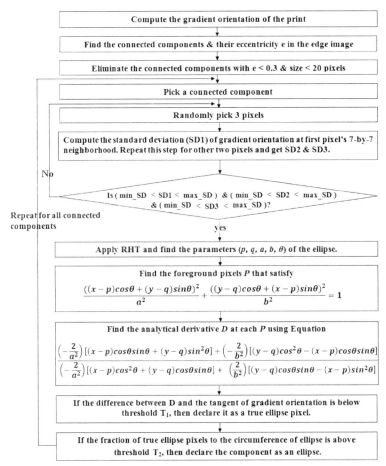

| Compute the gradient orientation of the print |

| Find the connected components & their eccentricity e in the edge image |

| Eliminate the connected components with e < 0.3 & size < 20 pixels |

| Pick a connected component |

| Randomly pick 3 pixels |

| Compute the standard deviation (SD1) of gradient orientation at first pixel's 7-by-7 neighborhood. Repeat this step for other two pixels and get SD2 & SD3. |

No

Is (min_SD < SD1 < max_SD) & (min_SD < SD2 < max_SD) & (min_SD < SD3 < max_SD)?

Repeat for all connected components

yes

| Apply RHT and find the parameters (p, q, a, b, θ) of the ellipse. |

Find the foreground pixels P that satisfy

$$\frac{((x-p)cos\theta + (y-q)sin\theta)^2}{a^2} + \frac{((y-q)cos\theta + (x-p)sin\theta)^2}{b^2} = 1$$

Find the analytical derivative D at each P using Equation

$$\frac{\left(-\frac{2}{a^2}\right)[(x-p)cos\theta sin\theta + (y-q)sin^2\theta] + \left(-\frac{2}{b^2}\right)[(y-q)cos^2\theta - (x-p)cos\theta sin\theta]}{\left(-\frac{2}{a^2}\right)[(x-p)cos^2\theta + (y-q)cos\theta sin\theta] + \left(\frac{2}{b^2}\right)[(y-q)cos\theta sin\theta - (x-p)sin^2\theta]}$$

| If the difference between D and the tangent of gradient orientation is below threshold T_1, then declare it as a true ellipse pixel. |

| If the fraction of true ellipse pixels to the circumference of ellipse is above threshold T_2, then declare the component as an ellipse. |

Algorithm 2: MRHT

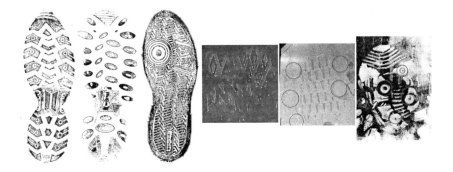

Fig. 6. Detected lines, circles and ellipses are shown for 3 known prints on the left and 3 crime scene marks on the right

There are three types of nodes (lines, circles and ellipses) and nine types of edges (line-to-line, line-to-circle, line-to-ellipse, circle-to-line, circle-to circle, circle-to-ellipse, ellipse-to-line, ellipse-to-circle and ellipse-to-ellipse) in this representation, which are denoted as L2L, L2C, L2E, C2L, C2C, C2E, E2L, E2C, E2E edges. To tackle the case of nodes being missing or incorrectly detected due to noise, occlusion and incompleteness, a *fully-connected directed graph* is adopted. This means that there is a directed edge from each node to all other nodes. To distinguish one node from the other and one pair of nodes from another pair, node and edge attributes have been carefully designed to describe the spatial relationship between nodes in terms of distance, relative position, relative dimension and orientation, and are tabulated in Table 2. All these attributes have been normalized within the range [0, 1]. This description is *invariant* to scale, rotation, translation and *insensitive* to noise and degradations. Figure 7 describes the two cases of relative position for L2L, L2C and C2E. Sample ARG for a footwear print is shown in Figure 8.

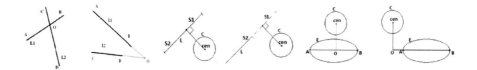

Fig. 7. Relative Position Definition for L2L, L2C and C2E

4   Footwear Print Distance (FPD)

The quality of clusters depends highly on the similarity measure used by the clustering algorithm so the similarity measure has to be accurate and robust. A distance metric, called the Earth Mover's Distance (EMD) [13] has been proposed and investigated for content-based image retrieval.

We propose *Footwear Print Distance* (FPD), which is derived from EMD, to compute the similarity between footwear prints. Let $FP = (V, E, A, W, N)$ be a footwear print with N nodes, where $V = \{V_i\}_{i=1}^{N}$, $E = V \times V$, $A = A_N \cup A_E$, $A_N = \bigcup_{i=1}^{N} A_{Ni}$, $A_E = \bigcup_{i=1}^{N} \bigcup_{j=1}^{N} A_{Eij}$, $W = \{W_i\}_{i=1}^{N}$. A_N, A_E and W denote node attribute, edge attribute and weights respectively. Let $FP_1 = (V_1, E_1, A_1, W_1, N_1)$ be the first print with N_1 nodes; $FP_2 = (V_2, E_2, A_2, W_2, N_2)$ the second print with N_2 nodes; and $C = [c_{ij}]$ be the *unit* cost matrix where c_{ij} is the **unit** matching cost between $V_{1i} \in V_1$ and $V_{2j} \in V_2$, which is defined as follows. If V_{1i} is a line and V_{2j} is a circle/ellipse or vice-versa, then $c_{ij} = 1$ else c_{ij} is computed as an EMD [13] in which the distance between any two nodes is defined as a weighted Euclidean distance between their node and edge attributes. Each node is assigned *equal* weight to enforce a *one-to-one* correspondence between nodes, i.e. $W_{1i} = W_{2j} = \frac{1}{\max(N_1, N_2)}$, $1 \leq i \leq N_1$, $1 \leq j \leq N_2$.

Table 2. Node & Edge Attributes

L2L

Att	Definition	Normalization
N-a	$\dfrac{abs(L1.\theta - L2.\theta)}{180}$	-
N-rs	$\dfrac{L1.len}{L1.len + L2.len}$	-
rd	$\dfrac{dist(L1.m, L2.m)}{L1.len + L2.len}$	$2(\sigma(rd) - 0.5)$
pd	$\dfrac{dist(L1.m, L2)}{L1.len + L2.len}$	$2(\sigma(pd) - 0.5)$
rp_1	$\dfrac{min(OA, OB)}{max(OA, OB)}$	$\dfrac{rp1 + 1}{2}$
rp_2	$-\dfrac{min(|OA|, |OB|)}{max(|OA|, |OB|)}$	$\dfrac{rp2 + 1}{2}$

L2E

e	$E.e$	-
N-rs	$\dfrac{L.len}{L.len + E.ER}$	-
rd	$\dfrac{dist(L.m, E.cen)}{L.len + E.ER}$	$2(\sigma(rd) - 0.5)$
rp1	$\dfrac{min(OA, OB)}{max(OA, OB)}$	$\dfrac{rp1 + 1}{2}$
rp2	$-\dfrac{min(|OA|, |OB|)}{max(|OA|, |OB|)}$	$\dfrac{rp2 + 1}{2}$
N-ro	$\dfrac{abs(L.\theta - E.\theta)}{180}$	-

C2E

e	$E.e$	-
N-rs	$\dfrac{C.r}{C.r + E.ER}$	-
rd	$\dfrac{dist(C.cen, E.cen)}{C.r + E.ER}$	$2(\sigma(rd) - 0.5)$
rp	$\dfrac{min(OA, OB)}{max(OA, OB)}$	$\dfrac{rp + 1}{2}$

C2C

Att	Definition	Normalization
N-rs	$\dfrac{C1.r}{C1.r + C2.r}$	-
rd_1	$\dfrac{dist(C1.cen, C2.cen)}{C1.r + C2.r}$	$\dfrac{rd1}{rd1 + 10/rd1}$
rd_2	$\dfrac{dist(C1.cen, C2.cen)}{max(|C1.r - C2.r|, 10^{-3})}$	$\dfrac{rd2}{rd2 + 10/rd2}$

L2C

N-rs	$\dfrac{L.len}{C.r + L.len}$	-
rd	$\dfrac{dist(C.cen, L)}{C.r}$	$\dfrac{rd}{rd + 10/rd}$
rp	$\dfrac{min(S1, S2)}{max(S1, S2)}$	$\dfrac{rp + 1}{2}$

C2L

N-rs	$\dfrac{C.r}{C.r + L.len}$	-
rd	$\dfrac{dist(C.cen, L)}{C.r}$	$\dfrac{rd}{rd + 10/rd}$

E2E

e_ratio	$\dfrac{E1.e}{E1.e + E2.e}$	-
$f(\Delta e)$	$\dfrac{E1.e - E2.e + 1}{2}$	-
rd	$\dfrac{dist(E1.cen, E2.cen)}{E1.ER + E2.ER}$	$\dfrac{rd}{rd + 10/rd}$
N-rs	$\dfrac{E1.ER}{E1.ER + E2.ER}$	-
N-ro	$\dfrac{abs(E1.\theta - E2.\theta)}{90}$	-
rp	$rp(E1.major\text{-}axis, E2.major\text{-}axis)$	$\dfrac{rp + 1}{2}$

Symbols Used & its Definition

L: Line segment
C: Circle
E: Ellipse
cen: Centre
Dist: Euclidean distance
rs: Relative size
r: Radius
Len: Length
rp: Relative position
θ: Orientation
E: eccentricity
Att: attributes
ER: $\sqrt{a \cdot b}$
N: Normalized
mid: mid-point
$\sigma(x)$: $\dfrac{1}{1+e^{-x}}$
pd: perpendicular distance
Ellipse:
a: Semi-major axis.
b: Semi-minor axis.
p, q: centre
max: maximum
| |: absolute
abs: absolute

Node Attributes

Node	Attributes	Definition	Node	Attributes	Definition	Node	Attributes	Definition
Circle	Completeness	Standard deviation of the angle that on-circle pixels make w.r.t. center	Circle	Quality	$\dfrac{Number\ of\ pixels\ on\ circle}{Circumference\ of\ circle}$	Ellipse	Eccentricity	$\sqrt{1 - \dfrac{b^2}{a^2}}$

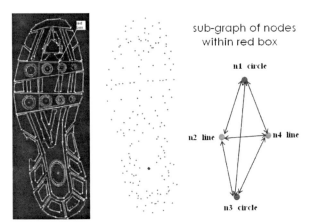

Fig. 8. Extracted features of a shoeprint shown in Fig. 5(a), its ARG and sub-graph of nodes within red box. The ARG is fully connected and its edges are omitted for clarity.

The goal is to calculate a node correspondence matrix $M = [m_{ij}]$, where m_{ij} denotes the amount of weight transferred from V_{1i} to V_{2j}, which minimizes the total matching cost $Cost(FP_1, FP_2, M) = \sum_{i=1}^{N_1} \sum_{j=1}^{N_2} m_{ij} * c_{ij}$, subject to the following constraints:

$$m_{ij} \geq 0, \quad 1 \leq i \leq N_1, 1 \leq j \leq N_2 \tag{1}$$

$$\sum_{j=1}^{N_2} m_{ij} \leq W_{1i}, 1 \leq i \leq N_1 \tag{2}$$

$$\sum_{i=1}^{N_1} m_{ij} \leq W_{2j}, 1 \leq j \leq N_2 \tag{3}$$

$$\sum_{i=1}^{N_1} \sum_{j=1}^{N_2} m_{ij} = \min(\sum_{i=1}^{N_1} W_{1i}, \sum_{j=1}^{N_2} W_{2j}) \tag{4}$$

Once the correspondence matrix is found, the FPD is defined as the overall cost normalized by the sum of all the weights transferred from FP_1 to FP_2.

$$FPD(FP_1, FP_2) = \frac{\sum_{i=1}^{N_1} \sum_{j=1}^{N_2} m_{ij} * c_{ij}}{\sum_{i=1}^{N_1} \sum_{j=1}^{N_2} m_{ij}} \tag{5}$$

5   Clustering Footwear Prints

Clustering algorithms can be generally divided into partition-based, density-based and hierarchical based methods [14]. Existing clustering algorithms like K-means, Hierarchical Clustering, and Expectation Maximization requires similarity matrix consisting of pair-wise distance between every footwear prints in the dataset. Building similarity matrix for a large dataset is computationally expensive. Hence, to cluster the entire dataset we propose using *recurring patterns* as fixed cluster center.

Recurring patterns (shown in Fig.9(a)) such as wavy pattern, concentric circles etc. are common in footwear prints and can be used to represent a group of similar prints. These patterns are simple in structure and graphs constructed from them have less number of nodes. Hence, recurring patterns can be used as query to fetch all similar prints from the database. This drastically reduced the computation and did not require similarity matrix. Though this clustering method requires domain knowledge to determine the recurring patterns, it avoids the problems of deciding the number of clusters beforehand (unlike K-means).

From visual inspection, 25 recurring patterns (shown in Figure9(a)) were determined and used as cluster representatives. FPD between each database print and every cluster representative was calculated. Then each print was assigned to the nearest representative, for which the FPD is below threshold T. If FPD between a print and cluster representatives are greater than T, then the print remains as a single cluster. In our experiments, T was set to 0.15. 1410 shoeprints were fitted in to these 25 clusters. Remaining 1250 prints were so unique that each of them was a cluster by itself. Sample clusters are shown in Figure 9(b).

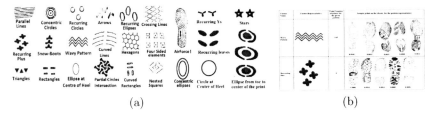

(a)   (b)

Fig. 9. (a) Cluster Representatives. (b) Sample Clusters.

6   Experiments and Results

A database of 2660 known prints and 100 crime scene marks was used for experiments. Each known print has the meta data such as brand and model of the footwear, which is useful for linking a suspect's footwear to a crime scene mark. In the clustered database, crime scene mark was first matched against every cluster representative to find the closest cluster, and then matched against each print in that cluster and the top n matches are retrieved. Retrieval results for 4 sample marks are shown in Figure 10.

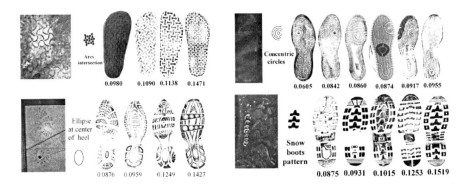

Fig. 10. Crime Scene marks, their closest cluster and closest matches from the cluster

The system's performance has been evaluated using 100 real crime scene marks and 1400 degraded prints, which were obtained by applying combinations of affine transformation, partitioning and noise degradation on certain database prints. Cumulative Match Characteristic (CMC) [2] was chosen as the performance metric because it can answer the question "What is the probability of a match in the first n percent of the sorted database?". The probability of a match (cumulative match score) is estimated by the proportion of times a matching footwear print appears in the first n percent of the sorted database. SIFT [15] being a robust image matching algorithm, we compared our system with SIFT. The CMC curve of our system *before* clustering and of SIFT are shown in Fig. 11. CMC curve *remains the same* before and after clustering but clustering makes significant improvement in the retrieval speed, which is shown in Table 3.

Table 3. Retrieval speed

No. of Crime Scene marks used for experiments	Average Time Taken for Retrieval Before Clustering	Average Time Taken for Retrieval after Clustering
100	120 minutes	10 minutes

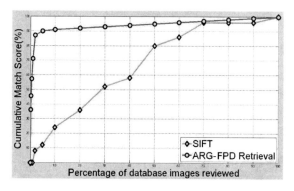

Fig. 11. CMC of Our System and SIFT on Retrieval of Crime Scene Marks

Table 4. Comparison of ARG-FPG with the State-of-the-art

State-of-the-art	Query from the learning set : similar to one in learning set						Experiments using Real Crime Scene marks	Shortcoming	Dataset
	Full print			Partial print					
	CMS at 1%	CMS at 5%	CMS at 10%	CMS at 1%	CMS at 5%	CMS at 10%			
Chazal et al.[2] (Using Power Spectral Density)	64	87	90	50	70	77	-	Lacks Scaling invariance.	475 prints from dataset of Forensic Science Laboratory, Dublin, Ireland
Zhang et al. [3] (Using Edge Direction Histogram)	85.4	95	97.44	-	-	-	-	Not tested with partial prints.	512 prints from Foster & Freeman Dataset
Pavlou et al. [4] (Using Gradient Location and Orientation Histogram)	86	90	93	85	90	92	-	Not tested with real crime scene marks	368 prints provided by Forensic Science Services dataset, UK
Crookes et al. [5] (Using Local Image Features)	100	100	100	100	100	100	-	Tested with only synthesized SoCs	500 clean prints and 50 degraded prints
Crookes et al. [5] (Using phase only correlation)	100	100	100	100	100	100	-	Lacks rotational invariance	100 clean prints and 64 synthetic scene images
Gueham et al. [6] (Using Advanced Correlation Filters)	-	-	-	95.68	-	-		Tested only with 100 prints	100 prints from Foster & Freeman Dataset
Dardil et al. [7] (Using texture)	-	-	-	-	-	-	CMS at 10% is 73 % CMS at 5% is 40 % CMS at 1% is 10%	Tested only with 87 known prints and 30 real crime SoC's	87 known prints and 30 real crime scenes from ENSFI group
ARG-FPD Approach	100	100	100	100	100	100	CMS at 10% is 91% CMS at 5% is 90% CMS at 1% is 71%		1400 degraded prints, 100 real crime scenes & 2660 known prints

Dardil et al. [7] are the only one who have worked with real crime scene marks. They have reported that 73% of the real crime scene marks were found in the top 10% of database prints but they have tested their system with only 87 known prints and 30 real crime scene marks. From CMC of our system, it is clear that, 91% of matching prints for the crime scene marks were found in the top 10% of the database prints. Table 4 compares our work with the state of the art techniques and our system performed better than the others for full prints, partial prints and real crime scene marks. Accuracy of 100% with degraded full and partial prints demonstrates the invariance of our system to affine transformation and robustness against noise and degradations.

7   Conclusion

The proposed Attributed Relational Graph representation of footwear prints works well with crime scene marks. Our system is invariant to affine transformation and robust against noise and various image degradations. Performance of the system clearly shows that fundamental shapes in shoes are one of the most reliable features, ARG is a robust descriptor of these features and FPD is an ideal similarity measure to match partial and degraded prints. Clustering using recurring patterns is a promising method to cluster footwear prints and it certainly enhances the retrieval speed with same accuracy.

References

1. Bouridane, A.: Imaging for Forensics and Security: From Theory to Practice. Springer, New York (2009)
2. De Chazal, P.D., Flynn, J., Reilly, R.: Automated processing of shoeprint images based on the fourier transform for use in forensic science. IEEE Transaction on Pattern Analysis and Machine Intelligence, 341–350 (2005)
3. Zhang, L., Allinson, N.: Automatic shoeprint retrieval system for use in forensic investigations. In: 5th Annual UK Workshop on Computational Intelligence (2005)
4. Pavlou, M., Allinson, N.M.: Automatic extraction and classification of footwear patterns. In: Proc. Intelligent Data Engineering and Automated Learning (2006)
5. Crookes, D., Bouridane, A., Su, H., Gueham, M.: Following the Footsteps of Others: Techniques for Automatic Shoeprint Classification. In: 2nd NASA/ESA Conference on Adaptive Hardware and Systems (2007)
6. Gueham, M., Bouridane, A., Crookes, D.: Automatic classification of Partial Shoeprints using Advanced Correlation Filters for use in Forensic Science. In: International Conference on Pattern Recognition, pp. 1–4. IEEE Press, Los Alamitos (2008)
7. Dardi, F., Cervelli, F., Carrato, S.: A Texture based Shoe Retrieval System for Shoe Marks of Real Crime Scenes. In: International Conference on Image Analysis and Processing, pp. 384–393. IEEE Press, Los Alamitos (2009)
8. Rui, Y., Huang, T.S., Chang, S.-F.: Image retrieval: Current techniques, promising directions, and open issues. J. Visual Communication and Image Representation 10, 39–62 (1999)
9. Nixon, M., Aguado, A.: Feature Extraction and Image Processing. Elsevier Science, Oxford (2002)
10. Hough, P.V.C.: Method and means for recognizing complex patterns, US Patent 3069654 (1962)
11. McLaughlin, R.: Randomized Hough transform: better ellipse detection. IEEE TENCON-Digital Signal Processing Applications, 409–414 (1996)

12. Sanfeliu, A., Fu, K.S.: A distance measure between attributed relational graphs for pattern recognition. IEEE Transactions on Systems, Man, and Cybernetics, 353–362 (1983)
13. Rubner, Y., Tomasi, C., Guibas, L.J.: The earth movers distance as a metric for image retrieval. International Journal of Computer Vision 40, 99–121 (2000)
14. Han, J., Kamber, M., Pei, J.: Data Mining: Concepts and Techniques. Morgan Kaufmann, San Francisco (2005)
15. Lowe, D.G.: Distinctive image features from scale-invariant keypoints. International Journal of Computer Vision 40, 91–110 (2004)

Improvement of Inkjet Printer Spur Gear Teeth Number Estimation by Fixing the Order in Maximum Entropy Spectral Analysis

Yoshinori Akao[*], Atsushi Yamamoto, and Yoshiyasu Higashikawa

National Research Institute of Police Science, Kashiwa, Chiba 2770882, Japan
akao@nrips.go.jp

Abstract. In this paper, we estimated the number of inkjet printer spur gear teeth from shorter pitch data strings than previous study by fixing the order in maximum entropy method (MEM). The purpose of this study is to improve the efficiency of inkjet printer model identification based on spur mark comparison method (SCM) in the field of forensic document analysis. Experiments were performed using two spur gears in different color inkjet printer models. The eight kinds of pitch data length whose length ranges from three to 10 rotations of spur gear was provided for analysis. The experimental results showed that proper teeth number was estimated from shorter pitch data string compared with the strategies based on minimum AIC estimate in our previous study. The estimation was successful from the short data length nearly equal to the condition of nyquist frequency. The proposed method was considered to improve the accuracy of printer model identification based on SCM.

Keywords: forensic document analysis, inkjet printer identification, spur mark comparison method, teeth number, maximum entropy method, AR order.

1 Introduction

Computational approaches have provided extremely effective solutions for problems in forensic document analysis [1, 2, 3, 4, 5, 6, 7]. However, various fraudulent documents, such as counterfeited banknotes, securities, passports, traveler's checks and driver's licenses, are still being created worldwide on computers and peripherals as a result of technological improvements. These technologies are also used to counterfeit documents such as wills, contracts, and receipts that can be used to perpetrate financial crimes.

Inkjet printer identification is becoming more prevalent in document analysis, and of the various computer peripherals, the number of inkjet printers is drastically increasing and it is becoming the most popular image output device for personal use [8]. In the first stage of forensic studies, the chemical or spectral properties of inkjet inks are the main focus [9, 10, 11].

---

[*] Corresponding author.

H. Sako, K. Franke, and S. Saitoh (Eds.): IWCF 2010, LNCS 6540, pp. 101–113, 2011.
© Springer-Verlag Berlin Heidelberg 2011

Tool marks have been extensively used in forensic science to link a known and a suspect item, and the items that created the markings [12]. Also in the field of forensic document analysis, examinations based on tool marks have been applied to photo-copiers [13, 14, 15], typewriters [16, 17, 18], and label markers [19]. The latent physical markings left on documents by printers and copiers have also been visualized by electrostatic detection devices [20].

Based on the philosophy of tool mark examination, the authors present a spur mark comparison method (SCM) [21, 22, 23], in which we compare the spur gears of an inkjet printer with the spur marks on printouts. Figure 1 is the overview of the paper conveyance mechanism (a) and a spur gear (b) of an inkjet printer. Spur gears are mechanisms that hold the paper in place as it passes through an inkjet printer [24], and spur marks are the indentations left on documents by the spur gears. In order to improve the feasibility of SCM, Furukawa *et al.* proposed a visualization method for spur marks using an infrared (IR) image scanner, and enhancing image quality by estimating a point spread function of the scanner [5, 25]. In SCM, two characteristic indices "pitch" and "mutual distance" are introduced to classify inkjet printer models. Figure 2 shows spur marks left on the printout of an inkjet printer. Two characteristic indices in SCM are explained in this figure.

Generally speaking, the greater the number of indexes, the classification result will be more precise. In our previous study [26], we proposed to extract the number of spur gear teeth from pitch data string. There is a periodicity in spur mark pitch data strings, as spur marks are formed by the same part of a spur gear at regular tooth number intervals. The teeth number of spur gears was successfully estimated within a deviation of one tooth from the pitch data string of 10 rotations of spur gear. The required length of pitch data string was shortened to 5 rotations of spur gear by our experiments [4].

In our previous study [4], a problem was indicated in the determination of the order in maximum entropy method (MEM) [27, 28]. The order needs to be higher than the teeth number of the spur gear. Although MAICE is a reasonable strategy for deter-mining the order in MEM based on maximum likelihood and the number of parame-ters, it was not always appropriate for the objective of this study—especially in the case of short pitch data string.

(a)   (b)

Fig. 1. Overview of the paper conveyance mechanism (a) and a spur gear (b) of an inkjet printer

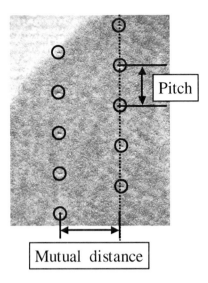

Fig. 2. Spur marks left on the printout of an inkjet printer. Two characteristic indices used in Spur mark Comparison Method (SCM), Pitch and Mutual distance, are explained

In this paper, we tried to estimate spur gear teeth number from shorter pitch data strings than in our previous study. In our new strategy, the order in MEM was set to the highest value of teeth number among various spur gears.

2 Materials and Method

2.1 Samples for Analysis

Samples for analysis were two spur gears from different model color inkjet printers. The specifications of these spur gears are shown in Table 1. The number of teeth on the spur gears is different. Spur marks from these spur gears were formed on pressure-sensitive film (Fujifilm, Prescale MS) by feeding the sheets of film into each printer. In this process, continuous spur mark lines of more than 10 spur gear rotations were sampled on the films.

The pitch data string of the spur mark lines was calculated from two-dimensional position data of the spur marks. The position of each spur mark was measured by a measurement microscope, which consisted of a two-axis micro-scanning stage (Chuo Precision Industrial, MSS-150) and a metaloscope (Nikon, Optiphoto 150). The micro-scanning stage was controlled to a resolution of 0.002 millimeters for each axis. Pitch data were calculated from the positional data of adjacent spur marks as shown in our previous study [29]. The length of a measured pitch data string was for 10 rotations of each spur gear.

Table 1. Specifications of spur gears

Spur gear	Manufacturer	Model	Number of teeth
A	Canon	BJF800	18
B	Seiko EPSON	PM-750C	24

Pitch data strings of limited length were prepared by extracting part of the pitch data string. In this study, eight pitch data lengths ranging from three to 10 rotations of spur gear were prepared. Each pitch data string was extracted from the head of the pitch data string for 10 rotations of a spur gear.

In this study, the pitch data strings of length N are represented as follows:

$$\{x_1, x_2, \cdots, x_i, \cdots, x_N\}. \tag{1}$$

2.2 Maximum Entropy Spectral Analysis of Pitch Data Strings

The spectral components of each pitch data string were analyzed by the maximum entropy method (MEM) [27, 28]. MEM spectral analysis is considered to provide robust estimation even in the case of short data length. The maximum entropy spectrum at frequency f [cycle per tooth] was represented as follows,

$$P(f) = \sigma_m \Big/ \left|1 + \sum_{k=1}^{m} a_k^{(m)} e^{-j \cdot 2\pi f k}\right|^2. \tag{2}$$

Each parameter in Eq. (2) was calculated by Burg's algorithm [27, 28] as follows,

$$\left.\begin{aligned}
\sigma_{m+1}^2 &= \sigma_m^2 \left(1 - k_m^2\right), \\
k_m &= -2 \sum_{i=m}^{N-1} e_i^{(m-1)} r_{i-1}^{(m-1)} \Big/ \sum_{i=m}^{N-1} \left(\left[e_i^{(m-1)}\right]^2 + \left[r_{i-1}^{(m-1)}\right]^2\right), \\
a_i^{(m)} &= a_i^{(m-1)} + k_m a_{m-i}^{(m-1)}, \\
e_i^{(m)} &= e_i^{(m-1)} + k_m r_{i-1}^{(m-1)}, \\
r_i^{(m)} &= r_{i-1}^{(m-1)} + k_m e_i^{(m-1)}, \\
e_i^{(0)} &= r_i^{(0)} = x_i : i = 0, 1, \cdots, N-1.
\end{aligned}\right\} \tag{3}$$

The order m in Eq. (2) is the order of autoregressive (AR) model shown below,

$$x_i + \sum_{k=1}^{m} a_k x_{i-k} = e_i. \tag{4}$$

MEM is analogous to the identification of AR model. In AR model, current value is determined by the regression of its past value to the extent of its order m.

In Eq. (4), $\{x_i\}$ is the data string sampled from stationary normal sequence, and $\{e_i\}$ stationary normal white noise. These assumptions are suitable for spur mark pitch data string by considering its nature.

In this study, AR order m was determined by following two strategies. The first strategy determines the AR order based on minimum AIC estimate (MAICE) [30]. AIC (Akaike's information criterion) [31] is widely used as a criterion for determining the number of parameters in statistical models, as it provides a reasonable model by balancing maximum likelihood against the number of parameters. In this study, AIC is represented as follows,

$$AIC = N \ln S_m^2 + 2m , \tag{5}$$

where,

$$S_m^2 = \sum_{i=m+1}^{N} \left(x_i + \gamma_{m,1} x_{i-1} + \gamma_{m,2} x_{i-2} + \cdots + \gamma_{m,m} x_{i-m} \right)^2 \Big/ (N - m) . \tag{6}$$

The second strategy is fixing AR order to the maximum value of spur gear teeth number. According to the transcendental information about spur gear to the extent of we were able to examine, the maximum value of teeth number was 48. In this strategy, we fixed AR order to 48 or the maximum value satisfying the condition of nyquist frequency determined from the data length N as follows,

$$m = \min\left[\frac{N}{2} - 1, 48 \right]. \tag{7}$$

In this study, we refer the first strategy as MAICE strategy, and the second one as MAX strategy.

2.3   Estimation of Teeth Number by Maximum Entropy Spectrum

The number of spur gear teeth was estimated by the maximum entropy spectrum. The peak frequency of the spectrum was assumed to provide a frequency corresponding to the number of teeth. The peak was searched in the range of the frequency that corresponds to teeth numbers 15 to 48, based on transcendental information about spur gears. In this paper, we considered the peaks to be a signal to noise ratio (SNR) higher than 7, and also full width at half maximum (FWHM) as less than 0.02 cycles per tooth.

3   Results and Discussion

Figure 3 shows image of spur marks sampled on pressure sensitive sheet of Spur gear A and Spur gear B respectively. There are two lines of spur marks impressed by adjacent spur gears of each spur gear. A line of spur marks measured for pitch data string is denoted by surrounding with a rectangular in this figure.

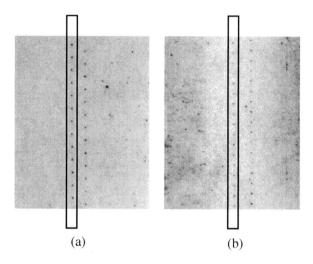

Fig. 3. Spur marks of (a) Spur gear A and (b) Spur gear B sampled on pressure-sensitive film. A line of spur marks measured for pitch data string is denoted by surrounding with a rectangular.

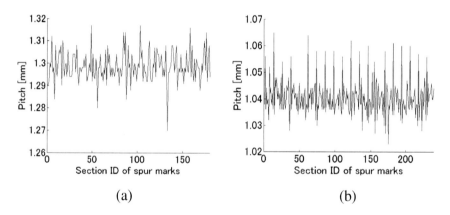

Fig. 4. Pitch data string for 10 rotations of spur gear; (a) Spur gear A and (b) Spur gear B

Figure 4 (a) shows spur mark pitch data string for 10 rotations of Spur gear A. The pitch of each spur gear was not constant, but was different according to the section of spur marks. It was difficult to acquire periodicity at a glance. Figure 4 (b) shows spur mark pitch data string for 10 rotations of Spur gear B. As same as the case of Spur gear A, pitch was different between the sections of spur marks. However a periodic feature was easily observed because of the long pitch that appears at constant interval.

Table 2 shows mean and standard deviation (S.D.) of the spur mark pitch data for 10 rotations of a spur gear. The mean of spur mark pitch was different between the two spur gears. The standard deviation was almost at the same level—smaller than 0.01.

Table 2. Mean and standard deviation (S.D.) of spur mark pitch data for 10 rotations of a spur gear

Spur gear	Mean [mm]	S.D. [mm]
A	1.298	0.006
B	1.040	0.007

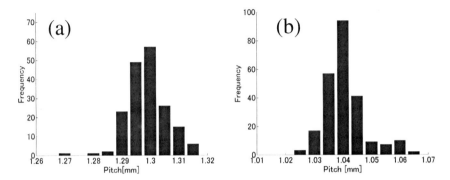

Fig. 5. Histogram of spur mark pitch data for 10 rotations of a spur gear; (a) Spur gear A and (b) Spur gear B

Figure 5 shows the histogram of the spur mark pitch data for 10 rotations of spur gear. The distribution of spur mark pitch was different between the two spur gears. In spur gear A, pitch data showed an almost Gaussian distribution around a mean value except for extremely short pitch data observed occasionally. However in spur gear B, a minor group of long pitch data around 1.06 millimeters was observed in addition to a major group of pitch data around 1.04 millimeters. The minor group of longer pitch in spur gear B was considered to be noticed as a periodic feature in Fig. 4 (b).

Table 3 lists the AR order in MEM determined by MAICE strategy or MAX strategy for Spur gear A. The AR order is listed for each length of spur mark pitch data. Concerning the MAICE strategy, AR order was higher than the number of spur gear teeth for the cases of pitch data longer than four rotations of spur gear. However AR order was lower than the number of spur gear teeth in a case where pitch data length was three rotations of spur gear. In MAX strategy, AR order was determined by Eq. (7) as listed in this table.

Table 4 lists the AR order in MEM determined by MAICE strategy or MAX strategy for Spur gear B. The AR order is listed for each length of spur mark pitch data. Concerning the MAICE strategy, AR order was higher than the number of spur gear teeth for the cases of pitch data longer than five rotations of spur gear. On the contrary, AR order was lower than the number of spur gear teeth in a case where pitch data length was shorter than four rotations of spur gear. In MAX strategy, AR order was determined by Eq. (7) as listed in this table.

Table 5 is the estimation result of teeth number of Spur gear A. The results are listed for each length of pitch data string. In the case of MAICE strategy, teeth

Table 3. AR order determined by MAICE or MAX method for each length of pitch data string sampled from Spur Gear A

Length of pitch data [Multiple of teeth number]	MAICE	MAX
3	16	26
4	18	35
5	20	44
6	20	48
7	24	48
8	19	48
9	19	48
10	19	48

Table 4. AR order determined by MAICE or MAX method for each length of pitch data string sampled from Spur Gear B

Length of pitch data [Multiple of teeth number]	MAICE	MAX
3	16	35
4	16	47
5	35	48
6	25	48
7	25	48
8	25	48
9	25	48
10	48	48

number was successfully estimated for the pitch data longer than five rotations of spur gear within a deviation of one tooth as shown in our previous study [4]. In the case of MAX strategy, teeth number was properly estimated from shorter pitch data string than the case of MAICE strategy. The required length was four rotations of spur gear.

Figure 6 shows MEM spectral distribution in MAX strategy for pitch data string shorter than five rotations of Spur gear A. The spectral peak at 18 teeth was obviously observed in the case of four and five rotations respectively. The SNR of spectral peak was higher in the case of five rotations than that of four rotations. However obvious spectral peak was not observed in the case of three rotations.

Table 6 is the estimation result of teeth number of Spur gear B. The results are listed for each length of pitch data string. In the case of MAICE strategy, teeth number was successfully estimated for the pitch data longer than five rotations of spur gear within a deviation of one tooth as shown in our previous study [4]. In the case of MAX strategy, teeth number was properly estimated from shorter pitch data string than the case of MAICE strategy. The required length was three rotations of spur gear.

Table 5. Teeth number of Spur gear A estimated for each length of pitch data string by MAICE or MAX method

Length of pitch data [Multiple of teeth number]	MAICE	MAX
3	-	-
4	-	18
5	19	18
6	18	18
7	18	18
8	18	18
9	18	18
10	18	18

Table 6. Teeth number of Spur gear B estimated for each length of pitch data string by MAICE or MAX method

Length of pitch data [Multiple of teeth number]	MAICE	MAX
3	-	24
4	-	23
5	24	24
6	24	23
7	25	24
8	25	24
9	24	24
10	25	25

Figure 7 shows MEM spectral distribution in MAX strategy for pitch data string shorter than five rotations of Spur gear B. The spectral peak was obviously observed around 24 teeth within a deviation of one tooth in all cases. The SNR of spectral peak was getting higher as the number of rotations increased.

These results show that MAX strategy provided successful estimation for shorter pitch data string than MAICE strategy. The minimum length of spur mark line required for successful estimation was approximately 93 mm and 75 mm of Spur gear A and Spur gear B respectively. This is adequately included within A6 documents, and also it is shorter than the width of many banknotes and security documents.

The reason of the improvement by MAX strategy was considered to be due to avoiding the failures in the process of AR order determination by MAICE in our previous study. As shown in Table 5 and Table 6, the order determined by MAICE was smaller than the teeth number of each spur gear in these cases. Therefore, the nature of pitch data strings for which the current value has a strong relation with the previous

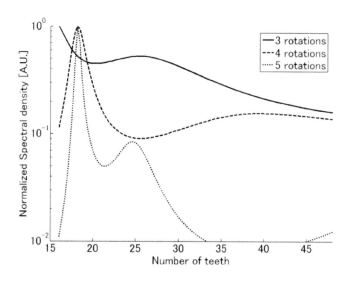

Fig. 6. MEM power spectrum of pitch data string for 3, 4 and 5 rotations of Spur Gear A

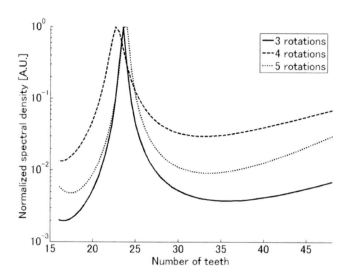

Fig. 7. MEM power spectrum of pitch data string for 3, 4 and 5 rotations of Spur Gear B

value for the same number as teeth was not adequately considered in these cases. Although MAICE is a reasonable strategy for determining the order in MEM based on maximum likelihood and the number of parameters, it was not always appropriate for the objective of this study—especially in the case of short pitch data string.

In general, MEM spectral analysis is considered to be effective even in the case of short data length. By taking MAX strategy, the ability of MEM spectral analysis was adequately utilized. Therefore, the result of this study indicates the proposed method can potentially be applied to forensic document examinations.

However in the case of three rotations of Spur gear A, teeth number was not properly estimated although AR order was higher than its teeth number. The background of this issue was considered that the periodicity of pitch data string was not so obvious as in the case of Spur gear B that the effect of noise obscured extracting the periodicity of pitch data string.

The results in this study showed that the estimation was successful even for the short data length nearly equal to the condition of nyquist frequency. Therefore the teeth number estimation based on the approach of frequency analysis of pitch data string was considered to be improved to the extent of its theoretical limit.

In order to apply the proposed method to actual forensic document evidence, the technique should be verified against the spur marks on normal paper documents. Another problem is the estimation from intermittent spur mark pitch data. In actual forensic document analysis, spur mark lines left on inkjet-printed evidence are not always continuous, but sometimes occur intermittently. A technique for interpolating intermittent spur mark pitch data will be required in future work.

4 Conclusion

In this paper, we estimated the number of spur gear teeth from shorter data length of spur mark pitch than in our previous study. The correct number of spur gear teeth was estimated from the data that corresponds to three or four rotations of spur gear. The estimation results were improved by fixing AR order to maximum value in MEM spectral analysis. The reason of the improvement in this study was considered to be due to avoiding the failures in the process of AR order determination by MAICE in our previous study. The proposed method was considered to improve the accuracy of printer model identification based on SCM in the field of forensic document analysis. These result showed that the estimation was successfully performed from the short data length nearly equal to the condition of nyquist frequency. Therefore the teeth number estimation based on the approach of frequency analysis of pitch data string was improved to the extent of its theoretical limit. In order to apply the proposed method to actual forensic document evidences, verification against the spur marks on normal paper documents should be performed. A technique for interpolating intermittent spur mark pitch data will extend the extent of the proposed method in future work.

References

1. Khanna, N., Mikkilineni, A.K., Chiu, G.T.C., Allebach, J.P., Delp, E.J.: Survey of Scanner and Printer Forensics at Purdue University. In: Srihari, S.N., Franke, K. (eds.) IWCF 2008. LNCS, vol. 5158, pp. 22–34. Springer, Heidelberg (2008)
2. Beusekom, J., Shafait, F., Breuel, M.: Document Signature Using Intrinsic Features for Counterfeit Detection. In: Srihari, S.N., Franke, K. (eds.) IWCF 2008. LNCS, vol. 5158, pp. 47–57. Springer, Heidelberg (2008)

3. Schulze, C., Schreyer, M., Stahl, A., Breuel, T.M.: Evaluation of Gray level-Features for Printing Technique Classification in High-Throughput Document Management Systems. In: Srihari, S.N., Franke, K. (eds.) IWCF 2008. LNCS, vol. 5158, pp. 35–46. Springer, Heidelberg (2008)

4. Akao, Y., Yamamoto, A., Higashikawa, Y.: Estimation of Inkjet Printer Spur Gear Teeth Number from Pitch Data String of Limited Length. In: Geradts, Z.J.M.H., Franke, K.Y., Veenman, C.J. (eds.) IWCF 2009. LNCS, vol. 5718, pp. 25–32. Springer, Heidelberg (2009)

5. Furukawa, T.: Detecting the Spur Marks of Ink-Jet Printed Documents Using a Multiband Scanner in NIR Mode and Image Restoration. In: Geradts, Z.J.M.H., Franke, K.Y., Veenman, C.J. (eds.) IWCF 2009. LNCS, vol. 5718, pp. 33–42. Springer, Heidelberg (2009)

6. Berger, C.E.H., Veenman, C.J.: Color Deconvolution and Support Vector Machines. In: Geradts, Z.J.M.H., Franke, K.Y., Veenman, C.J. (eds.) IWCF 2009. LNCS, vol. 5718, pp. 174–180. Springer, Heidelberg (2009)

7. Beusekom, J., Shafait, F., Breuel, T.: Automatic Line Orientation Measurement for Questioned Document Examination. In: Geradts, Z.J.M.H., Franke, K.Y., Veenman, C.J. (eds.) IWCF 2009. LNCS, vol. 5718, pp. 165–173. Springer, Heidelberg (2009)

8. Pan, A.I.: Advances in Thermal Inkjet Printing. In: Proceedings of the SPIE, vol. 3422, pp. 38–44 (1998)

9. Doherty, P.: Classification of Ink Jet Printers and Inks. J. Am. Soc. Quest. Doc. Exam. 1, 88–106 (1998)

10. Lewis, J.A., Kondrat, M.: Comparative Examination of Black Ink Jet Printing Inks. In: Proceedings of the 49th Annual Meeting of American Academy of Forensic Sciences, NewYork, February 17-22, p. 182 (1997)

11. Mazzella, W.D.: Diode Array Micro Spectrometry of Colour Ink-jet Printers. J. Am. Soc. Quest. Doc. Exam. 2, 65–73 (1999)

12. Davis, J.E.: An Introduction to Tool Marks, Firearms and the Striagraph, pp. 3–6. Bannerstone House, Springfield (1958)

13. Totty, R.N., Baxendale, D.: Defect Marks and the Identification of Photocopying Machines. J. Forensic Sci. 21, 23–30 (1981)

14. James, E.L.: The Classification of Office Copy Machines from Physical Characteristics. J. Forensic Sci. 32, 1293–1304 (1987)

15. Gerhart, F.J.: Identification of Photocopiers from Fusing Roller Defects. J. Forensic Sci. 37, 130–139 (1992)

16. Hardcastle, R.A.: Progressive Damage to Plastic Printwheel Typing Elements. Forensic. Sci. Int. 30, 267–274 (1986)

17. Moryan, D.D.: Cause of Typewriter Printwheel Damage Observed in the Questioned Document. J. Am. Soc. Quest. Doc. Exam. 1, 117–120 (1998)

18. Brown, J.L., Licht, G.: Using the ESDA to Visualize Typewriter Indented Markings. J. Am. Soc. Quest. Doc. Exam. 1, 113–116 (1998)

19. Mason, J.J., Grose, W.P.: The Individuality of Toolmarks Produced by a Label Marker Used to Write Extortion Notes. J. Forensic. Sci. 32, 137–147 (1987)

20. LaPorte, G.M.: The Use of an Electrostatic Detection Device to Identify Individual and Class Characteristics on Document Produced by Printers and Copiers—a Preliminary Study. J. Forensic. Sci. 49, 1–11 (2004)

21. Akao, Y., Kobayashi, K., Seki, Y.: Examination of spur marks found on inkjet-printed documents. J. Forensic Sci. 50, 915–923 (2005)

22. Akao, Y., Kobayashi, K., Sugawara, S., Seki, Y.: Discrimination of inkjet printed counter-feits by spur marks and feature extraction by spatial frequency analysis. In: van Renesse, R.F. (ed.) Optical Security and Counterfeit Deterrence Techniques IV, Proceedings of the SPIE, vol. 4677, pp. 129–137 (2002)
23. Akao, Y., Kobayashi, K., Seki, Y., Takasawa, N.: Examination of inkjet printed counter-feits by spur marks. In: Abstract of 4th Annual Meeting of Japanese Association of Sci-ence and Technology for Identification, Tokyo, p. 115 (1998) (in Japanese)
24. Maruyama, M.: inventor. Seiko Epson Corp., assignee.: Paper-pressing Mechanism for Ink Jet Printer. Japan patent 1814458, April 12 (1983)
25. Furukawa, T., Nemoto, N., Kawamoto, H.: Detection of Spur Marks Using Infrared Ray Scanner and Estimation for Out-of-Focus PSF. In: Abstract of 14th Annual Meeting of Japanese Association of Forensic Science and Technology, Tokyo, p. 190 (2008) (in Japa-nese)
26. Akao, Y., Kobayashi, K., Sugawara, S., Seki, Y.: Estimation of the number of spur teeth by determination of AR model order. In: Abstract of 6th Annual Meeting of Japanese As-sociation of Science and Technology for Identification, Tokyo, vol. 170 (2000) (in Japa-nese)
27. Burg, J.P.: Maximum entropy spectral analysis. In: 37th Annual International Meeting, Soc. of Explor. Geophys., Oklahoma City, Okla, October 31 (1967)
28. Burg, J.P.: Maximum Entropy Spectral Analysis. In: Ph.D dissertation, Stanford Univ. (1975)
29. Akao, Y., Kobayashi, K., Sugawara, S., Seki, Y.: Measurement of pitch and mutual dis-tance of spur marks by two-axes automatic scanning stage. In: Abstract of 5th Annual Meeting of Japanese Association of Science and Technology for Identification, Tokyo, p. 137 (1999) (in Japanese)
30. Akaike, H.: A new look on the statistical model identification. IEEE Trans. Automat. Contr. AC-19, 716–723 (1974)
31. Akaike, H.: Information theory and an extension of the maximum likelihood principle. In: Petrov, B.N., Csaki, F. (eds.) 2nd International Symposium on Information Theory, Akademiai Kiado, Budapest, pp. 267–281 (1973)

Detecting Indentations on Documents Pressed by Pen Tip Force Using a Near Infrared Light Emitting Diode (NIR LED) and Shape from Shading

Takeshi Furukawa

Forensic Science Laboratory, Ibaraki Prefectural Police H.Q.,
978-6 Kasahara, Mito, 3108550 Japan
tfurukawa@ieee.org

Abstract. We proposed the new method that detected indentations pressed by pen tip force on paper using an oblique near infrared (NIR) emitting by light emitting diodes (LEDs). According to conventional methods indentations were observed by document examiners' eyes using a microscope. However it is difficult to estimate depths of the indentations because human eyes only can observe shades and brightness made by indentations instead of measuring the depths of indentations. Using a confocal laser microscope is able to directly measure the depths of indentations. However this method needs to take long time and instruments are expensive. Using a NIR LED and an optical model called shape from shading resolved the issues of time and cost. It is useful for forensic document examiners to approximately evaluate the depths of indentations of handwriting by our proposal method because the method will be lead to convenient discrimination between forgery handwriting and genuine one.

Keywords: Handwriting, Indentations, NIR LED, Shape from shading.

1 Introduction

In a field of online authentication system a lot of attempts to utilize several parameters (e.g. pen tip velocity, pen tip acceleration and pen tip pressure) as indicators of hand-writing recognition had already been addressed by many computer scientists using sets of apparatus such as digitizer tablets. Now these efforts resulted in recognition devices of online handwriting character when data were inputted to tablet PCs. While turn ours eyes to a filed of forensic science evidences remained in real crime scenes were almost merely offline static handwriting on documents. We forensic document examiners observed handwriting using an optical microscope because we need to exploit traces that were left by dynamic hand movements such as pen tip pressure. However it is difficult to estimate how many quantifies were equivalent to observations by human eyes. We strongly desire to develop a new system that measures indentations pressed by pen tip force on documents because shapes of handwriting are easily faked by counterfeiters who overwrite forgeries of handwriting on a sheet of paper

H. Sako, K. Franke, and S. Saitoh (Eds.): IWCF 2010, LNCS 6540, pp. 114–125, 2011.

as watching transparently underneath genuine of handwriting. In this situation, several studies that combined online features with offline features were addressed. These studies were mainly classified into two categories. One is methods of measuring direct indicators indicating the pen tip force such as depths or profiles of indentations using confocal laser scanning microscopes or scanning electron microscopes (SEM) [1, 2]. The other is methods for measuring indirect indicators relating the pen tip force such as ink deposit or density of writing ink using image processing techniques [3, 4, 5, 6, 7, 8, 9, 10]. The former is ideal methods however the defect is that measuring area is too small and measuring time is too long. The latter is conventional methods however the ink density or deposit always does not have linear relationship with the pen tip force. In this paper we propose a new method for reconstructing indentations profiles using a near infrared (NIR) light emitting diode (LED) and an optical model (i.e. shape from shading). According to progress of charge coupled devices (CCDs) or complementary metal oxide semiconductor (CMOS) sensors we can easily acquire high grade digital photographs using flat bed image scanners or digital cameras. In the field of forensic science the sets of apparatus are widely used at laboratories. Especially flat bed image scanners are suitable for handwriting on documents as scanning it because these have fixed focus structure. In a field of forensic document examination image input devices are used by examiners instead of film cameras. We already have used NIR emitting by a multi band scanner in NIR mode to forensic document examination. One object we applied was spur marks spiked by spur gears of ink jet printers [11]. Other was detecting indentations pressed by pen tip force while writing handwriting characters [12]. In these applications there were several difficulties to use the multi band scanner. One is defocus due to differences of wave length of illumination (e.g. visible light, ultraviolet (UV) and NIR). Other is low resolution of a multi band scanner (i.e. 1600dpi) is not enough to express details of evidences. Recently iMeasure Inc, Japan has developed a new multi band scanner which has auto focus system to multi wave length and has high resolution (2400dpi). We can resolve above two difficulties using the new scanner however this scanner is expensive. In this paper we try to another more reasonable method. A multi band scanner uses NIR LEDs as illuminators. LEDs have several advantages compared to incandescent bulbs that have been used as illuminators for long time. One is low assumption of electronic power and is to avoid heat from light sources. Additionally its size is compact. We can acquire an image that includes indentations expressed as shade using the NIR LED. A lot of issues of shape from shading have been addressed by many researchers. These efforts resulted in proposing a lot of models [13, 14, 15]. In these methods, it was reported that reconstruction of profiles of unfolded books modified stitches using a flat bed scanner as an oblique light source [16, 17]. This study adopted Lambert model among many models. In next chapter we explained shortly the NIR LED and a method for reconstruction of profiles of indentations. At last we compared the indentation profile reconstructed using our proposal method with real measurement values of the indentation using a confocal laser scanning microscope.

2   Materials and Method

2.1   NIR LED and CCD Camera Used in the Experience

We used the NIR LED, (HDMISI8IR-940, HAYASHI WATCH-WORKS CO. Ltd, Japan). Fig.1 shows the overview of the device. Table 1 shows the specification of the NIR LED used. A CCD camera we used was an internal camera which was equipped in a video spectral comparator (VSC 6000, foster + freeman Ltd, UK). A long pass filer that cuts off the radiation under approximate 850nm wave length NIR was also used the VSC6000 attached system.

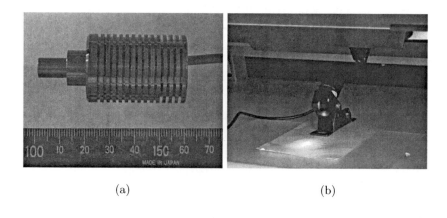

(a)   (b)

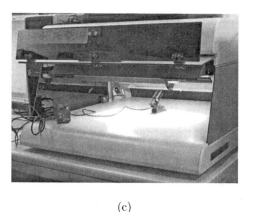

(c)

Fig. 1. Instruments overview. (a) is the near infrared light emitting diode (NIR LED) using in the experiment. (b) is an image of the NIR LED emitting photographed by a CCD camera. (c) is the NIR LED set in a video spectrum comparator (VSC6000).

Table 1. Specification of the NIR LED used in the experiment

Item	Details
Product name	Near infrared light emitting diode
Model number	HDMISI8IR-940, HAYASHI WATCH-WORKS
Central wave length	940nm
Half bandwidth	60nm
Material	GaAs
Price	Approx. JPY50000, Power supplier JPY35000
Power supply	HDC-700SV
Person in charge	Soushi TOMITA, Sales Div. Special Product Dept.

2.2 Samples for Analysis

Ball point pens have widely used in Japan instead of fountain pens. These black inks are almost composed of several color dyes that were transmitted by NIR. Figure 2 shows the two images of the line that was drawn by a ball point pen (BNH5-BK, Zebra, Japan) under illuminations of visible light and the NIR LED on five sheets of recycled paper. The left side image shows under the visible light from a fluorescent light tube. The right side shows under NIR from the LED. Figure 2 (b) shows the line that was drawn with the black ink ball point pen disappeared under the NIR LED illumination. In the image NIR separated the shade made by the indentation from the black ink on the paper surface. Our method resulted in the clear observation of the gray gradient of the shade. The gray scaled image contained the information of the indentation pressed by pen tip force. Table 2 shows that the conditions under which the samples of handwriting we used were written.

Table 2. Specification of paper and materials of underlay used

Paper	Underlay materials
Recycled paper (RECYCLE PAPER, NBSRICHO, Japan)	Top of OA Desk (Uchida, Japan)
	Five sheets of the recycled paper
Coated paper (Super fine paper, EPSON, Japan)	Rubber mat (ITO, Japan)

2.3 Observation of a Brightness Profile under the NIR LED Illumination

Figure 3 shows the brightness profile perpendicular to the horizontal line of the cross line handwriting stroke in Figure 2. The peak and the trough observed in the profile in Figure 3 correspond to high light and dark in the image obtained under the NIR illumination using the NIR LED. The profile was formed as shape of 'S'.

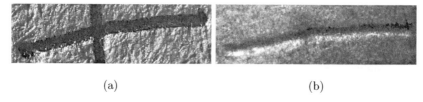

(a)   (b)

Fig. 2. Magnified images of handwriting drawn by a black ink ball point pen. (a) is image under the visible light illumination. (b) a is image under the NIR LED illumination.

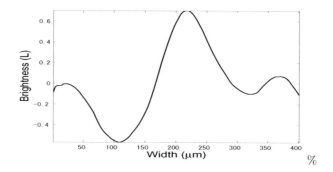

Fig. 3. The profile of brightness on the indentation under the NIR LED illumination

2.4   Measurement of Real Indentation Profile by a Confocal Laser Microscope

In order to verify an accuracy of a simulated indentation profile that was reconstructed by the shade the real indentation profiles of the handwritten trace were measured using a confocal laser scanning microscope (VF-7500, Keyence Ltd, Japan). Figure 4 shows a example of a profile of a indentation pressed by the pen tip force. The profile was so jaggy by fiber on paper that it was smoothed by a butter wise filter. The thick line shown in Figure 4 was the smoothed profile.

2.5   Application of Optical Model

Methods for reconstructing indentation profiles of handwriting on paper from NIR shade images were described below. In order to reconstruct indentation profiles across a width of a handwritten line we used a following simple conventional method of shape from shading in computer graphics. In a lot of optical models the Lambert model have widely used in computer vision in spite of proposing this model in 1790's. This model considers reflection of light from an object surface as a complete diffuse reflection. Accordingly while Lambert model was suitable to apply the reflection from the object that has a little roughness surface (e.g. paper, clay, and cloth) this model dose not befit objects that have bear specular surface. Lambert model is the empirical model however it is useful because most

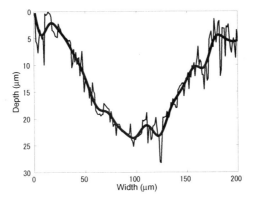

Fig. 4. The measurement real indentation profile and the smoothed profile. The thin line shows real measurement values. The thick line shows smoothed line by butter wise filter.

popular forms as several piece of paper contain a little rough surface. This model is indicated by the following equation.

$$I_d(V) = k_d \cdot L_d \cdot \cos\theta = k_d \cdot L_d \cdot (N \cdot L). \tag{1}$$

Where $I_d(V)$ is a intensity of sum total brightness from an object surface. K_d is a coefficient of diffuse reflection that each substances individually possess. L_d is an intensity of a light source. N is a vector of a normal line. V is a vector of a visual line. Figure 5 (a) shows a diagram that indicates relationship between an incident rays, a normal line, a reflect line and a visual line. When we reconstructed indentation profiles of handwriting we hypothesized the following four ideal prerequisites.

1. The paper surface has complete diffuse reflection properties.
2. Reflection properties of the paper surface were constant in all area.
3. The indentation profile of handwritten trace was approximated by the Gaussian function.
4. The angle between NIR incident ray and the visual (CCD) line was constantly $\pi/4$ (45 degree).

Figure 5 (b) shows a diagram of a profile of handwriting indentation on a document which was illuminated by the NIR LED. The diagram simply explained the optical relationship when the Lambert model was applied to the indentation surface. In the Figure 5 (b) the y-axis indicates the direction to which the light source illuminated. The z-axis indicates the depth of the indentation pressed by the pen tip force when the handwriting was drawn. Here, the following relationship was obtained.

ψ(d) was an angle between a light source line and a visual line. The angle was the constant $\pi/4$ obtained from prerequisite 4. ϕ was an angle between a light source line and a normal line. θ was an angle between the normal line and the

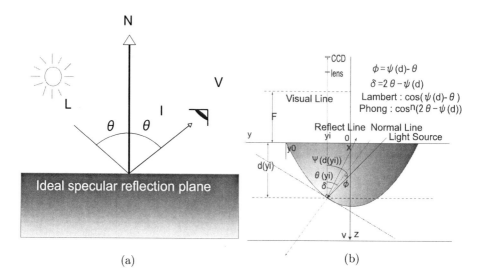

(a)   (b)

Fig. 5. Compared the brightness profile simulated to the real profile. (a) is the diagram of Lambert model. (b) is the diagram applied the Lambert model for the relationship between the indentation and the NIR LED incident.

visual line. Intensity of brightness that reflected from surface of indentations was cosine of an angle between a light source line and a normal line by the definition of the Lambert model.

Figure 6 shows the profile was obtained by measuring the indentation using a confocal laser scanning microscope. In the Figure 6 the thin line indicates the raw values measured and the thick line indicates the approximated curve by Gaussian.

2.6   Comparison between Simulated Brightness Profile and Real Profile

The following equation (2) is obtained because indentation profiles were approximated by Gaussian curves.

$$f(x) = a \cdot \exp\left(-\frac{x^2}{b^2}\right). \tag{2}$$

'x' denoted a position along a horizontal axis in indentations, 'a' denoted depths of indentations and 'b' denoted widths of indentations. After Gaussian curves were differentiated tangential lines to the indention profiles were obtained. By being approximated indentation profiles by Gaussian curves and by differentiated this curves tangential lines to indentation profiles were obtained. By inversed tangential lines normal lines were acquired because normal lines were orthogonal

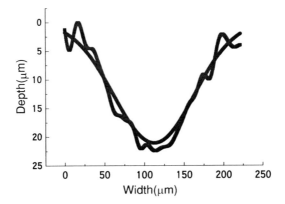

Fig. 6. The indentation profiles approximated with the Gaussian function

to tangential lines. As mentioned above calculations we acquired normal lines
and angles between normal lines and the visual lines (see Eq. 3).

$$\theta = \tan^{-1}\left\{ -\frac{2a}{b^2}x \cdot \exp\left(-\frac{x^2}{b^2}\right)\right\}. \tag{3}$$

Also angles of between NIR LEDs illuminating lines and the normal lines were
calculated by below equation (see Figure 5).

$$\phi = \frac{\pi}{4} - \theta. \tag{4}$$

Intensity of brightness on indentations surface was cosine of ϕ. Accordingly following function was obtained.

$$f(x) = \frac{\sqrt{2}}{2}(\cos\theta + \sin\theta). \tag{5}$$

We simulated brightness profiles from indentations surface. Figure 7 shows the
example of the simulated result. The left profile indicated the simulated profile.
The right profile indicated the real measurement profile. The both profiles were
similar to the each other.

2.7   Reconstruction of Indentation Profiles

Before now, we simulated brightness profiles of handwriting using the NIR LED
and the Lambert model. In turn we reconstructed the profile of the indentation
from the brightness profile. Accordingly, the following estimated function was
obtained and tried to minimize this function. L was an estimated value. F was
a real measured data and f was the fitting function descried above in following
Eq. 6.

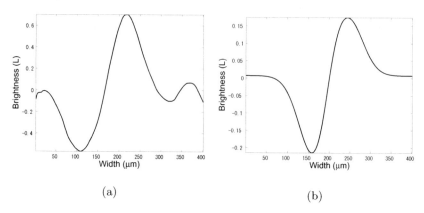

(a)   (b)

Fig. 7. Compared the brightness profile simulated to the real profile. (a) is real profile, (b) is simulated one.

$$L = \left\{ \bar{F} - f(x) \right\}^2.$$
(6)

The widths of the indentations were determined with the real measurement values by the confocal laser scanning microscope. The depths of the indentations were shifted from 1 μm to 100 μm. The depths estimated were able to be obtained in this way.

3   Results and Discussion

Using above method the reconstructed indentation profiled were shown in Figure 8.The comparing the indentation profile simulated by the proposal method to the real indentation profiles measured by the confocal laser scanning micro- scope indicated that the both profiles were on weak consistent with the each other. For the first step to reconstruct the dynamic behavior of handwriting we proposed the new approach using the NIR LED and the Lambert model. We were able to obtain the image in which the lines disappeared was acquired using the NIR LED as an illuminator because NIR was able to transmit inks of black ball point pens. And this process resulted in separating the shade made by in- dentation from the gradation of ball point pen inks. The indentation profile was implied in the shade image as gray scale gradation value. We reconstructed the indentation profile from the shade image using the Lambert model. Finally the pseudo profile was compared to the real indentation profile that was measured by the confocal laser scanning microscope. The result of the simulation was on weak consistent with the real indentation profile. The reasons of inconsistent were considered to following points;

1. The paper surface was not complete the diffuse surface but also contains the specular components.
2. The fitting approximated function (the Gaussian curve) was inappropriate.

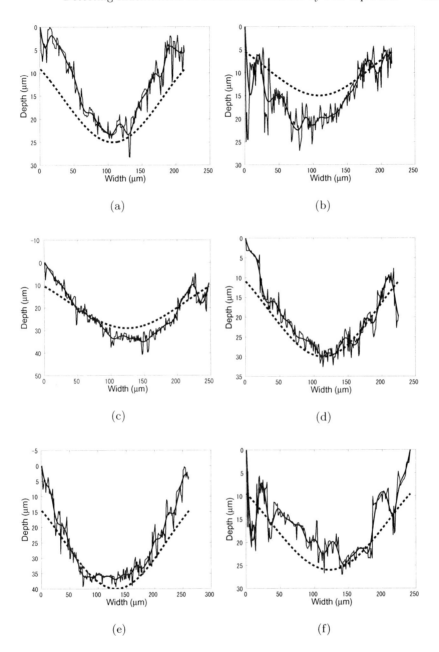

Fig. 8. Comparison of indentation profiles reconstructed with real profiles. The dotted line shows the reconstructed profiles. The solid line shows real profiles.(a) is written on the recycled paper on the top of desk. (b) is on the coated paper on the top of desk. (c) is on the recycled paper on the five sheets of paper. (d) is on the coated paper on the five sheets of paper. (e) is on the recycled paper on the rubber mat. (f) is on the coated paper on the rubber mat.

In future a Phong model and a Lognormal Gaussian model is going to be applied our method to improve the accuracy of the reconstruction.

We should take the much device to the method to use practical applications that could measure indentations pressed by pen tip forces. This method could be helped for forensic document examiners to investigate dynamic behaviors that remained in handwriting.

Acknowledgments. This study was supported by the Grant-in-Aid for Encouragement of Scientists (KAKENHI, 22919009-2010) from Japan Society for the Promotion of Science (JSPS).

References

1. Akao, Y., Sugawara, S., Seki, Y.: 3D measurement and visualization of handwritten trace by ballpoint pen using confocal laser scanning microscope. In: Abstract of 7th Annual Meeting of Japanese Association of Science and Technology for Identification, vol. 175 (2001) (in Japanese)
2. Berx, V., Kinder, J.D.: The application of profilometry in the analysis of the 'crossing lines' problem". In: Proceedings of the Conference of American Society of Questioned Document Examiners (1996)
3. Abuhaiba, S.I., Ahmed, P.: Restoration of temporal information in off-line Arabic handwriting. Pattern Recognition 26(7), 1009–1017 (1993)
4. Ammar, M., Yoshida, Y., Fukumura, T.: A new effective approach for off-line verification of signature by using pressure differences. In: Proceeding 8th ICPR (International Conference on Pattern Recognition), Paris, France, pp. 566–569 (1986)
5. Doermann, D.S., Rosenfeld, A.: Recovery of Temporal Information from Static Images of Handwriting. International Journal of Computer Vision 15(1-2), 143–164; Earlier: Computer Vision and Pattern Recognition CVPR 1992, pp. 162–168 (1995)
6. Feminani, J., Rowe, J., Razdan, A.: 3D aspects of offline signatures. In: Proceedings of the 11th Conference of the International Graphonomics Society (IGS 2003), pp. 233–236 (2003)
7. Franke, K., Grube, G.: The automatic extraction of pseudodynamic information from static images of handwriting based on marked grayvalue segmentation. Journal of Forensic Document Examination 11, 17–38 (1998)
8. Franke, K., Bünnemeyer, O., Sy, T.: Ink texture analysis for writer identification. In: Proceeding 8th International Workshop on Frontiers in Handwriting Recognition (IWFHR), pp. 268–273 (2002)
9. Franke, K., Rose, S.: Ink-Deposition Model: The relation of writing and ink deposition processes. In: Proceeding 9th International Workshop on Frontiers in Handwriting Recognition (IWFHR), pp. 173–178 (2004)
10. Kato, Y., Yasuhara, M.: Recovery of drawing order from single-stroke handwriting images. IEEE Transaction, Pattern Analysis and Machine Intelligence 22(9), 938–949 (2000); Comm. Pure Appl. Math. 33, 609–633 (1980)
11. Furukawa, T.: Detecting the spur marks of ink-jet printed documents using a multi-band scanner in NIR mode and image restoration. In: Geradts, Z.J.M.H., Franke, K.Y., Veenman, C.J. (eds.) IWCF 2009. LNCS, vol. 5718, pp. 33–42. Springer, Heidelberg (2009)

12. Furukawa, T.: Detecting indentations pressed by pen tip force on writing paper using infrared scanner. In: Proceedings of 64th American Society of Questioned Document Examiners (ASQDE 2006), pp. 19–24 (2006)
13. Blinn, J.F.: Models of light reflection for computer synthesized pictures. In: ACM Computer Graphics (SIGGRAPH 1977), vol. 19(10), pp. 542–547 (1977)
14. Phong, B.T.: Illumination for computer generated pictures. CACM (Communications of the Association for Computing Machinery) 18(6), 311–317 (1975)
15. Torrance, K.E., Sparrow, E.M.: Theory for offspecular reflection from roughened surface. Journal of Optic Society of America 57(9), 1105–1114 (1967)
16. Trowbridge, T.S., Reiz, K.P.: Average irregular representation of a rough surface for ray reflection. Journal of the Optical Society of America 65(5), 531–536 (1975)
17. Wada, T., Ukida, H., Matsuyama, T.: Shape from shading with interreflections under proximal light source-3D shape reconstruction of unfolded book surface from a scanner image. In: Proceedings of 5th International Conference on Computer Vision, vol. 66 (1995)
18. Wada, T., Ukida, H., Matsuyama, T.: Shape from shading with interreflections under a proximal light source: Distortion-Free copying of an unfolded book. International Journal of Computer Vision 24(2), 125–135 (1997)

Similar Partial Copy Detection of Line Drawings Using a Cascade Classifier and Feature Matching

Weihan Sun and Koichi Kise

Graduate School of Engineering, Osaka Prefecture University
1-1 Gakuen-cho, Sakai, Osaka, 599-8531 Japan
sunweihan@m.cs.osakafu-u.ac.jp
kise@cs.osakafu-u.ac.jp

Abstract. Copyright protection of image publications is an important task of forensics. In this paper, we focus on line drawings, which are represented by lines in monochrome. Since partial copies and similar copies are always applied in plagiarisms of line drawings, we propose combining the technique of object detection and image retrieval to detect similar partial copies from suspicious images: first, detecting regions of interest (ROIs) by a cascade classifier; then, locate the corresponding source parts from copyrighted images using a feature matching method. The experimental results have proved the effectiveness of proposed method for detecting similar partial copies from complex backgrounds.

Keywords: Line drawing, Copyright protection, Object detection, Image retrieval, Similar copy, Partial copy.

1   Introduction

The development of computer techniques offers us methods to store images in digital mode and distribute quickly through the Internet. In contrast of conveniences, it also causes copyright problems of images. Such as comics, graphs and logos, line drawings are an important part of image publications. Line drawings are a type of images that consist of distinct straight and curved lines in monochrome or few colors placed against plain backgrounds. Because of simplicities of line drawings, it is easy to create similar drawings. Practically, illegal users usually copy the important part and apply them as a part of their own drawings, which are called partial copies. Therefore, for protecting the copyright of line drawings, we should consider the detection of similar copies and partial copies, which bring more challenges to their copyright protection.

In our previous research, we proposed applying the technique of image retrieval to detect partial copies of line drawings [1]: copyrighted line drawings are collected in a database, and suspicious images are treated as queries. By applying MSER (Maximally Stable Extremal Regions) [2] as a region detector and HOG (Histograms of Oriented Gradients) [3] as a feature detector, we achieved detecting both printed and handwritten partial copies from complex

H. Sako, K. Franke, and S. Saitoh (Eds.): IWCF 2010, LNCS 6540, pp. 126–137, 2011.
© Springer-Verlag Berlin Heidelberg 2011

backgrounds. However, because of enormous volume of line drawing publications which require copyright protection, the problems of database overload and low detection speed prevent the method to be utilized in practice.

Considering not the whole image requires copyright protection, the key to solve these problems is only to store important parts in our database. In addition, based on the important parts in the database, the similar copies should also be able to be detected. However, which part is the important part? This is a quite controversy problem. Here, let us focus on one of the most important line drawing publications: comics, in which faces of characters might be the parts which requires copyright protection.

To detect such important parts (regions of interest (ROIs)), we propose applying an object detection technique. There are many researches about object detection, such as the detection of face, pedestrian, vehicle and so on [3,4,5]. Viola et al. [6] proposed a framework to train a cascade classifier, by which rigid objects can be detected with fast detection speed and low false positive rate. However, since terrific transformation in faces of comic characters, the effectiveness for detecting comic faces has not been proved. In this paper, we apply Viola-Jone framework to line drawings and prove it is available for detecting the faces of comic characters. Furthermore, we built a database using detected parts and achieved the detection of similar parts by applying a method of feature matching.

The rest parts of this paper is arranged as: Section 2. describes our proposed method. Experiments and results is shown in Section 3. Finally, Section 4. is conclusions and future works.

2   Proposed Method

2.1   Overview

As shown in Fig. 1, the processing of the proposed method is divided into two parts: ROI detection and similar part detection. In the part of ROI detection, we propose applying the method of object detection to detect possible faces of comic characters. Then, in the part of similar part detection, the detected parts from copyrighted images are collected to build a database. The parts extracted from suspicious images are treated as queries. By matching the features of queries and the database, the part which is similar with each query is reported.

2.2   ROI Detection

To detect faces of comic characters, we propose applying Viola-Jones detection framework. In this framework, positive samples (images contain the object) and negative samples (non-object images) are collected. Then, features are extracted from these samples and marked with their response (1:object, 0:non-object). After that, the most characteristic features are selected. Based on a threshold, a decision tree can be built for each feature, which is called a classifier. By arranging such classifiers in a cascade structure, we can get a cascade classifier.

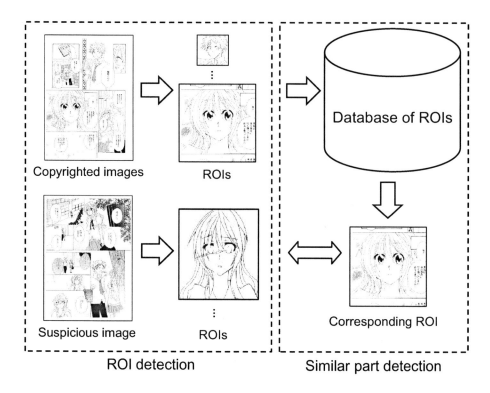

Fig. 1. Processing of the proposed method

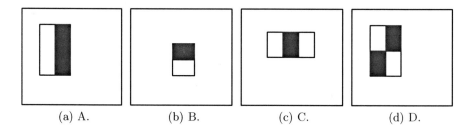

(a) A.   (b) B.   (c) C.   (d) D.

Fig. 2. Example of using Haar-like features

Feature extraction. Viola et al. applied Haar-like features in their method. More specifically, they utilized four kinds of features. As show in Fig. 2, the Haar-like feature is represented by the difference of sums of pixel values within adjacent rectangles. Since the size of rectangles changes from 1 pixel to the whole detecting region (detector). We will have $162,336$ features for a detector with the size of 24×24 pixels.

To speed up the calculation of Haar-like features, Viola et al. proposed applying integral image. The integral image at location x, y contains the sum of the pixels above and to the left of x, y, inclusive:

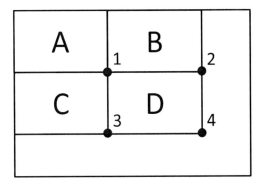

Fig. 3. Calculation using integral image. The value at location 1 (ii_1) is the sum of the pixels in rectangle A, ii_2 is A+B, ii_3 is A+C, ii_4 is A+B+C+D. Therefore, the sum pixels in D can be computed as $ii_4 + ii_1 - ii_2 - ii_3$.

$$ii(x, y) = \sum_{x' \leq x, y' \leq y} i(x', y')$$

where $ii(x, y)$ is the integral image and $i(x, y)$ is the original image. As shown in Fig. 3, we can get the sum of pixels for any region by 3 times' calculations. Therefore, the Haar-like features can be calculated in a constant time.

Also other features can be applied to the Viola-Jones framework. A more precise description of objects' characteristics can lead to a higher detection rate. In addition, since the construction of cascade classifiers demands many samples, the speed of feature calculation has an important effect on training time.

Feature selection. Since the Haar-like feature set is over-complete, Adaboost [7] is utilized for choosing the features. AdaBoost is a machine learning method to combine weak classifiers into a strong classifier by an iterative algorithm. The specific algorithm is shown in Fig. 4. In each loop, a weak classifier with the lowest error rate is generated, and the samples which failed to be classified will be assigned a larger weight to increase the precision of following classifiers. Finally, weak classifiers (with weights which depend on accuracy) are added to be a strong classifier. In Viola-Jones framework, weak classifiers are decision trees built by different features in one detector. According to a certain threshold, weak classifiers predict the results (1: positive, 0 negative).

Construction of cascade classifiers. Furthermore, the framework imports a cascade structure to increase the detection performance while reducing computation time. As shown in Fig. 5, only the sub-windows predicted true can go to next layers.

The Adaboost algorithm is applied to build such a cascade automatically. The specific algorithm is shown in Fig. 6. By reducing the threshold of classifiers,

1. Given example images $(x_1,y_1),...,(x_n, y_n)$ where $y_i = 0$ for negative samples and $y_i = 1$ for positive samples.
2. Initialize weights $w_{1,i} = \frac{1}{2m}, \frac{1}{2l}$ for each sample, where m and l are the number of negatives and positives respectively.
3. For t = 1,...,T:
   (a) Normalize the weights, $w_{t,i} \leftarrow \frac{w_{t,i}}{\sum_{j=1}^{n} w_{t,j}}$
   (b) Select the best weak classifier with respect to the weighted error

$$\epsilon_t = min_{f,p,\theta} \sum_i w_i|h(x_i, f, p, \theta) - y_i|$$

   (c) Define $h_t(x) = h(x, f_t, p_t, \theta_t)$ where f_t, pt_t, and θ_t are the minimizers of ϵ_t.
   (d) Update the weights:

$$w_{t+1,i} = w_{t,i}\beta_t^{1-e_i}$$

   where $e_i = 0$ if sample x_i is classified correctly, $e_i = 1$ otherwise, and $\beta_t = \frac{\epsilon_t}{1-\epsilon_t}$.
4. The final strong classifier is:

$$C(x) = \begin{cases} 1 & \sum_{t=1}^{T} \alpha_t h_t x \geq \frac{1}{2} \sum_{t=1}^{T} \alpha_t \\ 0 & \text{otherwise} \end{cases}$$

Fig. 4. Boosting algorithm

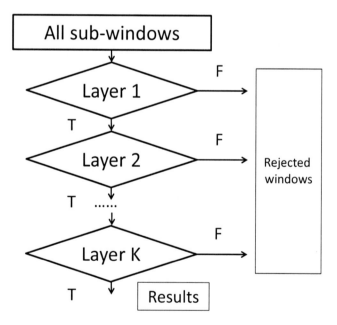

Fig. 5. Detection using cascade classifiers

- User selects values for f, the maximum acceptable false positive rate per layer and d, the minimum acceptable detection rate per layer.
- User Selects target over all false positive rate, F_{target}.
- P = set of positive samples
- N = set of negative samples
- $F_0 = 1, D_0 = 1$
- $i = 0$
- while $F_i > F_{target}$
  - $i \leftarrow i + 1$
  - $n_i = 0, F_i = F_{i-1}$
  - while $F_i > f \times F_{i-1}$
    * $n_i \leftarrow n_i + 1$
    * Use P and N to train a classifier with n_i features using AdaBoost
    * Evaluate current cascaded classifier on validation set to determine F_i and D_i.
    * Decrease threshold for the ith classifier until the current cascaded classifier has a detection rate of at least $d \times D_{i-1}$ (this also affects F_i)
  - $N \leftarrow \emptyset$
  - If $F_i > F_{target}$ then evaluate the current cascaded detector on the set of non-face images and put any false detections into the set N

Fig. 6. Cascade detector training algorithm

it is easy to achieve a high detection rate with a high false positive rate. The detection rate(D) and false positive rate(F) of final cascade classifier will be

$$D = \prod_{i=1}^{K} d_i \ , \quad F = \prod_{i=1}^{K} f_i$$

where d_i, f_i represent detection rate and false positive rate for each layer respectively, K is the number of cascade layers. For example, for a 10 layers cascade classifier, if d_i is set to be 0.995 and f_i is set to be 0.3 for each layer. For the final cascade classifier, the detection rate will be about 0.95(since $0.995^{10} \approx 0.95$) and the false positive rate will be about 6×10^{-6} (since $0.3^{10} \approx 6 \times 10^{-6}$), by which can lead satisfied detections.

Detection of ROIs. We apply sliding window technique to detect sub-windows in different scale. The detecting sub-windows are normalized into the same size of detector. After detecting all sub-windows of the whole image, we apply the union-find algorithm to group detected sub-windows. To make detected parts contain more information, the sub-windows are enlarged as k times large as the detected parts to be ROIs. In following parts of this paper, we set $k = 4$ by considering the balance between information and noisy in such regions.

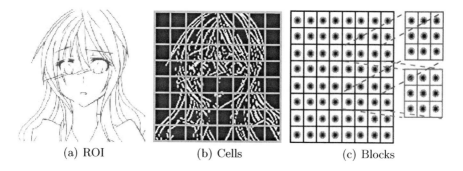

(a) ROI   (b) Cells   (c) Blocks

Fig. 7. Region instruction of HOG features

2.3   Similar Part Detection

In the processing of similar part detection, we propose applying the HOG feature descriptor to describe the ROIs, and matching the pair of parts whose features are near each other.

Feature extraction. We apply HOG to describe the detected ROIs, and extract one HOG feature from each ROI. As shown in Fig. 7(b), first calculate the gradient magnitude and the direction at each pixel, and divide each ROI into 8×8 cells evenly. Then, as shown in Fig. 7(c), the gradient directions are quantized into 9 bins. Thus we get a vector of 9 dimensions for each cell by calculating the gradient direction histogram based on the gradient strength. Next, combine the cells into overlapped blocks as 3×3 cells per block. The vector for each block is composed of vectors of cells, and the vector of each ROI consists of all normalized vectors of blocks. Therefore we extract a vector of $9 \times 3 \times 3 \times 6 \times 6 = 2916$ dimensions.

Matching. Matching of queries and parts in database is based on the distance between their feature vectors. The pair of image parts which are nearest with each other is reported as result.

To speed up the searching of feature vector closed to each other, we apply ANN (Approximate Nearest Neighbor Search) [8]. ANN is a method to find the approximate nearest neighbor by using the k-d tree. To increase the matching speed, ANN searches the feature space shrunk by the factor $1/(1+\epsilon)$. Considering the detetion speed and detection accuracy, we set ϵ to 1 empirically.

3   Experiments

3.1   ROI Detection

First, we did an experiment to test the effectiveness of comic face detection.

To train the cascade classifier, we collect $3,000$ frontal faces of comic characters from 20 kinds of comics. As shown in Fig. 8, most of the faces are cropped

Fig. 8. Examples of positive samples used for training. They are from Rurouni Kenshin, Neon Genesis Evangelion, Hoshin Engi, H2, Hunter × Hunter, JoJo's Bizarre Adventure, Lucky Star, Master Keaton, Maison Ikkoku, Miyuki, Monster, Planetes, Rosario + Vampire, Rough and Slam Dunk.

from just above the eyebrows to chin, and normalized to 24 × 24 pixels as our positive samples. For the negative samples, we prepare backgrounds from comic pages without faces.

As the validate set, we chose 201 comic pages (700 × 1, 000 pixels) which are not utilized in the training part. There are 705 faces in the validate set.

Considering the training time, we set the cascade as 20 layers with 0.995 detection rate and 0.5 false positive rate for each layer.

The experimental results are shown in Table 1. By the cascade classifier (trained by 3, 000 positive samples and 8, 000 negative samples), we got 658 parts, in which contain 584 true faces. Examples of detection are shown in Fig. 9. The average detection time is 492 ms per image (CPU: 2.5 GHz, RAM: 4 GB).

Table 1. Face detection result

Number of detected parts	658
Number of detected faces	584
Precision	88.7%
Recall	82.8%

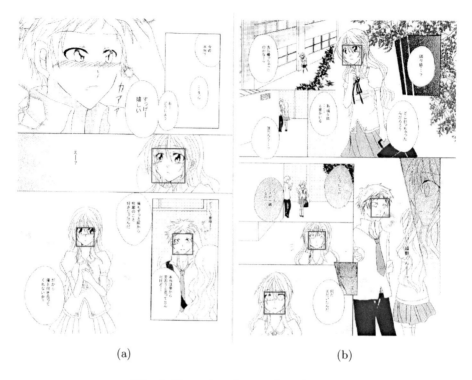

(a)
(b)

Fig. 9. Examples of comic face detection

From the results, we can see the Viola-Jones framework is also applicable for detecting comic character's faces. Although faces of comic characters contain more variations comparing with real faces of human beings, there are still some discriminative features. As shown in Fig. 10, we can recognize the shape of face from the mean image of positive samples.

3.2 Similar Part Detection

Next, we tested the similar part detection of the proposed method.

As the copyrighted images, we utilized $7,682$ comic pages ($700 \times 1,000$ pixels, from volume 1 and volume 2 of 21 kinds of comics). The cascade classifier trained in the first experiment was applied detecting the possible face parts from images. From the copyrighted images, we detected $19,509$ possible face parts, and built a database with these parts.

As the query images, we chose 201 comic pages (from volume 3 of each kind comic), which contain 705 faces in total. Of course, for the same comic, the main character should appear in different volume but always with various kinds of different poses and face expressions, which are treated as similar copies in our experiments.

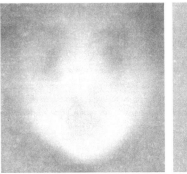 

(a) Mean image of positives   (b) Mean image of negatives

Fig. 10. Mean images of training samples

The experimental results are shown in Table 2. The correct matching is defined as a matched pair that belong to the same character of the same comic. All the detected parts (including right faces and non-face) are treated as queries. This means the errors of ROI detection are also included in this experimental results. Since the evaluation is strict, the precision and recall are about 50%. The examples of correct matching are shown in Fig. 11. We can see the proposed method can detect similar parts with certain range of transformations.

Table 2. Results of similar part detection

Number of detected parts	658
Number of correct matching	348
Precision	52.9%
Recall	49.4%

The examples of failure are shown in Fig. 12. There are several reasons for the failures:

– Since we just utilize two volumes of each kind of comic, there are some faces of queries, which are not included in our database. For example, as shown in Fig. 12(a), some faces are with strange expressions, and some faces not from main characters as Fig. 12(b) shown.
– There are some similar features between different comic characters. Such as Fig. 12(c) and Fig. 12(d). the characters are very similar in different comic drawn by the same author.
– Some errors are caused in ROI detection. As shown in Fig. 12(e) and Fig. 12(f), the parts extracted from query are not faces.

The detection time is 68 ms per part (CPU: 2.5 GHz, RAM: 4 GB).

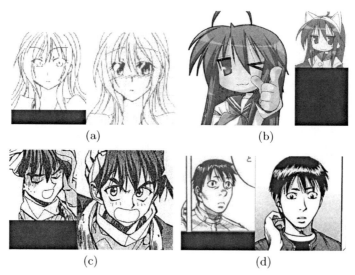

Fig. 11. Examples of correct detected similar pairs. (left : parts from queries, right : parts from database). They are from Lucky Star, Hoshin Engi and Planetes.

Fig. 12. Examples of failure in similar part detection. (left : parts from queries, right : parts from database) They are from Neon Genesis Evangelion, Hoshin Engi, Master Keaton, Miyuki, Monster, Slam Dunk and Rough.

4   Conclusion and Future Works

In this paper, we propose a method to detect illegal copies of line drawings. By applying a cascade classifier and feature matching, we have achieved the detection of similar partial copies from complex backgrounds to some extent.

There are some remaining work for us in the future including:

- detection of other kinds of ROIs beside comic faces,
- increase the detection rate of ROIs,
- describe the difference in detail of ROIs,
- enlarge the database of copyrighted images.

Acknowledgement

This research was supported in part by the Grant-in-Aid for Scientific Research (B)(22300062) from Japan Society for the Promotion of Science (JSPS).

References

1. Sun, W., Kise, K.: Detecting Printed and Handwritten Partial Copies of Line Drawings Embedded in Complex Backgrounds. In: International Conference on Document Analysis and Recognition, pp. 341–345 (2009)
2. Matas, J., Chum, O., Urban, M., Pajdla, T.: Robust Wide Baseline Stereo from Maximally Stable Extremal Regions. In: British Machine Vision Conference, pp. 384–393 (2002)
3. Dalal, N., Triggs, B.: Histograms of Oriented Gradients for Human Detection. In: IEEE Conference on Computer Vision and Pattern Recognition, vol. 1, pp. 886–893 (2005)
4. Zhu, Q., Avidan, S., Yeh, M., Cheng, K.: Fast Human Detection Using a Cascade of Histograms of Oriented Gradients. In: IEEE Conference on Computer Vision and Pattern Recognition, vol. 2, pp. 1491–1498 (2006)
5. Schneiderman, H., Kanade, T.: A statistical Method for 3D Object Detection Applied to Faces and Cars. In: IEEE Conference on Computer Vision and Pattern Recognition (2000)
6. Viola, P., Jones, M.: Robust Real-Time Face Detection. International Journal of Computer Vision 57(2), 137–154 (2004)
7. Freund, Y., Schapire, R.: A Decision-Theoretic Generalization of On-Line Learning and an Application to Boosting. Journal of Computer and System Sciences 55(1), 119–139 (1997)
8. Arya, S., Mount, D., Silverman, R., Wu, A.Y.: An optimal algorithm for approximate nearest neighbor searching. Journal of the ACM 45(6), 891–923 (1998)

Detection of Malicious Applications on Android OS

Francesco Di Cerbo[1], Andrea Girardello[2],
Florian Michahelles[2], and Svetlana Voronkova[1]

[1] Center for Applied Software Engineering, Free University of Bolzano-Bozen,
Bolzano-Bozen, Italy
{fdicerbo,svoronkova}@unibz.it
[2] Information Management, ETH Zurich
Zurich, Switzerland
{agirardello,fmichahelles}@ethz.ch

Abstract. The paper presents a methodology for mobile forensics analysis, to detect "malicious" (or "malware") applications, i.e., those that deceive users hiding some of their functionalities. This methodology is specifically targeted for the Android mobile operating system, and relies on its security model features, namely the set of permissions exposed by each application. The methodology has been trained on more than 13,000 applications hosted on the Android Market, collected with AppAware. A case study is presented as a preliminary validation of the methodology.

Keywords: Mobile Forensics, Android OS, Security.

1 Introduction

The amount and the significance of personal data stored on cellular phones, PDA's and Smart Phones is equal to those carried by computers, due to the use of numerous cloud synchronization services like Funambol [1], Microsoft ActiveSync[2], Apple MobileMe[3]. This aspect is particularly relevant, as mobile phones are also used when committing crimes: in many cases, for instance, wiretapping gives valuable benefits to investigations. This results in a growing attention on mobile devices involved in crimes, as a valuable source of information. Thus, there is also a strong interest in the evolution of digital forensics techniques. Mobile phones contain sensible data, that in a trial could be precious to demonstrate innocence or guilt. With "sensible (or sensitive) data", we refer to a broad definition of information that are relating to race or ethnic origin, political opinions, religious beliefs, physical/mental health, trade union membership, sexual life or criminal activities. They include communications log, SMS, MMS, contacts list, appointments, tasks and so on.

Evidence discovered during a mobile device analysis might have a vital importance for the case investigation. Here evidence is interpreted as information of probative value that is stored or transmitted in binary form [4]. Digital forensics is generally defined as a branch of e-discovery that examines how the extraction

H. Sako, K. Franke, and S. Saitoh (Eds.): IWCF 2010, LNCS 6540, pp. 138–149, 2011.

of digital evidence can aid in crime investigations and identification of potential suspects [5]. In some cases, as it happens on regular desktop systems, criminals may use mobile applications to conduct frauds, i.e., stealing home banking and other sensible credentials from mobile phones: this kind of applications are generally called "malware". In those situations, some evidences and insights on the crime are contained in an application, therefore it is necessary to identify it precisely, in order to gather as much information as possible.

The methodology we propose is a mobile forensics technique, aimed at supporting a forensics analyst to detect applications that deal with sensible data in a way that could be defined as "suspicious", i.e., not aligned with respect to the trends of all other applications, that are part of a significant dataset of safe applications.

In the following Sections 2 and 3 we will provide a short overview on mobile forensics and on Android OS, especially on its key issues that are significant for the mobile forensics science. In Section 4 it will be presented AppAware, the application we used to collect data on Android applications, and finally Section 5 and 6 will cover the proposed methodology, and a use case based on real applications. Section 7 contains the final remarks and future perspectives.

2   Mobile Forensics

The mobile forensics science as a part of digital forensics focuses on recovering digital evidence from a mobile phone under forensically sound conditions using accepted methods [6]. The mobile forensics techniques and methodologies focus mainly of 3 different areas [7]:

- *SIM card forensics*: it aims to extract the data stored on this physical item and provide so called primary image of it.
- *Digital data acquisition*: extraction of data carried by flash memory of mobile device using through filesystem
- *Physical data acquisition*: extraction of full memory image bit-by-bit.

Although the goals of computer forensics and mobile forensics are basically the same, the examiners consider mobile forensics to be much more complicated. The key issues that cause a trouble for investigators is the uniqueness of mobile device and its pervasive nature. Each cell phone manufacturer sets up his own standards, uses particular operating system, hardware and software [8]. Therefore information acquisition from such devices in a forensically sound manner becomes a real challenge. Digital forensics techniques are usually divided into 2 main groups [8]: *post mortem analysis*: when the device is switched off; *live analysis*: techniques performed on the device that is turned on.

However, both techniques differ in many aspects from the traditional methods when it comes to the cell phone investigation. Post mortem analysis (also called off-line analysis) of small scale device becomes more complex than computer examination, due to the fact that mobile devices contain an internal clock, which continuously changes data stored in the cell phone's flash memory. Therefore, it is impossible to reproduce a consistent bit-to-bit image of the entire memory. Considering the live forensic, device connectivity plays a vital role [9]. It is necessary to keep the device isolated from any networks during the analysis time, otherwise it may lead to the loss of some information that could be beneficial for the investigation. However, in the case of mobile devices, the preservation of this requirement is more difficult, because of the expanded connectivity options (i.e., the possibility to deal with cellular network, and through it with Internet services).

3   Android OS

Android OS (referred as "Android") delivers a complete set of software for mobile devices: an operating system, middleware and key mobile applications [10]. It enables the developers to take advantage of all functionalities and features included in the handset to create innovative and sophisticated mobile applications. Each Android application runs in its own process on Dalvik, a custom virtual machine designed for embedded use. Android relies on modified Linux Kernel version 2.6 for core system services such as security, memory management, process management, network stack, and driver model [11]. It also includes a set of Java libraries that provide the functionalities available in standard Java Programming Language, and C/C++ libraries such as SQLite relational database management system, 3D libraries, Media Libraries etc.

3.1   Android Security Model - A Permission-Based Approach

Android's security model combines the standard Linux OS features that control the security at the process level and the permission based mechanism. The permission [11] is a right that a developer has to declare in its application to be able to interact with the system or access the components of other applications. As each program is executed as a distinguished process, typically applications neither read nor write each other's data or code. Sharing data between applications must be done explicitly. However, after a permissions request, an application has access to the protected features of Android to which each permission refers. A permission is generally simple text string assigned to a predefined list of functionalities of the system, i.e., "INTERNET" to connect to the Internet, "READ_SMS" to read SMS messaging, and so on. Permissions have to be statically defined in the application package, so that during the deployment, a user could grant them to the application, or abort the process. In Listing 1.1, it is shown an example of a permission to write data to the SD card:

```
<permission xmlns:android=
    "http://schemas.android.com/apk/res/android"
  android:name="com.isecpartners.android.
     WRITE_EXTERNAL_STORAGE"
```

```
android : description="@string/access_sd_card"
android : protectionLevel="normal"
android : label="@string/access_perm_label">
</permission>
```

Listing 1.1. An example of an Android OS security permission

Each permission contains the following attributes: name, description, label and the protection level.

3.2   Android Threads

As an open source handset that relies on Linux Kernel, Android is considered to be a secure platform. Despite the Android malware market is still in an infancy stage, detection of some malfunction on Android Market had proven that it can be easily exploited by attackers.

Recently, a report of SMobile [13] considering 48,694 applications, found 29 of them to be possibly spyware available on the Android Market, while for other 383 it is possible to access authentication credentials stored on the mobile phone. The cited analysis has some commonalities with the case study presented in Section 6, as both of them use applications' permissions as a privileged source of information on mobile applications. The report confirms the urgency of developing anti-malware systems and checks, as well as forensics methodologies to be used against those applications in a trial. In particular, in [13] it is proposed that a number of specific permissions combinations can lead to declare applications as notable, suspicious or spyware. SMobile methodology is not fully disclosed, therefore a precise comparison with our approach cannot be developed. However, from what is disclosed, SMobile methodology seems different from the one proposed here, even if the identification of "notable permissions" and their identification into Android applications (i.e. permissions that allow to access sensible data stored on the phone) seems to be similar to the concept of sensible data access profile, which is defined later.

An example of Android malware is an application called "DROID09", that was discovered on Android Market in January of 2010 [12]. The application "pretended" to be a useful online banking utility, which was supposed to connect the user to its bank web page and process the transactions. However, it turned out that it was only facilitating a web browser connection and actually stealing online banking credentials of the users. Indeed it is not known how exactly the application was performing the fraud, how long it has been in Android Market and how many users installed it, until this application was removed.

However, in order to develop efficient forensics tools there should be a clear definition of what kind of applications should be considered as suspicious in Android. Applications can be considered spyware if they have the ability to spy the users sensitive data in a specific way by capturing them and transmitting it outside the local system.

4   AppAware

Today most mobile operating systems provide users with an application portal
where they can search for applications published by third-party developers. However, finding new apps is not an easy task. Application portals offer thousands
of applications and users often have to go through countless titles to find what
they are looking for. AppAware [14] is a mobile application that tries to solve
this issue by allowing users to discover mobile applications in a serendipitous
manner. AppAware captures and shares installations, updates, and removals of
Android programs in real-time. AppAware also offers statistics to discover the
top installed, updated or removed applications.

This service provides also a new way to let user implicitly rate applications
and thus define their acceptance. This acceptance is represented by a meter
colored from red to green. When the gauge points toward the green range the
acceptance is excellent, yellow range for good acceptance and red range if almost
no AppAware user is keeping the application installed. The assumption behind
this approach is that excellent/good applications are not removed once installed,
whereas applications that are removed from the device are not liked/ considered
useful according to users.

The AppAware system has a client-server architecture. The client component is the Android mobile application, which represents AppAware's graphical
user interface (GUI) and allows following installations, updates and removals
of applications shared by other users. The client application is also monitoring
the Android OS, thus being able to detect installations, updates and removals
of applications, even those not installed from the official Android Market. The
applications monitored are more than 42,000 at the time of writing.

5   The Methodology

The methodology we propose aims at the detection of suspicious applications,
using Android security permissions, especially those connected with personal
information: credentials, contacts, calendar events, email, SMS/MMS and so on.

As remarked in Section 3.2, each application needs to declare explicitly the
permissions it needs, with respect to the operating system or to other applications. This security constraint allows to discriminate exactly what data will be
accessed, as the Android security model will prevent any other access from being actually performed. We propose the definition of profiles related to sensible
data access, each of them distinguished by a specific set of permissions. Comparing the permissions requested by an application, with the reference model of
sensible data access profiles, it is possible to detect if an application has different security requirements with respect to other applications in the same profile.
In this way, an analyst could detect unexpected anomalies. The method is not
going to clearly determine the maliciousness of a certain application, it simply
signals to the forensics analyst a situation that could require additional specific
investigations. In this way, it is possible to identify applications that hide their

real features, pretending to be a game, for instance. The methodology could be used also by standard users, to detect if an application permission request is coherent with respect to those of direct competitors. However, this perspective is still being considered and it is not part of this work.

A limitation of our approach is the impossibility to identify suspicious software that exploits Android vulnerabilities, e.g., using Android native code. This possibility has been recently demonstrated by Oberheide [16], and as no permissions are needed to access internal Android API, no methodology based on permission analysis can effectively identify the mentioned applications.

The method is composed by the following steps:

1. definition of a number of applications' classification profiles, associated to the manipulation of sensitive data types, managed on an Android mobile phone;
2. assessment of the permissions declared by a significant set of applications belonging to different classification profiles;
3. mining of association rules on the basis of the different classification profiles;
4. definition of a reference set of permissions for each classification profile.

To apply our method, we start with the definition of a set of classification profiles, to describe applications that manage or have access to sensible data. This classification (shown in Table 1) is based on the analysis of the default set of Android permissions, and takes into account features that are connected with each sensible data category profile. To analyze an application, multiple profiles could be considered, according to the specific functionalities offered by the application.

As second step, we conducted an assessment of the permissions requested by the most common applications. In order to perform this step, we used AppAware. In this way, at present we collected information on 13,098 selected applications (on over 42,000). We selected the dataset among application not reported to be malicious in users'comments, and from which we had permissions data. Both features are provided by the AppAware features. Moreover, the considered applications are distributed worldwide, and of almost any category available on the Android Market. This allows us to state that the sample considered is heterogeneous enough for our purposes.

For each application, we recorded the permissions that were declared at the installation on the device of AppAware users.

The third step was to analyze the dataset with the Apriori algorithm [17] (using the tool Weka[15]), with different parameters, in order to group the applications according to their similarity of requested permissions. Apriori is a technique used in association rules mining, and it is a process of discovering frequent patterns, associations and correlations between sets of items in database. The rule mining process has two main steps:

a. find all frequent itemsets. A frequent itemset is an itemset whose support is greater than the minimum support. The support of an itemset is a measure of how often the itemset occurs in a given set of transactions;

b. generate the association rules that have high confidence, from the frequent itemsets identified in the first step. Confidence is a measure of how often items Y appear in transaction that contain items X.

The Apriori algorithm performs these 2 steps using a "bottom up" approach, where frequent subsets are extended one item at a time, and groups of candidates are tested against the data. The result of the Apriori analysis is a list of itemsets, grouped by the number of simultaneous features. See the following Section 6 for an exemplification.

The fourth step is the identification of the most relevant clusters of applications, on the basis of the support. From this, it is also possible to consider the set of rules that depends directly on the selected clusters. It is possible to state that the clusters represent a typical configuration for applications that deal with the particular sensitive data profile in consideration.

6   Case Study

In order to show a use case of the described forensics analysis methodology, we consider two applications, MobileSpy and MobileStealth, known to be spyware by design [12]. Both applications access sensible information on an Android device, and are able to send to a criminal the data collected. Table 2 shows the capabilities possessed by MobileSpy and MobileStealth, while their permissions are shown in Table 3.

The features of MobileSpy and MobileStealth are absolutely peculiar, and cases of users that intentionally wish to expose all their private data to others are considered very rare by the authors.

Our case study assumes that both applications have been found on a mobile device: data gathered through them might have been used to commit a crime, such as a non-legitimate bank transfer, and a forensics analyst has to identify the source of the information leak.

The analyst, having created a forensics copy of the device, will start her activities retrieving the list of all application deployed on the mobile phone, together with all permissions requested for each application. To this purpose, we developed an application, called AForensics: it is an Android application that looks up for third-party applications installed on a device, and retrieves their permission information. AForensics gathers permissions that third-party applications request from Android, and permissions declared by applications. Moreover, it also collects complementary information, like services, broadcast receivers and content providers that each application defined.

Once executing AForensics, the analyst shall receive an XML file, that contains, among data about other applications, the node shown in Listing 1.2.

```
<application name="MobileSpy" package="x.y.z"
        version="j.k.1">
    <requested-permission permission="android.permission.
        ACCESS_FINE_LOCATION" />
```

```
<requested−permission  permission=" android . permission .
   READ_CONTACTS" />
<requested−permission  permission=" android . permission .
   READ_SMS" />
<requested−permission  permission=" android . permission .
   WRITE_SECURE_SETTINGS" />
<requested−permission  permission=" android . permission .
   READ_PHONE_STATE" />
....
</application>
```

Listing 1.2. The XML snippet representing an excerpt of permission requested by the MobileSpy application

Table 1. Secure information profiles and relative permissions

Category	Android Permissions
Contacts	WRITE_SYNC_SETTINGS, WRITE_CONTACTS, READ_CONTACTS, MANAGE_ACCOUNTS, GET_ACCOUNTS, ACCOUNT_MANAGER
SMS-MMS messages	WRITE_SYNC_SETTINGS, WRITE_SMS, VIBRATE, SET_ORIENTATION, SEND_SMS, RECEIVE_SMS, RECEIVE_MMS, READ_SMS, FLASHLIGHT, BROADCAST_SMS
Call Log	VIBRATE, PROCESS_OUTGOING_CALLS, FLASHLIGHT, CALL_PHONE, CALL_PRIVILEGED
Audio & Video	WRITE_EXTERNAL_STORAGE, SET_ORIENTATION, RECORD_AUDIO, MODIFY_AUDIO_SETTINGS, GLOBAL_SEARCH, FLASHLIGHT, BLUETOOTH, BLUETOOTH_ADMIN, CAMERA
Tasks & Calendar	WRITE_CALENDAR, REORDER_TASKS, READ_CALENDAR, GLOBAL_SEARCH, GET_TASKS, BLUETOOTH_ADMIN
Browser History	WRITE_SYNC_SETTINGS, WRITE_HISTORY_BOOKMARKS, READ_HISTORY_BOOKMARKS
Images	WRITE_EXTERNAL_STORAGE, SET_WALLPAPER_HINTS, SET_WALLPAPER, SET_ORIENTATION, READ_FRAME_BUFFER, GLOBAL_SEARCH, FLASHLIGHT, BLUETOOTH, BLUE-TOOTH_ADMIN, CAMERA
Phone Settings	WRITE_SYNC_SETTINGS, WRITE_SECURE_SETTINGS, WRITE_GSERVICES, WRITE_APN_SETTINGS, SET_WALLPAPER, SET_WALLPAPER_HINTS, SET_ORIENTATION, READ_SYNC_STATS, READ_SYNC_SETTINGS, READ_PHONE_STATE, MODIFY_AUDIO_SETTINGS, FLASHLIGHT, ACCESS_CHECKIN_PROPERTIES, CHANGE_CONFIGURATION, DEVICE_POWER
Email & services related to web	WRITE_SYNC_SETTINGS, WRITE_GSERVICES, USE_CREDENTIALS, SET_ORIENTATION, MANAGE_ACCOUNTS, GLOBAL_SEARCH, GET_ACCOUNTS, FLASHLIGHT, AC-CESS_COARSE_LOCATION, ACCESS_FINE_LOCATION, ACCESS_NETWORK_STATE, ACCESS_WIFI_STATE, AC-COUNT_MANAGER, CHANGE_NETWORK_STATE, INTERNET

Table 2. Functionalities of MobileSpy and MobileStealth applications

MobileSpy	MobileStealth
monitor SMS messages	recording of surrounding
view inbound and outbound call details	SMS logging
access GPS location	contact details
view all websites visited from the device	picture logging
expose a web interface to view and manage the captured logs	GPS Tracking

Table 3. Permissions for applications MobileSpy and MobileStealth. All permissions belong to the *android.permission* package, except for *_HISTORY_BOOKMARKS, part of *com.android.browser.permission*.

MobileSpy	MobileStealth
RECEIVE_SMS	RECEIVE_BOOT_COMPLETED
SEND_SMS	READ_CONTACTS
READ_CONTACTS	RECEIVE_SMS
INTERNET	INJECT_EVENTS
READ_PHONE_STATE	PROCESS_OUTGOING_CALLS
ACCESS_FINE_LOCATION	READ_SMS
READ_CALENDAR	CHANGE_WIFI_STATE
RECEIVE_BOOT_COMPLETED	WRITE_SETTINGS
READ_SMS	READ_PHONE_STATE
WRITE_SMS	READ_LOGS
WRITE_CONTACTS	ACCESS_FINE_LOCATION
ACCESS_NETWORK_STATE	DISABLE_KEYGUARD
MODIFY_PHONE_STATE	INTERNET
ACCESS_COARSE_LOCATION	ACCESS_NETWORK_STATE
WRITE_CALENDAR	ACCESS_WIFI_STATE
READ_HISTORY_BOOKMARKS	WRITE_SECURE_SETTINGS
WRITE_HISTORY_BOOKMARKS	

The analyst should now compare the application permissions listed in Table 3 obtained with AForensics, with the reference models of application permissions discussed in Section 5.

To perform this comparison, the analyst could use the full AppAware dataset, or extract a subset of applications that belongs to the same or similar sensible data profiles. In this case, a subset could be generated considering applications that request READ_SMS, READ_CONTACTS and READ_PHONE_STATE permissions. If the second option is chosen, this leads to the creation of a subset, composed by 140 applications. The subset analysis gives a set of tables, containing the typical profiles of applications that manage user contacts. The full result presents 11 tables, considering itemsets that request from 1 to 11 permissions at the same

Table 4. Most relevant itemsets at the L7 of Apriori algorithm

Itemsets
RECEIVE_SMS, READ_CONTACTS, READ_SMS, INTERNET, READ_PHONE_STATE, SEND_SMS, WRITE_SMS
RECEIVE_SMS, READ_CONTACTS, READ_SMS, INTERNET, READ_PHONE_STATE, CALL_PHONE, WRITE_SMS
READ_CONTACTS, READ_SMS, INTERNET, READ_PHONE_STATE, CALL_PHONE, WRITE_CONTACTS, WRITE_SMS
RECEIVE_SMS, READ_CONTACTS, READ_SMS, INTERNET, READ_PHONE_STATE, WRITE_CONTACTS, WRITE_SMS
READ_CONTACTS, READ_SMS, INTERNET, READ_PHONE_STATE, CALL_PHONE, SEND_SMS, WRITE_SMS
READ_CONTACTS, READ_SMS, INTERNET, VIBRATE, READ_PHONE_STATE, SEND_SMS, WRITE_SMS
RECEIVE_BOOT_COMPLETED, RECEIVE_SMS, READ_CONTACTS, READ_SMS, INTERNET, READ_PHONE_STATE, WRITE_SMS

time (identified as "L1" to "L11"). The number of elements in each itemset varies from 4 (L11) to 3702 (L5). An excerpt of one of these tables resulting from the Apriori analysis is shown in Table 4, representing L7 itemset. Each row in Table 4 represents a group of 7 permissions.

It is clear that the permission sets of MobileSpy and MobileStealth do not appear in Table 3, and the authors have checked that such a permission set does not appear in any of the sets generated in the full analysis output.

In the cases of MobileSpy and MobileStealth, however, to declare the applications as suspicious it is sufficient to notice that, for instance, the pair READ_CONTACS and INJECT_EVENTS is present only once on the whole dataset, by a software development library. The difference between MobileStealth/MobileSpy and a software library corroborates a legitimate suspicion on the application; moreover, considering any other requested permission, the number of similar applications decreases to 0.

7   Conclusions

We presented a methodology for the detection of malicious applications in a forensics analysis. Malicious applications in this context are those that have access capabilities to sensible data, and transmission capabilities as well, at the same time deceiving the users, by pretending to offer services that typically do not require such capabilities, or to make a legitimate use of them. The methodology relies on the comparison of the Android security permission of each application, with a set of reference models, for applications that manage sensitive data. An extensive validation of the methodology is in progress, but we are facing difficulties due to limited information and data publicly available so far. In this research we only considered a rather simple analysis technique, namely association rules. Association rules are easy to apply and provide a first understanding of the problem at hand.

Some authors however report problems with their use, among them the potentially large number of groups and rules obtained, which may confuse the interpretation.

While there are solutions to some of these issues [18] in our future work we plan to investigate further data mining methods, for example classification and clustering algorithms. Classification is useful for predicting to which class an application with a given feature vector belongs, given that we can define our classes beforehand. Clustering of similar feature vectors could be used for defining classes as a first step. In the future, we plan to apply standard data mining and pattern recognition techniques (for instance [19]) to simplify the analysis process for the analyst. Particular attention will be devoted to the identification of the "best" learners for predicting the classification membership of new applications (see for example [20]).

Our ultimate objective is to implement a general model for an automated or semi-automated forensics system, which could detect application with abnormal permission requests, such as the previous case study of MobileSpy/MobileStealth. Such a system should be periodically re-trained (by performing the above steps) and therefore it shall be able to evolve over time. We are also considering to include the outcome of the research directly into AppAware, in order to warn all Android end users about suspicious software before installing it.

References

1. Funambol inc.: Funambol Open Source Mobile Cloud Sync and Push Email, http://www.funambol.com
2. Microsoft: ActiveSync, Windows Phone Synchronization, http://www.microsoft.com/windowsmobile/en-us/help/synchronize/device-synch.mspx
3. Apple inc.: Apple - MobileMe, http://www.apple.com/mobileme/
4. Scientific Working Groups on Digital Evidence and Imaging Technology: Combined Master Glossary of Terms (retrieved on July 2, 2010)
5. Robbins, J.: An Explanation of Computer Forensics, PC Software Forensics, http://www.computerforensics.net/forensics.htm (retrieved on July 2, 2010)
6. Jansen, W., Ayers, R.: Guidelines on Cell Phone Forensics. NIST Special Publication 800-101 (2007), http://csrc.nist.gov/publications/nistpubs/800-101/SP800-101.pdf (retrieved on July 2, 2010)
7. Kim, K., Hong, D., Chung, K., Ryou, J.: Data Acquisition from Cell Phone using Logical Approach. Proceedings of the World Academy of Science, Engineering and Technology 26 (2007)
8. Rizwan, A., Dharaskar, R.V.: Mobile Forensics: an Overview, Tools, Future trendsand Challenges from Law Enforcement perspective, http://www.iceg.net/2008/books/2/34_312-323.pdf (retrieved on July 2, 2010)
9. Carrier, B.D.: Risks of live digital forensic analysis. Commun. ACM. 49, 56–61 (2006)
10. Open Handset Alliance: Android, http://www.openhandsetalliance.com/android_overview.html (retrieved on July 2, 2010)

11. Android Community: What is Android?, `http://developer.android.com/guide/basics/what-is-android.html` (retrieved on July 2, 2010)
12. Vennon, T.: Android Malware, A Study of Known and Potential Malware Threats, `http://threatcenter.smobilesystems.com/wp-content/plugins/download-monitor/download.php?id=6` (published February 24, 2010)
13. Vennon, T., Stroop, D.: Android Malware, A Study of Known and Potential Malware Threats, June 21 (2010), `http://threatcenter.smobilesystems.com/wp-content/uploads/2010/06/Android-Market-Threat-Analysis-6-22-10-v1.pdf` (published June 21, 2010)
14. Girardello, A., Michahelles, F.: Explicit and Implicit Ratings for Mobile Applications. In: 3. Workshop Digitale Soziale Netze and der 40. Jahrestagung der Gesellshaft fr Informatik, Leipzig (September 2010)
15. Hall, M., Frank, E., Holmes, G., Pfahringer, B., Reutemann, P., Witten, I.H.: The WEKA data mining software: an update. SIGKDD Explor. Newsl. 11, 110–118 (2009)
16. Oberheide, J.: Remote Kill and Install on Google Android, `http://jon.oberheide.org/blog/2010/06/25/remote-kill-and-install-on-google-android/` (retrieved on July 2, 2010)
17. Orlando, S., Palmerini, P., Perego, R.: Enhancing the *apriori* algorithm for frequent set counting. In: Kambayashi, Y., Winiwarter, W., Arikawa, M. (eds.) DaWaK 2001. LNCS, vol. 2114, pp. 71–82. Springer, Heidelberg (2001)
18. Garca, E., Romero, C.: Drawbacks and solutions of applying association rule mining in learning management systems. In: Proceedings of the International Workshop on Applying Data Mining in e-Learning (ADML 2007), pp. 14–22 (2007)
19. Duda, R.O., Hart, P.E., et al.: Pattern classification. Wiley-Interscience, Hoboken (2001)
20. Moser, R., Pedrycz, W., et al.: A comparative analysis of the efficiency of change metrics and static code attributes for defect prediction. In: Proceedings of the 30th International Conference on Software Engineering, pp. 181–190 (2008)

JPEG Quantization Tables Forensics: A Statistical Approach

Babak Mahdian[1], Stanislav Saic[1], and Radim Nedbal[2]

[1] Institute of Information Theory and Automation of the ASCR, Czech Republic
{mahdian,ssiac}@utia.cas.cz
[2] Institute of Computer Science of the ASCR, Czech Republic
radned@seznam.cz

Abstract. Many digital image forensics techniques using various fingerprints which identify the image source are dependent on data on digital images from an unknown environment. As often software modifications leave no appropriate traces in image metadata, critical miscalculations of fingerprints arise. This is the problem addressed in this paper. Modeling information noise, we introduce a statistical approach for noise-removal in databases consisted of "unguaranteed" images. In this paper, employed fingerprints are based on JPEG quantization tables.

Keywords: Image forensics, image forgery detection, hypergeometric distribution, jpeg quantization tables.

1 Introduction

Verifying the integrity of digital images and detecting the traces of tampering without using any protecting pre–extracted or pre–embedded information have become an important and hot research field of image processing [1, 2].

One of the typical ways of determining the image integrity is by matching the image being analyzed with its acquisition device via device fingerprints. Having no access to a higher number of acquisition devices we have to rely on popular photo sharing sites to get a sufficiently large training set for extracting fingerprints. When using images from such sites, we face a real problem: uncertainty about the image's history. As these images could be processed and re–saved by an editing and image uploading software (for instance for contrast enhancing or down-sizing) and by taking into account that many pieces of software do not leave typical traces in metadata, we may face miscalculations of fingerprints. This is the problem addressed in this paper. Modeling information noise in such databases, we introduce a statistical approach for removal of this noise.

JPEG photographs in photo-sharing sites contain various important metadata. Among others, they are taken by (camera) *users* with *cameras*, which encode them by means of *quantization tables* (QTs). As different image acquisition devices and software editors typically use different JPEG QTs [3, 4], we employ here QTs as device fingerprints.

H. Sako, K. Franke, and S. Saitoh (Eds.): IWCF 2010, LNCS 6540, pp. 150–159, 2011.

It should be pointed out that a typical acquisition device uses some family of QTs very often whereas some others very rarely, and, most importantly, there is a (unknown) set of QTs that it uses never. And this is exactly the set that is of a great interest as for the image integrity. Indeed, it is easily seen that it can be exploited to negate it. Also note that a simple threshold based approach to determine the above set is unlikely to be feasible as the QT distribution is far from uniform for most acquisition devices. Therefore we propose a more sophisticated approach that is believed to deal with the non-uniformity of QT distribution effectively. Specifically, it allows to condition a threshold value for determining the above set on the QT distribution.

2   Related Work

There are a number of papers dealing with detection of artifacts brought into the JPEG image by the quantization procedure and corresponding QTs. The artifacts were used to detect the doubly/multiply compressed JPEG images. For example, see [5–12].

For instance, Jan Lukáš and Jessica Fridrich [5] presented a method for estimation of primary quantization matrix from a double compressed JPEG image. The paper presents three different approaches from which the Neural Network classifier based one is the most effective. Tomáš Pevný and Jessica Fridrich [6] proposed a method based on support vector machine classifiers with feature vectors formed by histograms of low–frequency DCT coefficients. Dongdong Fu et al. [7] proposed a statistical model based on Benford's law for the probability distributions of the first digits of the block–DCT and quantized JPEG coefficients. Weiqi Luo et al. [8] proposed a method for detecting recompressed image blocks based on JPEG blocking artifact characteristics. Babak Mahdian and Stanislav Saic [9] proposed a method for detection double compressed JPEG images based on histograms properties of DCT coefficients and support vector machines. Alin C. Popescu and Hany Farid [10] proposed a double JPEG Compression technique by examining the histograms of the DCT coefficients. In [11], Zhenhua Qu et al. formulated the shifted double JPEG compression as a noisy convolutive mixing model to identify whether a given JPEG image has been compressed twice with inconsistent block segmentation.

The mentioned methods are directly dependent on quantization tables and mostly they need them to be different in the image acquisition device and the software. Unfortunately, when leaving the lab conditions and applying these methods in real–life conditions, typically they produce considerably higher false positive rates than which are reported in papers [1]. Furthermore they efficiency is high only under limited conditions. These drawbacks mostly are caused by high variety of real–life image textures and properties (size and frequency of uniform regions, etc.).

To our best knowledge, there are two papers directly analyzing the potential of QTs to separate images that have been processed by software from those that have not.

Hany Farid [4, 13] using a database of one million images analyzed the potential of JPEG QTs to become a tool for source identification. He found out that while the JPEG QTs are not unique, they are effective at narrowing the source of an image to a single camera make and model or to a small set of possible cameras. His approach was based on equivalence classes.

Jesse D. Kornblum [3] examined several thousand images from various types of image acquisition devices and software. This allowed him to categorize the various types of QTs and discuss the implications for image forensics.

By comparison, being based on sophisticated statistical considerations, our approach aims at minimizing sensitivity to the data noise. As a result, in this sense, we provide a more robust tool for source identification.

3   Basics of JPEG Compression

Typically, the image is first converted from RGB to YCbCr, consisting of one luminance component (Y), and two chrominance components (Cb and Cr). Mostly, the resolution of the chroma components are reduced, usually by a factor of two [14]. Then, each component is split into adjacent blocks of 8×8 pixels. Blocks values are shifted from unsigned to signed integers. Each block of each of the Y, Cb, and Cr components undergoes a discrete cosine transform (DCT). Let $f(x, y)$ denotes a 8×8 block. Its DCT is:

$$F(u, v) = \frac{1}{4} C(u) C(v)$$
$$\sum_{x=0}^{7} \sum_{y=0}^{7} f(x, y) \cos \frac{(2x+1)u\pi}{16} \cos \frac{(2y+1)v\pi}{16}, \tag{1}$$

where

$$(u, v \in \{0 \cdots 7\});$$
$$C(u), C(v) = 1/\sqrt{2} \quad \text{for} \quad u, v = 0; \tag{2}$$
$$C(u), C(v) = 1 \qquad \text{otherwise.}$$

In the next step, all 64 $F(u, v)$ coefficients are quantized. Then, the resulting data for all blocks is entropy compressed typically using a variant of Huffman encoding (there also can be other forms of entropy coding like arithmetic, etc.). The quantization step is performed in conjunction with a 64–element quantization matrix, $Q(u, v)$. Quantization is a many–to–one mapping. Thus it is a lossy operation. Quantization is defined as division of each DCT coefficient by its corresponding quantizer step size defined in the quantization matrix, followed by rounding to the nearest integer:

$$F^Q(u, v) = round(\frac{F(u, v)}{Q(u, v)}), \quad u, v \in \{0 \cdots 7\} \tag{3}$$

Generally, the JPEG quantization matrix is designed by taking the visual response to luminance variations into account, as a small variation in intensity is more visible in low spatial frequency regions than in high spatial frequency regions. Typically, JPEG images contain one quantization table for the luminance band and one common quantization table for chrominance bands [14]. These tables are saved in the jpeg files header.

4   Basic Notations and Preliminaries

Suppose that any camera is determined uniquely by a pair of attributes make mk and model md^1. Given a ternary relation, denoted S, a subset of the ternary Cartesian product $Cm \times Qt \times U$ of the set Cm of all the cameras, the set Qt of all QTs, and the set U of (all the potential) camera end users, we interpret a triplet $\langle cm, qt, u \rangle$ from S as the QT qt that has been OBSERVED to encode an image taken by the (camera) user u with a camera cm.

Assuming that S stores data from the Internet for instance, it provides noisy information. Indeed, some (unknown amount of) triplets from S result from a software manipulation of some photographs. Here, we assume (cf. Assumption 2) that most (or typical) software manipulations affect QTs. Accordingly, $\langle cm, qt, u \rangle \in S$ does not necessarily entail that qt is the QT that has been employed by a camera cm to encode an image taken by the (camera) user u. In fact, qt might be the QT employed by a software application to encode the image that was taken originally with a camera cm, which, however, had encoded the image originally by means of a QT different from qt. This is the noise inherent in S.

To represent noise-free information, we introduce a virtual, binary relation, denoted R, that is a subset of the binary Cartesian product $Cm \times Qt$. A pair $\langle cm, qt \rangle$ from R is interpreted as the QT qt that (in reality, which is unknown) is employed to encode some image taken by a camera cm. The other way round, $\langle cm, qt \rangle \notin R$ entails that cm never employs qt to encode an image.

5   Image Database

To create S, we needed to download and process a large number of images. Keeping at disposition a variety of popular photo–sharing servers from which photos can by downloaded, we have opted for Flickr, one of the most popular photo sharing sites. We downloaded two millions images labeled as "original." Nevertheless, as has been pointed out, Flickr, in fact, is an "uncontrolled arena." In other words, there is no guarantee that the image at hand is coming from the camera model information as indicated by metadata. To minimize the noise, as discussed in the previous section, we have discarded images with illegible metadata, a software tag signifying traces of some known photo processing software, or inconsistencies in original and modification dates or between quoted and actual width and height. Also, we discarded images without 3–channel colors. All

---

[1] In general, other sets of appropriate attributes can be considered, e.g., size, orientation, format, etc.

these operations, reduced the number of "original" images to 798,924. Our strategy was to maximize $|Cm|, |Qt|, |U|$ and, at the same time, to minimize the noise in S.

We believe that the frequency of original images in this remaining set is much higher than noise (images processed by software).

6   A Statistical Approach for Noise Removal

In general, the question arises: Given observed information, represented as S, what can be concluded about reality, represented as R? Specifically, given S, can we objectively quantify a "confidence" that the QT as found in the image file may correspond to the one used by the camera upon capturing? Indeed, we present an approach based on statistical hypothesis testing that enables to make a lower estimation of this confidence.

In brief, we utilize a statistical analysis of information noise inherent in S. Noisy information generally is contained in any set of tuples from S. Specifically, given a "testing" pair $t_0 = \langle cm_0, qt_0 \rangle$, our default position is that all the triplets from S containing attribute values cm_0 and qt_0 represent noisy information only. Accordingly, we set out the null hypothesis

H_0:   "t_0 is not included in R"

and introduce a *test statistic* T, which, in general, is a numerical summary of S that reduces S to a set of values that can be used to perform the hypothesis test. Specifically, T quantifies the noisy information. Last, we determine the upper estimation p of observing a value v for T that is at least as extreme as the value that has been actually observed. That is, the probability of observing v or some more extreme value for T is no more than p.

The test statistic is defined as the mapping $T: Cm \times Qt \longrightarrow \mathbb{N}_0$ that maps each pair $\langle cm, qt \rangle$ from the binary Cartesian product $Cm \times Qt$ to the cardinality (a value from the set of nonnegative integers, denoted $\mathbb{N}_0$) of the set of all and only those users who, in accordance with S, have taken some image with a camera cm that has encoded it by means of qt. In symbols:

$$T(cm, qt) = \text{card}\{u \mid \langle cm, qt, u \rangle \in S\} \tag{4}$$

for any pair $\langle cm, qt \rangle$ from $Cm \times Qt$.

The rationale behind using the above test statistic is based on the ASSUMPTION OF PROPORTIONALITY:

Assumption 1. Given a pair $\langle cm, qt \rangle$ of a camera cm and a QT qt, the amount of noisy information in S concerning $\langle cm, qt \rangle$ is directly proportional to the number of (observed) distinct users (in S) who have taken an image encoded by means of qt with cm.

Speaking in broad terms, we conclude that the number of these users is too big to be attributed exclusively to an information noise if the number exceeds a specified significance level. To determine this significance level, we introduce mappings in terms of which we define the exact *sampling distribution* of T. It will be seen that, under the above and the undermentioned assumptions, this exact sampling distribution of T is the *hypergeometric distribution* that is relative to an appropriate set of cameras.

Observe that H_0 implies that any image that, in accordance with its metadata, has been taken with a camera cm_0 and encoded by means of qt_0 must in fact have been modified with a software application. Moreover, consider the following assumption of software manipulations.

Assumption 2. Software manipulations usually do not change image metadata concerning a camera.

Essentially, this assumption states that any image that, in accordance with its metadata, has been taken with a camera, say cm, indeed, has been taken with that camera. Consequently, $T(cm, qt)$ is interpreted as the number of all distinct users from S who have taken an image with a camera cm, which, IN ACCORDANCE WITH S, has encoded the image by means of qt. However, taking into account possible software manipulations, qt, in the reality that is OUT OF ACCORD WITH S, might have been employed by a software application used by a user to modify the image in question. Specifically, provided that H_0 is true, $T(cm_0, qt_0)$ is interpreted as the number of all distinct users from S who have taken an image with a camera cm_0, but, CONTRARY TO S, not cm_0 but a software application, used by a user to modify the image, has encoded the image by means of qt_0.

Next, C denoting a subset of Cm, we introduce the following mappings:

$$G\colon Cm \longrightarrow \mathbb{N}_0, \tag{5}$$

$$N\colon 2^{Cm} \longrightarrow \mathbb{N}_0, \tag{6}$$

$$n\colon Qt \times 2^{Cm} \longrightarrow \mathbb{N}_0. \tag{7}$$

defined by the following respective rules:

$$G(cm) = \mathrm{card}\{u \mid \langle cm, qt, u \rangle \in S\}, \tag{8}$$

$$N(C) = \sum_{cm \in C} G(cm), \tag{9}$$

$$n(qt, C) = \sum_{cm \in C} T(cm, qt). \tag{10}$$

$G(cm)$ is interpreted as the number of all (observed) distinct users (i.e., from S) who have taken an image with a camera cm. Accordingly, $N(C)$ is the summation of these numbers (of all distinct users from S) for all cameras from the set C. That is, each user is added in $N(C)$ k-times if he or she has taken images with k distinct respective cameras from C. Last, $n(qt, C)$ is the summation of the numbers of all (observed) distinct users (from S) who have taken an image with a respective camera from the set C, whereas the image is encoded by means of

qt: either, in accordance with S, the camera, or, out of accord with S, a software application, used by a user to modify the image, has employed qt to encoded the image. That is, each user is added in $n(qt, C)$ k-times if he or she has taken images with k distinct respective cameras from C, whereas the image is encoded by means of qt.

Specifically, suppose a set C including only cameras that never employ qt_0 to encode an image. Then $n(qt_0, C)$ is interpreted as the summation of the numbers of all (observed) distinct users (from S) who have taken an image with a camera from the set C, whereas the image is encoded by means of qt_0 by a software application, used by a user to modify the image. Moreover, suppose that the camera cm_0 is included in C. Indeed, in accordance with H_0, cm_0 is a camera that never employs qt_0 to encode an image.

Note that, for large S, $G(cm)$ is proportional to the number of all images taken with a given camera cm. In particular, CONSIDERING ONLY IMAGES TAKEN WITH CAMERAS FROM C, the $G(cm_0)$ to $N(C)$ ratio, $\frac{G(cm_0)}{N(C)}$, is interpreted as the probability that an image has been taken with a camera cm_0 (by a user, say u_1). Similarly, $G(cm_0) - 1$ to $N(C)$ ratio, $\frac{G(cm_0)-1}{N(C)}$, could by interpreted as the probability that an image has been taken with a camera cm_0 by a user, say u_2, different from the user u_1. However, observe that this interpretation is correct only if the following assumption is adopted.

Assumption 3. Given any camera cm from C and a set U_{cm} of users who have taken an image with a camera cm, the probability p_u that an image has been taken by a user u is (approximately) equal to $\frac{1}{G(cm)}$ for any user u from U_{cm}.

Then, disregarding all images that have been taken by considered users u_1, u_2 with respective cameras (identified as cm_0), $1 - \frac{G(cm_0)-2}{N(C)}$, is interpreted as a probability that an image has been taken with a camera from C (but distinct from cm_0) by a user, say u_1'. To put it another way, knowing that a given image has not been taken with a camera cm_0 by a user u_1 or u_2, the probability the image has been taken (by any user) with a camera from C (but distinct from cm_0) is equal to $1 - \frac{G(cm_0)-2}{N(C)}$. In general, continuing the above train of thoughts, $\frac{G(cm_0)-k}{N(C)-\ell}$ is interpreted as a probability that, disregarding images that have been taken by any of $k+\ell$ considered users with respective cameras from C, an image has been taken with a camera cm_0. $1 - \frac{G(cm_0)-k}{N(C)-\ell}$ is interpreted analogously. Now the following proposition is clear upon reflection.

Proposition 1 (Sampling distribution of test statistic). Consider a mapping

$$F \colon \mathbb{N}_0 \times Cm \times Qt \times 2^{Cm} \longrightarrow \langle 0, 1 \rangle \tag{11}$$

that coincides with the hypergeometric (cumulative) distribution function, whose *probability mass function* is defined as follows:

$$h(x; n, G, N) = \frac{\binom{G}{x}\binom{N-G}{n-x}}{\binom{N}{n}}, \tag{12}$$

where, by abuse of notation,

$$n = n(qt, C) \; , \qquad\qquad G = G(cm) \; , \qquad\qquad N = N(C) \; .$$

Then $F(x, cm_0, qt_0, C)$ is the sampling (discrete cumulative) distribution of $T(cm_0, qt_0)$ under H_0 if C includes cm_0 and only those cameras that never employ qt_0 to encode an image:

$$C \subseteq \{ cm \mid \langle cm, qt_0 \rangle \notin R \} \; . \tag{13}$$

Most importantly, note that

$$p = 1 - F\big(T(cm_0, qt_0), cm_0, qt_0, C\big) \tag{14}$$

is the *p-value* that is interpreted as the probability of obtaining a test statistic at least as extreme as $\mathrm{T}(mk_0, qt_0)$, which is uniquely determined by S (i.e., the observed data), assuming that the null hypothesis H_0 is true. It presents the probability of incorrectly rejecting H_0.

Finally, we discuss an important subtlety of the condition (13) imposed on C in the above proposition. In fact, this condition is hard to fulfill as R is unknown. However, the following corollary is easily verified:

Corollary 1. Failing to fulfill (13) results in an upper estimation of the *p*-value.

To see the assertion of the corollary, observe that failing to fulfill (13) increases $n(qt_0, C)$ defined by (10) but, due to Assumption 2, affects neither $G(cm)$ for any cm from C and thus nor $N(C)$. It follows from properties of the hypergeometric distribution that its (cumulative) distribution function is inversely proportional to n for fixed but arbitrary x, G, and N. Consequently, for cm_0, qt_0 and fixed but arbitrary x, $F(x, cm_0, qt_0, C)$ has a global maximum at C if (13) holds. Now it is immediate that failing to fulfill (13) OVERVALUES p (defined as (14)) the probability estimation that the null hypothesis will be rejected incorrectly.

Note that rejecting H_0 entails accepting the alternative hypothesis, namely that t_0 is included in R, which means that qt_0 may be employed by a camera cm_0 to encode an image. Consequently, the confidence of accepting the alternative hypothesis can be quantified by the value $1 - p$ with rigorous interpretation, and the presented statistical approach results in a lower estimation of this value.

7   Experimental Results

We have carried out an experiment on 1000 randomly selected JPEG non-modified images taken by 10 cameras (100 images per camera) to demonstrate the efficiency of the proposed approach. For every image, we have repeated a statistical test procedure with the significance level (the probability of mistakenly rejecting the null hypothesis) set to 1%. All the cameras from S has been included in the set C, the parameter of the sampling distribution of test statistic T. Consequently, in accordance with the corollary, we have obtained a rather coarse upper estimation of the *p*-value, the probability of incorrectly rejecting H_0.

Results are shown in Tab. 1. The column denoted by "*orig*" refers to non-modified (i.e., original) images. Modified images have been simulated by re-saving original images so that randomly selected QTs (randomly for each image) used by popular software like Adobe Photoshop and GIMP (the column denoted by "*misc*") have been employed to encode them. Respective numbers of non-rejecting H_0 are shown, i.e., the numbers of images, whose originality cant be confirmed statistically from our data.

Table 1. Data in each cell are obtained using 100 JPEG images

cm	size	orig	misc
Canon EOS 20D	3504×2336	0	37
Canon EOS 50D	4752×3168	0	34
Canon PowerShot A75	2048×1536	0	28
Konica KD-400Z	2304×1704	0	16
Nikon Coolpix P80	1280×960	0	14
Nikon E990	2048×1536	5	10
Olympus C740UZ	2048×1536	2	7
Olympus X450	2048×1536	1	23
Panasonic DMC-LX2	3840×2160	0	19
Sony DSC-W40	2816×2112	2	16

8 Discussion

Denoising a DB (database) of QTs of JPEG images from "unguaranteed" sources is a complex task. Cameras and pieces of software often have complicate and unpredictable behavior. Many cameras compute QTs on the fly (based on the scene). Furthermore, a huge number of cameras and software employ standard IJG QTs. There also are devices using a particular set of QTs very widely and another set of QTs very rarely.

Many pieces of software modify images (for instance, enhance the contrast or rotate the image) without leaving any traces in image's JPEG file metadata. This makes difficult the task of obtaining acquisition devices's fingerprints from a DB consisting of images coming from an uncontrolled environment.

It is apparent that QTs cannot uniquely identify the source effectively. Despite this they provide valuable information, supplemental in the forgery detection task. This has been shown in the previous section.

We point out that our results are affected by the C parameter in the aforementioned fashion. In particular, a careful selection of cameras (to be included in C) based on an appropriate heuristics, is supposed to improve results remarkably. Specifically, it is expected to lower the probability of incorrectly rejecting H_0 concerning QTs of non-modified images, resulting in lower values in the column referred to as "*orig*.'

The approach presented is general and can straightforwardly be applies to other features forming devices fingerprints.

Acknowledgments. This work has been supported by the Czech Science Foundation under the projects No. GACR 102/08/0470 and GACR P202/10/P509. This work has been supported by the Institutional Research Plan AV0Z10300504 "Computer Science for the Information Society: Models, algorithms, Applications" and Institute for Theoretical Computer Science project no. 1M0021620808 (1M0545).

References

1. Mahdian, B., Saic, S.: A bibliography on blind methods for identifying image forgery. Signal Processing: Image Communication 25, 389–399 (2010)
2. Farid, H.: A survey of image forgery detection. IEEE Signal Processing Magazine 2(26), 16–25 (2009)
3. Kornblum, J.D.: Using jpeg quantization tables to identify imagery processed by software. In: Proceedings of the Digital Forensic Workshop, August 2008, pp. 21–25 (2008)
4. Farid, H.: Digital image ballistics from JPEG quantization, Tech. Rep. TR2006-583, Department of Computer Science, Dartmouth College (2006)
5. Fridrich, J., Lukas, J.: Estimation of primary quantization matrix in double compressed jpeg images. In: Proceedings of DFRWS, Cleveland, OH, USA, August 2003, vol. 2 (2003)
6. Fridrich, J., Pevny, T.: Detection of double–compression for applications in steganography. IEEE Transactions on Information Security and Forensics 3(2), 247–258 (2008)
7. Fu, D., Shi, Y.Q., Su, W.: A generalized benford's law for jpeg coefficients and its applications in image forensics. In: SPIE Electronic Imaging: Security, Steganography, and Watermarking of Multimedia Contents, San Jose, CA, USA (January 2007)
8. Luo, W., Qu, Z., Huang, J., Qiu, G.: A novel method for detecting cropped and recompressed image block. In: IEEE International Conference on Acoustics, Speech and Signal Processing, Honolulu, HI, USA, vol. 2, pp. 217–220 (April 2007)
9. Mahdian, B., Saic, S.: Detecting double compressed jpeg images. In: The 3rd International Conference on Imaging for Crime Detection and Prevention (ICDP 2009), London, UK (December 2009)
10. Popescu, A.C.: Statistical Tools for Digital Image Forensics, Ph.D. thesis, Ph.D. dissertation. Department of Computer Science, Dartmouth College, Hanover, NH (2005)
11. Qu, Z., Luo, W., Huang, J.: A convolutive mixing model for shifted double jpeg compression with application to passive image authentication. In: IEEE International Conference on Acoustics, Speech and Signal Processing, Las Vegas, USA, April 2008, pp. 4244–1483 (2008)
12. Kihara, M., Fujiyoshi, M., Wan, Q.T., Kiya, H.: Image tamper detection using mathematical morphology. In: ICIP, vol. (6), pp. 101–104 (2007)
13. Farid, H.: Digital image ballistics from JPEG quantization: A followup study, Tech. Rep. TR2008-638, Department of Computer Science, Dartmouth College (2008)
14. Pennebaker, W.B., Mitchell, J.L.: JPEG Still Image Data Compression Standard. Kluwer Academic Publishers, Norwell (1992)

Discovering Correspondences between Fingerprints Based on the Temporal Dynamics of Eye Movements from Experts

Chen Yu, Thomas Busey, and John Vanderkolk

Indiana University
1101 East 10th Street, Bloomington, IN, 47405
{chenyu,busey}@indiana.edu

Abstract. Latent print examinations involve a process by which a latent print, often recovered from a crime scene, is compared against a known standard or sets of standard prints. Despite advances in automatic fingerprint recognition, latent prints are still examined by human expert primarily due to the poor image quality of latent prints. The aim of the present study is to better understand the perceptual and cognitive processes of fingerprint practices as implicit expertise. Our approach is to collect fine-grained gaze data from fingerprint experts when they conduct a matching task between two prints. We then rely on machine learning techniques to discover meaningful patterns from their eye movement data. As the first steps in this project, we compare gaze patterns from experts with those obtained from novices. Our results show that experts and novices generate similar overall gaze patterns. However, a deeper data analysis using machine translation reveals that experts are able to identify more corresponding areas between two prints within a short period of time.

Keywords: fingerprint, Cognitive and Behavioral Studies, Computational data analysis, Data mining.

1 Introduction

The goal of our study is to use computational techniques derived from machine translation to explore the temporal dynamics of complex visual processing tasks in fingerprint examinations. These examinations involve a process by which a latent print, often recovered from a crime scene, is compared against a known standard or sets of standard prints. Despite advances in automatic pattern matching technology [2,3], latent prints are still compared by human experts. In the United States and in many other countries there is no fixed number of matching points or details that is mandated by the courts or forensic science community [1]. This implicitly gives the examiners some latitude in terms of the details they choose to use in order to determine whether the two prints come from the same source. For example, instead of relying on matching minutiae, the examiner is free to use what details and patterns they feel are relevant, including what is known as first level detail of general direction of ridges, second level specific ridge paths, and third level detail or the texture and shape of individual ridge elements.

H. Sako, K. Franke, and S. Saitoh (Eds.): IWCF 2010, LNCS 6540, pp. 160–172, 2011.
© Springer-Verlag Berlin Heidelberg 2011

While most computational fingerprint projects focus on building automatic pattern recognition systems, the goal of the present study is different. Here we aim at a better understanding of human fingerprint expertise which will not only provide useful evidence to justify the use of fingerprints in count but also provide principles and insights to develop better automatic recognition systems to reach expert-level performance (especially for latent prints). To achieve this goal, we developed a mobile sensing system to collect moment-by-moment eye gaze data from fingerprint experts, and then develop and use computational approaches to analyzing such data to gain a better understanding of their fingerprint examination practices. From the scientific perspective, compared with other forensic evidence (e.g. DNA), there is less known about the information content in fingerprints or statistics such as the likelihood of a random correspondence. On the one hand, we know fingerprint images are information-rich: even twins with identical DNA have different fingerprints [4]. On the other hand, experts may choose to rely on different sources of information depending on the circumstances and their training, which may raise issues with respect to the nature of the evidence presented in court. There exist no explicit standards for what information shall be used in latent print examinations. A recent National Academy of Sciences report [1] was somewhat critical of the language used by examiners when testifying about their results, and called for more training and research on the nature of the latent print examinations. The report revealed weaknesses in our current knowledge about what information experts rely on when performing identifications and exclusions. Part of the difficulty resides in the fact that much of the processes of perception are unconscious and can be difficult to translate into language and examinations may be subject to extra-examination biases [5]. The aim of the present study is to systematically study fingerprint experts to understand better what cognitive and perceptual processes support their matching decisions. We are particularly interested in the temporal dynamics of the search process as one marker of expertise. From engineering and applied perspectives, understanding where experts look would also provide useful insights on how to build computational systems that can either perform similar tasks or assist human experts to better perform such tasks.

2 Related Work

There are several different approaches to automatic fingerprint recognition [2,3]. Su et al. [6] presented a novel individuality evaluation approach to estimating the probability of random correspondence (PRC) based on the distribution of three fingerprint features: ridge flow, minutiae and minutiae together with ridge points. Ratha et al. [8] generated multiple cancelable identifiers from fingerprint images and those identifiers can be cancelled and replaced when compromised, showing that feature-level cancelable biometric construction is practicable in large biometric deployments. Tuyls et al. [7] applied template protection schemes to fingerprint data by splitting the helper data in two parts; one part determines the reliable components and the other part allows for noise correction on the quantized representations.

The goal of the present study is not to develop an automatic fingerprint recognition system. Instead, we intend to address fundamental research questions on human fingerprint examination using computational analysis techniques to discover how human fingerprint experts conduct a pattern matching task given both inked and latent prints and what visual features on the fingerprints they used which will shed light on building expert-like automatic fingerprint systems. To the best of our knowledge, this is the first study to use eye tracking to understanding the expertise fingerprint examiners (to our knowledge), eye tracking techniques have been successfully applied in several other scientific fields to assess implicit knowledge from human experts in certain domains. The field of mammography research has adopted similar eye tracking methodologies. Krupinski et al. [9] have used eye tracking to investigate not only what features radiologists rely on when inspecting mammograms, but also to suggest cognitive mechanisms such as holistic processing when experts are viewing mammograms. A similar work with chest x-rays demonstrated that dwell times were longer on missed tumors than at other locations, suggesting that errors in radiology are due to identification problems rather than detection problems. The field of questioned documents has also benefited from an eye tracking approach [13] as well, which has helped to delimit the visual features that experts rely on when comparing signatures. All of those applications of eye tracking indicate the promise of using eye movement data in fingerprint examination studies.

3 Experiment and Data

The first challenge to achieve our research goal is to collect behavioral data from fingerprint experts. As noted earlier, assessing implicit knowledge from human experts is a non-trivial task as such knowledge cannot be inferred from survey or questionnaire by asking experts where they look and why they look at there. Humans generate about 3 eye fixations per second to gather visual information from their environment. If we assume that experts move their eyes equally frequently, they must produce a large number of eye fixations in a print examination and clearly they cannot recall precisely which areas in the print they just visit moment by moment. Meanwhile, we know their eyes are not random; instead they actively collect visual information that is then fed into their brain for their decision making. In light of this, our solution is to collect momentary eye movement data from latent print examiners and use advanced computational techniques to analyze such data to lead to a better understanding of their expertise.

Eye tracking has become an important in behavioral studies as well as in human-computer interaction and marketing studies. There are several commercial eye tracking systems available in the market (e.g., Tobii eye tracking system, www.tobii.com). However, in practice, gathering data from experts poses a particular challenge since they work in different police or FBI branches throughout the U.S. and most commercial eye tracking systems can only be used in a laboratory environment.

To solve this problem, we developed a portable eye tracking system that is based on an open-source hardware design [10], allowing us to recruit experts at forensic identification conferences and collect gaze data from them. Participants were seated approximately 60 cm (~24 inches) away from a 21" LCD monitor. The fingerprint images were presented side-by-side on a 21" LCD monitor at a resolution of 1580 x 759 pixels. The monitor itself was set to its native resolution of 1680 x 1050 pixels. As shown in Figure 1, participants wore our head-mounted eye tracker which used two small cameras to monitor the eye and the view of the scene respectively according to the hardware proposed by [10]. Both cameras are mounted on a pair of lightweight safety glasses. One infrared light is located next to the eye-camera in order to illuminate the eye properly. This light provides us a constant spot of white light known as the first corneal reflection, which will be used for further offline analysis using the *ExpertEyes* software, an open source approach for analyzing eye-tracker data http://code.google.com/p/experteyes/wiki/ExpertEyes) developed by our research group. This image processing software takes two video streams from two cameras and generate (x,y) coordinates indicating where a person is looking in the scene camera. Further, we developed another program to convert (x,y) coordinates in the scene camera into (x,y) coordinates on the print image by detecting the location of the monitor in the scene camera's view. In this way, our system captures, moment by moment, which area in a print a person is fixating.

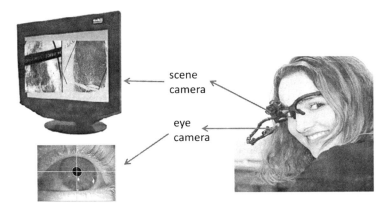

Fig. 1. Our eye tracking system consists of two cameras -- the eye camera captures eye images while the scene camera captures the visual information from the first-person view (in this case, fingerprints on a computer screen). Our custom software relies on image processing techniques to infer where a participant looks on the computer screen.

In our experiments, participants included both experts and novices. We include novices to establish a baseline for comparision. Even though novices do not have fingerprint expertise, our human visual system is still quite powerful to detect the similarities between visual stimuli. Therefore, the data from experts would allow us to distinguish between general capabilities in human visual system and true fingerprint expertise in experts.

Human observers (e.g. experts or novices) were asked to visually examine a set of fingerprints one by one and decided whether the two simultaneously-displayed fingerprints match each other or not. There was no particular instruction about where they should look during the matching task so that they could freely move their eyes. The typical latent print examination can take hours or even days to complete for difficult prints. Examiners will sometimes start with an inspection of the latent print, which may be augmented by photographs, notes or drawings. They then move on to the inked print, which helps prevent situations in which they may begin to see details in the latent print that are shared with the ink print. Our statistical analyses, however, require a relatively large number of images in order to ensure reliable results, and we wanted to gather a complete dataset from each participant. As a result, we decided to limit the amount of time that each participant could spend on each fingerprint to avoid corrupting our database with uninformative eye movements as they waited for the next print.

There were two datasets used in the present study. Dataset 1 was collected from a task in which participants were asked to examine 35 pairs of inked and latent prints. Each trial of examination took 20 seconds and then they moved to the next image pair. The stimuli for this study were taken from National Institutes of Standards and Technology Special Database 27. The print stimuli in dataset 2 consisted of two clear images that were scanned at a 1000-dpi from clear inked prints collected from members of the Bloomington Indiana community. Participants were allowed to review two prints individually for 5 seconds on each, and they had 10 seconds to review two prints displayed simultaneously. There were 12 fingerprint experts and 12 novices in each study. Experts were recruited at forensic identification conferences in Nevada, Illinois and Indiana, while the novices were members of the Bloomington, Indiana community. Figure 2 illustrates an example stimulus in dataset 1, along with the eye fixations and eye trace for participants. Our eye tracker generates gaze data at the sampling rate of 30Hz. In total, there were approximately 504,000 gaze data points in each dataset.

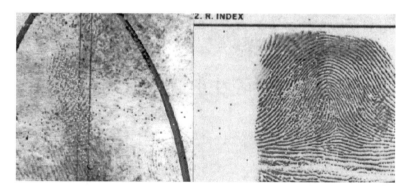

Fig. 2. Latent/inked pair from dataset 1, with fixations from all experts overplotted as green dots, and fixations from all novices overplotted as red dots. The green dots tend to be clustered in the upper-right portion of the inked print (right image), which corresponds to the area of high detail in the latent print. However, novices have a much wider distribution of fixations, including in regions that have very poor image quality.

4   Method

Given the high spatial and temporal resolutions of our eye tracking data, the technical challenge is to discover meaningful patterns from those rich datasets. Our computational data analysis consists of four steps as illustrated in Figure 3: 1) temporal fixation finding: reducing the continuous time series of raw gaze data into a sequence of eye fixations defined mostly by the speed of eye movements over time; 2) spatial clustering to calculate Regions-of-Interest (ROIs): clustering (x,y) gaze data points into several clusters/ROIs based on the spatial distribution of gaze data on the prints; 3) alignment: segmenting the ROI sequences into ink-latent fixation pairs based on temporal proximity; 4) using a machine translation method to compute the correspondences between ROIs in the inked and latent prints. As a result, we extract the patterns of which corresponding areas that experts examine back and forth between two prints and which areas that novices pay attention to when conducting the same matching task. In the following, we will provide technical details of each component briefly described above.

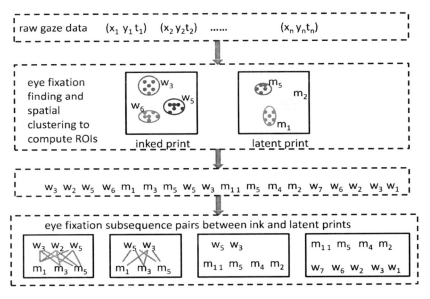

Fig. 3. The overview of our data analysis approach consisting of four stages

4.1 Temporal Fixation Finding

We have developed our own algorithm of eye fixation finding which is composed of four steps: 1) First, we computed the magnitude of velocity from raw eye movement data (x,y); 2) we next used a pre-defined threshold to segment the whole continuous stream into several big segments that correspond to dramatic eye location changes; 3) we analyzed each big segment and re-segmented each into individual segments that correspond to small eye position changes. Those small segments may or may not correspond to fixations; 4) Finally, we took spatial information into account by merging small segments (detected from Step 3) if they were spatially close to each other (e.g. eyes moving around an area with a certain speed). After the above four steps, we successfully segmented a continuous eye movement stream into several eye fixations by integrating both temporal (the speed of eye movement, etc.) and spatial (the overall spatial changes of eye gaze location) information.

4.2 Spatial Clustering

Given raw (x,y) coordinates from Step 1, the next step is to group those data points into several clusters – the regions that participants frequently visit. We used Hierarchical agglomerative clustering [11]. The basic idea is to treat each eye fixation location as a singleton cluster at the beginning and then successively merge (or *agglomerate*) pairs of clusters until all clusters have been merged into several prototype clusters. We took the centroid of each cluster as a ROI. The criterion used to terminate the clustering algorithm is the minimal distance required to group two data points. In the present study, the distance was set to be 20 pixels which match to a visual angle of 0.5 degrees.

4.3 Temporal Alignment

Now that we have a sequence of ROIs extracted from participants' gaze data, some over one image and the rest on the other. Our goal is to calculate correspondences between gazed regions in one image with gazed regions in the other image as participants conducted the matching task. To do so, we view this task as similar to machine translation in natural language processing [12]. The general idea of machine translation is this: assume that we have parallel texts from two languages, for example, "Harry Potter and the Order of the Phoenix" in both English and French, the goal of machine translation is to infer which two words in the two languages correspond. This inference can be done based on statistical information, such as how frequent "egg" in English and "oeuf" in French co-occur together and how frequent "egg" appears without "oeuf". Intuitively, if a word in English always co-occurs with another word in French and that word in English appears only when the other word in French appears, then those two words are likely to correspond to each other. Most often an assumption in machine translation is a sentence-level assignment – which sentence in English maps to which one in French is known. Say it in other way, we have sentence pairs from two languages and use this data to infer word correspondences.

In the fingerprint matching task, we conceptualize ROIs from one image as words in English, and ROIs on another print as words in French. Based on this conceptualization, the aim here is to find which gazed region in one print maps to which gazed region in the other print. To achieve this, we also need to segment continue gaze data generated by participants into "sentence" pairs. This is done based on the observation that participants may generate a few fixations on one image, switch to examine another image with more fixations to search for corresponding areas on the other image. In light of this, and as showed at the bottom of Figure 3, we first divided a whole sequence into several subsequences using the visual attention switches between two prints as breaking points, and then grouped those subsequences into several pairs based on temporal proximity. The outcome of this alignment is a set of fixation sequence pairs from which we further calculated which fixated area in one image maps to what fixated area in the other image in the next step. We call each pair of two fixation subsequences on two prints a searching instance as we assume that participants were comparing and matching regions between two prints through those eye fixations on both prints. Figure 3 shows four searching instances extracted from a continue ROI sequence. To the degree to which experts will find matching features in both prints we will be able to discover these through machine translation.

4.4 Machine Translation

The general setting of the final step is as follows: suppose we have one ROI set from one image $X = \{w_1, w_2, \dots, w_N\}$ and the other ROI set from the other image $Y = \{m_1, m_2, \dots, m_M\}$, where N is the number of ROIs in one print and M is the number of ROIs in the other print. Let S be the number of searching instances. All gaze data are in a dataset $\chi = \left\{(S_w^{(s)}, S_m^{(s)}), 1 \leq s \leq S\right\}$, where for each searching instance, $S_w^{(s)}$ consists of r ROIs $w_{u(1)}, w_{u(2)}, \dots, w_{u(r)}$, and $u(i)$ can be selected from 1 to N. Similarly, the corresponding gaze sequence on the other print $S_m^{(s)}$ includes l possible ROIs $m_{v(1)}, m_{v(2)}, \dots, m_{v(l)}$ and the value of $v(j)$ is from 1 to M. In the example in Figure 3, there are four searching instances (bottom row of Figure 3) that provide that data to determine which ROI in one image should be mapped with one or several co-occurring ROIs in the other image. The computational challenge here is to build several one-to-one mappings from many-to-many possible mappings within multiple searching instances as not all of the ROIs (generated by participants) within an instance can reliably map to the other ROIs on the other image. We suggest that to figure out which ROI in one image goes to which ROI in the other image, a good solution shouldn't consider the mapping of just a single ROI-ROI pair, but instead we should estimate all these possible mappings simultaneously. Thus, we attempt to estimate the mapping probabilities of all of these pairs so that the best overall mapping is achieved. In doing so, the constraints across multiple searching instances and the constraints across different ROI-ROI pairs are jointly considered in a general system which attempts to discover the best ROI-to-ROI mappings based on the overall statistical regularities in the whole eye fixation sequence.

Formally, given a dataset χ, we use the machine translation method proposed in [12] to maximize the likelihood of generating/predicting one set of ROIs from one image given a set of ROIs from the other image:

$$P\left(S_m^{(1)}, S_m^{(2)}, \dots, S_m^{(S)} \middle| S_w^{(1)}, S_w^{(2)}, \dots, S_w^{(S)}\right)$$
$$= \prod_{s=1}^{S} \sum_a p(S_m^{(s)}, a|S_w^{(s)})$$
$$= \prod_{s=1}^{S} \frac{\epsilon}{(r+1)^l} \prod_{j=1}^{l} \sum_{i=0}^{r} p(m_{v(j)}|w_{u(i)}) \quad (1)$$

where the alignment a indicates which ROI in one image is aligned with which ROI in the other image. $p(m_{v(j)}|w_{u(i)})$ is the mapping probability for a ROI-ROI pair and ϵ is a small constant. This is equivalent to predicting or generating a French sentence given an English sentence.

To maximize the above likelihood function, a new variable $c\left(m_m\middle|w_n,S_w^{(s)},S_m^{(s)}\right)$ is introduced which represents the expected number of times that any particular ROI w_n in one subsequence $S_w^{(s)}$ generates any specific ROI m_m in the other subsequence $S_m^{(s)}$:

$$c\left(m_m\middle|w_n,S_w^{(s)},S_m^{(s)}\right) = \frac{p\left(m_{v(j)}\middle|w_{u(i)}\right)}{p\left(m_m\middle|w_{u(1)}\right) + \cdots + p\left(m_m\middle|w_{u(r)}\right)}$$
$$\times \sum_{j=1}^{l} \delta(m_m, v(j)) \sum_{i=1}^{r} \delta(w_n, u(i)) \tag{2}$$

where δ is equal to 1 when both of its arguments are the same and equal to zero otherwise. The second part in Equation (2) counts the number of co-occurring times of w_n and m_m. The first part assigns a weight to this count by considering it across all the other ROIs in the same searching instance. By introducing this new variable, the computation of the derivative of the likelihood function with respect to the mapping probability $p(m_m|w_n)$ results in:

$$p(m_m|w_n) = \frac{\sum_{s=1}^{S} c\left(m_m\middle|w_n,S_w^{(s)},S_m^{(s)}\right)}{\sum_{m=1}^{M}\sum_{s=1}^{S} c\left(m_m\middle|w_n,S_w^{(s)},S_m^{(s)}\right)} \tag{3}$$

As shown in Algorithm 1, the method sets an initial $p(m_m|w_n)$ to be flat distribution, and then successively compute the occurrences of all ROI-ROI pairs $c\left(m_m\middle|w_n,S_w^{(s)},S_m^{(s)}\right)$ using Equation (2) and the mapping probabilities using Equation (3). In this way, our method runs multiple times and allows for re-estimating ROI-ROI mapping probabilities. The detailed technical descriptions can be found in [12].

Algorithm 1. Estimating ROI-ROI mapping probabilities

Assign initial values for $p(m_m|w_n)$ based on co-occurrence statistics.
repeat
         E-step: Compute the counts for all ROI-ROI pairs using equation 2.
         M-step: Re-estimate the mapping probabilities using equation 3.
until the mapping probabilities converge.

----

5   Results

As the first steps of this project, we focus on comparing gaze patterns between experts and novices. The first set of results is to compare overall gaze fixation statistics between the expert and novice groups. In dataset 1, we found no differences in terms of the average duration of each fixation for the two groups (M_{expert}= 185.51ms M_{novice}=183.50; p>0.5). In addition, we measured the proportion of the overall fixation duration (within a 20-second trial) and again the results showed no differences (M_{expert}= 11.04 sec M_{novice}=10.96 sec; p>0.5). The results derived from dataset 2 are almost identical with those from data set 1. Thus, we couldn't distinguish between experts and novices based on their overall eye movement patterns. One plausible reason is that participants in both groups were actively engaged in the pattern matching task and therefore their overall eye movement pattern were driven by low-level visual saliency of fingerprints and were controlled by the same neural architecture in the brain [14]. However, if this is the case, we expect that a deeper computational data analysis based on machine translation described earlier may reveal the differences between two groups. In particular, our research questions are 1) whether experts' gaze patterns are more consistent than those from novices; 2) whether experts can identify more ROI-ROI pairs within a short period of time; and 3) whether those pairs identified by experts or novices are actually correct.

Indeed, the results of the machine translation analysis applied to experts and novices are very clear. Our method produced all of the possible ROI-ROI mappings between fixations on the two images. We chose two criteria to select reliable ROI-ROI pairs. First, the co-occurring frequency is at least 2, meaning that a participant at least looked at one region in one image and subsequently look at another region in the other region twice. Second, the overall mapping probability $p(m_m|w_n)$ needs to be greater than 0.4. Based on this selection, the experts have an average of 17.1 reliable mappings/links found, while the novices have an average of 7.1 links found ($t(34)$=-6.73; p <0.001, sd = 8.84) from dataset 1. For dataset 2 with clean prints, we found a similar result. The machine translation found an average of 11.1 links for experts and 8.3 links for novices ($t(29)$=-3.18; p <0.01, sd = 4.59). Figures 4 (from dataset 1) and 5 (from dataset 2) show examples from both experts and novices. This demonstrates that the temporal dynamics for experts are much better as input to the machine translation algorithm in terms of assigning corresponding links between the two images. Within a short period of time, experts can manage to find more corresponding pairs than novice do.

Are those pairs visually spotted by either experts or novices are actually correct correspondences? Did expert do a better job in finding correct correspondences than novices did? To address those questions, we asked an expert to independently place corresponding marks on the pairs of clean prints in dataset 2 (the latent/inked pairs from dataset 1 did not have sufficient details to allow this procedure with high accuracy). We then used a second order polynomial function to map every point on the left print to a corresponding point in the right print for each print pair. As shown in Figure 5, each link (highlighted by red lines) has a ground-truth location (indicated by green dots) on the right print that is the matching location for the left side of the link. We computed the distance between this true matching location and the location obtained for each correspondence pair discovered by the machine translation algorithm. We found that both groups produce similar deviations. The mean for experts was 53.8 pixels, and the mean for novices was 51.2 pixels. These values were not significantly different ($t(29)$<1). This deviation is about 1 degree of visual angle which for our images corresponds to about 2 ridge widths in distance. This is perhaps a surprisingly small number given that the machine translation algorithm does not know about space directly.

Taken together with the results of the number of reliable pairs found, the converging evidence is that both experts and novices can identify matching locations (corresponding ROIs, etc.) between two (clear) prints, However, experts can find more of those pairs than novices do. In addition, our results also demonstrate the power of our data analysis method based on machine translation. Given large datasets of eye movement data, our method can successfully extract meaningful patterns that are not apparent from simple methods (e.g. computing the average fixation during or the total fixation time). Specially, this approach allows us to compute matching locations between two fingerprints based on gaze data generated by participants. Thus, the method fits quite well with the fingerprint matching task which may explain the reason of its success.

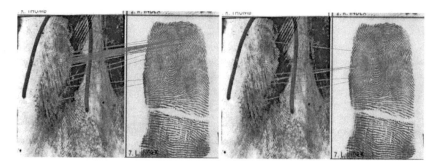

Fig. 4. The corresponding regions from Data Set 1 with inked and latent prints. Left: an example result from experts. Right: an example result from novices.

Fig. 5. The corresponding regions from Dataset 2. Left: an example result from experts. Right: an example result from novices.

6   Conclusions

The focus on the present study is not to build an automatic fingerprint system. Instead, we intend to address fundamental questions on fingerprint examination. Most fingerprint examination practices still heavily rely on human expertise to confirm and double check the results produced by automatic systems, especially in harder cases with latent prints. A more complete understanding of human fingerprint expertise will serve at least two important purposes. First, the results can be used as scientific evidence to justify human fingerprint practices. Second, the insights and principles gained by computational analyses of expert's gaze data can be incorporated into automatic recognition systems to improve the performance of those systems. Toward this goal, we developed and used an eye tracking device to record momentary gaze data from both fingerprint experts and novices. We then applied machine learning techniques to extract gaze patterns from both groups. We found that experts are able to identify more corresponding pairs than novices do within a short period of time and use that information to make correct judgments, showing the promise of this research direction. In our future work, we plan to further analyze image regions identified by our current system to infer what visual features are encoded in those regions. In addition, the technical contribution of the present paper is to introduce a machine translation method to compute correspondences between two prints based on gaze data generated by human experts. In this way, our approach can be viewed as human-guided machine learning as experts' gaze are used as supervisory signals to the automatic correspondence detection system.

Acknowledgement

This research was supported by NIJ grants NIJ 2005-MU-BX-K076 and NIJ 2009-DN-BX-K226. The authors would like to thank Dean Wyatte, Francisco Parada, and Ruj Akavipat for their help with data collection and analysis.

References

1. National Academy of Sciences: Strengthening Forensic Science in the United States: A Path Forward. The National Academies Press, Washington D.C. (2009)
2. Maltoni, D., Maio, D., Jain, A., Prabhakar, S.: Handbook of Fingerprint Recognition. Springer, New-York (2003)
3. Maio, D., Maltoni, D., Cappelli, R., Wayman, J.L., Jain, A.K.: FVC2000: Fingerprint Verification Competition. IEEE Trans. PAMI 24(3), 402–412 (2002)
4. Srihari, S.N., Cha, S., Arora, H., Lee, S.J.: Discriminability of Fingerprints of Twins. Journal of Forensic Identification 58(1), 109–127 (2008)
5. Dror, I.E., Charlton, D., Peron, A.E.: Contextual information renders experts vulnerable to making erroneous identifications. Forensic Science International 156(1), 74–78 (2006)
6. Su, C., Srihari, S.R.: Probability of Random Correspondence for Fingerprints. In: Proc. Third International Workshop on Computational Forensics, The Hague, Netherlands. Springer, Heidelberg (2009)
7. Tuyls, P., Akkermans, A.H.M., Kevenaar, T.A.M., Schrijen, G.-J., Bazen, A.M., Veldhuis, R.N.J.: Practical biometric authentication with template protection. In: Kanade, T., Jain, A., Ratha, N.K. (eds.) AVBPA 2005. LNCS, vol. 3546, pp. 436–446. Springer, Heidelberg (2005)
8. Ratha, N.K., Chikkerur, S., Connell, J.H., Bolle, R.M.: Generating cancelable fingerprint templates. IEEE Trans. Pattern Analysis and Machine Intelligence 29(4), 561–572 (2007)
9. Krupinski, E.A.: Visual scanning patterns of radiologists searching mammograms. Academic Radiology 3(2), 137–144 (1996)

10. Babcock, J.S., Pelz, J.: Building a lightweight eye tracking headgear. In: Eye Tracking Research and Applications Symposium, ETRA 2004, pp. 109–113 (2004)
11. Jain, A.K., Dubes, R.C.: Algorithms for Clustering Data. Prentice Hall, New Jersey (1998)
12. Brown, P.F., Stephen, A., Pietra, D., Pietra, V.J.D., Mercer, R.L.: The Mathematics of Statistical Machine Translation: Parameter Estimation. Computational Linguistics 19, 263–311 (1994)
13. Dyer, A.G., Found, B., Rogers, D.: Visual attention and expertise for forensic signature analysis. Journal of Forensic Sciences 51(6), 1397–1404 (2006)
14. Duchowski, A.T.: Eye tracking methodology: theory and practice, 2nd edn. Springer, London (2007)

Latent Fingerprint Rarity Analysis in Madrid Bombing Case

Chang Su and Sargur N. Srihari

University at Buffalo, Amherst NY, 14260 USA
{changsu,srihari}@buffalo.edu

Abstract. Rarity of latent fingerprints is important to law enforcement agencies in forensics analysis. While tremendous efforts have been made in 10-print individuality studies, latent fingerprint rarity continues to be a difficult problem and has never been solved because of the small finger area and poor impression quality. The proposed method is able to predict the core points of latent prints using Gaussian processes and align the latent prints by overlapping the core points. A novel generative model is also proposed to take into account the dependency on nearby minutiae and the confidence of minutiae in the probability of random correspondence calculation. The new methods are illustrated by experiments on the well-known Madrid bombing case. The results show that the probability that at least one fingerprint in the FBI IAFIS databases (over 470 million fingerprints) matches the bomb site latent is 0.93 which is large enough to lead to misidentification.

Keywords: latent fingerprints, rarity, generative models.

1 Introduction

On March 11, 2004, terrorists in Madrid bombed a passenger train, killing 191 people. The Spanish National Police (SNP) sent the FBI latent fingerprints recovered at the bomb site. Personnel from the FBI Latent Print Unit "coded" the prints by marking minutiae on each latent print to permit computer compare the prints with over 470 million prints in the Integrated Automated Fingerprint Identification (IAFIS) databases. The FBI examiners conducted comparison of the latent prints to the candidate prints that IAFIS listed, and believed they had a match for a latent print (LFP 17) with one of the candidate prints belonged to a lawyer named Brandom Mayfield. Fig. 1(a) shows the latent print LFP17 and the Mayfield's fingerprint in FBI's records is given in Fig. 1(b). Fingerprint examiner in Spain agreed that Mayfield's print and the LFP 17 shared similarity, but the numerous dissimilarities kept them from declaring a match. The FBI responds to the SNP's concerns by providing charted enlargements of the identification showing 15 numbered level 2 similarities in both prints. Shortly thereafter, FBI arrested Mayfiled. In the meantime, the police in Spain announced that the crime-scene latent belong to an Algerian suspect, Ouhname Daoud (Fig. 1(c)). FBI examiners subsequently realized that their individualization was in error and apologized to Mayfield [1].

H. Sako, K. Franke, and S. Saitoh (Eds.): IWCF 2010, LNCS 6540, pp. 173–184, 2011.

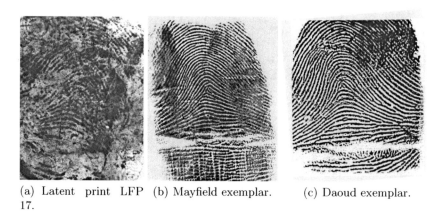

(a) Latent print LFP 17.   (b) Mayfield exemplar.   (c) Daoud exemplar.

Fig. 1. Fingerprint evidence in Madrid bombing case: (a) crime scene latent print LFP 17, (b) Mayfield's inked fingerprint, and (c) Daoud's inked fingerprint

The Madrid bombing case highlights the challenges of fingerprint evidence due to the doubts of their validity and reliability for personal identification. These challenges are based on the lacking of sound theoretical conclusion to support the claim that a particular area of friction ridge skin is the only possible source of a particular latent print. In other words, all other possible sources should been eliminated as possible sources of the latent print. This is obviously an enormously ambitious knowledge claim, and it necessarily raises an important question which concerns rarity.

Latent fingerprint rarity can be formulated as the probability that a randomly chosen fingerprint will be falsely identified as the source of a particular latent print. Rather than measuring the degree of variability of latent prints which come from small size of friction ridge skins, sustained attention has been devoted to 10-print fingerprint individuality. Much of it has focused on demonstrating or asserting the mere fact of the absolute non-duplication of complete fingertip-sized areas of friction ridge skin. This is true of both of the two major strands of fingerprint research. Anatomical research focused on detailing the formation of friction ridge skin, while occasionally commenting that this process was sufficiently complex to support an assumption of non-duplication as a working principle [2]. Statistical research focused on estimating the probability that exact duplicate areas of friction ridge skin (usually complete fingertips) exit. All models try to quantify the uniqueness property, e.g. the probability of false correspondence. These models can be classified into three categories: fixed probability [3], relative measurement [4], and most recently, generative models. Generative models are used to learn the distribution of fingerprint features such as minutiae. A couple of generative models have been proposed. Pankanti et al. [5] modeled the minutiae as uniformly and independently distributed. Zhu et al. [6] proposed a mixture model to account for the clustering tendency of minutiae. To model features other than minutiae, Su and Srihari [7] modeled the ridges by representing them as ridge points. Chen and Jain [8] proposed a model that incorporates minutiae, ridge and pore features. But all these models try to measure the degree of individuality for the complete fingerprints. The latent print rarity evaluation is different from complete fingerprints because of (i) lacking of information of the location of the latent print in its complete fingerprint,(ii) limited number of finger features, and (iii) greatly varying feature quality in latent fingerprints.

We proposes a method to compute probability of random correspondence for latent fingerprint evidences. Since minutiae is the most commonly used feature for representing fingerprints, we define the similarity between fingerprints based on the similarity of their minutiae. To determine which area of finger skin the latent print comes from, the latent print is aligned by overlapping the core points that represent the center area of the fingerprints. In particular, Gaussian processes are used to train the regression function for core point prediction. Minutiae dependency is important and tractable due to the limited size of minutiae sets. A novel generative model is proposed to model the distribution of minutiae as well as the dependency between them. The confidence of the minutiae is also taken into account in rarity measurement to deal with the greatly varying minutiae quality in latent fingerprints.

This paper is organized as follows. Section 2 describes the latent core point prediction using Gaussian processes. The generative model built on sequential minutiae data is described in section 3. Section 4 presents the evaluation of the rarity of latent fingerprints. The experimental results on Madrid bombing case are given in section 5. We summarize the paper in section 6.

2   Latent Fingerprint Registration

The fingerprint collected from the crime scene is usually only a small portion of the complete fingerprint. So the feature set extracted from the print only contains relative spatial relationship. It's obvious that feature sets with same relative spatial relationship can lead to different rarity if they come from the different areas of the fingertip. To solve this problem, we first predict the core points and then align the fingerprints by overlapping their core points. In biometrics and fingerprint analysis, core point refers to the center area of a fingerprint. In practice, the core point corresponds to the center of the north most loop type singularity. For fingerprints that do not contain loop or whorl singularities, the core is usually associated with the point of maxima ridge line curvature[9]. The most popular approaches proposed for core point detection is the Poincare Index (PI) which is developed by [10–12]. Another commonly used method [13] is a sine map based method that is realized by multi-resolution analysis. The methods based on Fourier expansion[14], fingerprint structures [15] and multi-scale analysis [16] are also proposed. All of these methods require that the fingerprints are complete and the core points can be seen in the prints. But this is not the case for all the fingerprints. Latent prints are usually small partial prints and do not contain core points. So there's no way to detect them by above computational vision based approaches.

We proposes a core point prediction approach that turns this problem into a regression problem [17]. Since the ridge flow directions reveal the intrinsic features of ridge topologies, and thus have critical impact on core point prediction. The orientation maps are used to predict the core points. A fingerprint field orientation map is defined as a collection of two-dimensional direction fields. It represents the directions of ridge flows in regular spaced grids. The gradients of gray intensity of enhanced fingerprints are estimated to obtain reliable ridge orientation [12]. Given an orientation map of a fingerprint, the core point is predicted using Gaussian processes. Gaussian processes dispense with the parametric model and instead define a probability distribution over functions directly. It provides more flexibility and better prediction. The advantage of Gaussian process model also comes from the probabilistic formulation[18]. Instead of representing the core point as a single value, the predication of the core point from Gaussian process model takes the form of a full predictive distribution.

Suppose we have a training set $\mathcal{D}$ of N fingerprints, $\mathcal{D} = \{(\mathbf{g}_i, y_i)|i = 1, \ldots, N\}$, where $\mathbf{g}$ denotes the orientation map of a fingerprint print and y denotes the output which is the core point. Suppose the orientation map of a input fingerprint is given by $\mathbf{g}^*$. The Gaussian predictive distribution of core point y^* can be evaluated by conditioning the joint Gaussian prior distribution on the observation $(G, \mathbf{y})$, where $G = (\mathbf{g}_1, \ldots, \mathbf{g}_N)^\top$ and $\mathbf{y} = (y_1, \ldots, y_N)^\top$. The core point $\hat{y}^*$ can be obtained by maximizing the predictive distributions with respect to $\mathbf{g}_i^*$. Thus the core point of the fingerprint is given by

$$\hat{y}^* = \mathbf{k}(\mathbf{g}_{MAX}^*, G)[K + \sigma^2 I]^{-1}\mathbf{y} \tag{1}$$

where σ^2 is the variance of the noise, K is the Gram matrix whose elements are given by covariance function $k(\mathbf{g}_i, \mathbf{g}_j)$, and $\mathbf{g}_{MAX}^*$ is the orientation map where the maximum predictive probability of core point can be obtained, given by

$$\mathbf{g}_{MAX}^* = \underset{\mathbf{g}^*}{\text{argmax}} \ p(m(y^*)|\mathbf{g}^*, G, \mathbf{y}) \tag{2}$$

Figure 2 shows the results of core point prediction and subsequent latent print registration given two different latent fingerprints. The latent fingerprints come from the NIST 27 [19] which contains latent fingerprints from crime scenes and their matching complete fingerprint mates. After the core points are determined, the fingerprints can be aligned by overlapping their core points. This is done by presenting the features in the Cartesian coordinates where the origin is the core point. Note that the minutia features mentioned in following sections have been aligned first.

3   Generative Model for Latent Prints

In order to estimate rarity, statistical models need to be developed to represent the distribution of fingerprint features. Previous generative models for fingerprints involve different assumptions: uniform distribution of minutia locations and directions [5] and minutiae are independent of each other [6, 8].

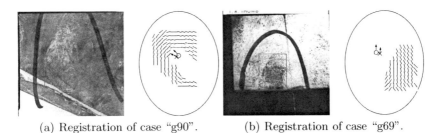

(a) Registration of case "g90".   (b) Registration of case "g69".

Fig. 2. Latent print localization: Left side images are the latent fingerprints (rectangles) collected from crime scenes. Right side images contain the predicted core points (crosses) and true core points (rounds) with the orientation maps of the latent prints. The position of the latent print in the complete print is also shown.

However, minutiae that are spatially close tend to have similar directions with each other [20]. Moreover, fingerprint ridges flow smoothly with very slow orientation change. The variance of the minutia directions in different regions of the fingerprint are dependent on both their locations and location variance [21, 22]. These observations on the dependency between minutiae need to be accounted for in eliciting reliable statistical models. The proposed model incorporates the distribution of minutiae and the dependency relationship between them.

Minutiae are the most commonly used features for representing fingerprints. They correspond to ridge endings and ridge bifurcations. Each minutia is represented by its location and direction. The direction is determined by the ridge at the location. Automatic fingerprint matching algorithms use minutiae as the salient features [23], since they are stable and are reliably extracted. Each minutia is represented as $\mathbf{x} = (s, \theta)$ where $s = (x_1, x_2)$ is its location and θ its direction.

In order to capture the distribution of minutiae as well as the dependencies between them, we first propose a method to define a unique sequence for a given set of minutiae. Suppose that a fingerprint contains N minutiae. The sequence starts with the minutia $\mathbf{x}_1$ whose location is closest to the core point. Each remaining minutia $\mathbf{x}_n$ is the spatially closest to the centroid defined by the arithmetic mean of the location coordinates of all the previous minutiae $\mathbf{x}_1, \ldots \mathbf{x}_{n-1}$. Given this sequence, the fingerprint can be represented by a minutia sequence $\mathbf{X} = (\mathbf{x}_1, \ldots, \mathbf{x}_N)$. The sequence is robust to the variance of the minutiae because the next minutia is decided by the all the previous minutiae. Given the observation that spatially closer minutiae are more strongly related, we only model the dependence between $\mathbf{x}_n$ and its nearest minutia among $\{\mathbf{x}_1, \ldots, \mathbf{x}_{n-1}\}$. Although not all the dependence is taken into account, this is a good trade-off between model accuracy and computational complexity. Figure 3(a) presents an example where $\mathbf{x}_5$ is determined because its distance to the centroid of $\{\mathbf{x}_1, \ldots, \mathbf{x}_4\}$ is minimal. Figure 3(b) shows the minutia sequence and the minutia dependencies (arrows) for the same configuration of minutiae.

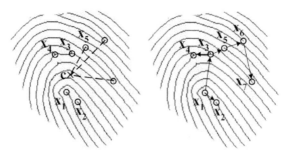

(a) Minutiae sequencing. (b) Minutiae dependency.

Fig. 3. An example showing the minutiae dependency modeling: (a) Given $\{\mathbf{x}_1,\ldots,\mathbf{x}_4\}$, the $\mathbf{x}_5$ is picked by comparing the distances to the centroid c. (b) The dependency between the sorted minutiae represented by arrows.

Based on the characteristic of fingerprint minutiae studied in [20–22], we know that the minutiae direction is related to its location and the neighboring minutiae. The minutiae location is conditional independent of the location of the neighboring minutiae given their directions. To address the probabilistic relationships of the minutiae, Bayesian networks are used to represent the distributions of the minutiae features in latent fingerprints. Figure 4 shows the Bayesian network for the distribution of the minutiae set given in Figure 3. The nodes $\mathbf{s}_n$ and θ_n represent the location and direction of minutiae $\mathbf{x}_n$. For each conditional distribution, a directed link is added to the graph from the nodes corresponding to the variables on which the distribution is conditioned.

In general, for a given latent fingerprint, the joint distribution over its minutiae set $\mathbf{X}$ is given by

$$p(\mathbf{X}) = p(\mathbf{s}_1)p(\theta_1|\mathbf{s}_1) \prod_{n=2}^{N} p(\mathbf{s}_n)p(\theta_n|\mathbf{s}_n,\mathbf{s}_{\psi(n)},\theta_{\psi(n)}) \tag{3}$$

where $\mathbf{s}_{\psi(n)}$ and $\theta_{\psi(n)}$ are the location and direction of the minutiae $\mathbf{x}_i$ which has the minimal spatial distance to the minutiae $\mathbf{x}_n$. So $\psi(n)$ is given by

$$\psi(n) = \operatorname*{argmax}_{i\in[1,n-1]} \|\mathbf{x}_n - \mathbf{x}_i\| \tag{4}$$

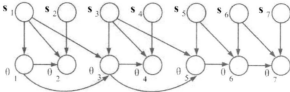

Fig. 4. The Bayesian network representing the conditional dependence over the minutiae shown in Figure 3

To compute above joint probability, there are three probability density functions need to be estimated:

1. Distribution of the location of minutiae: $f(\mathbf{s})$
2. Joint distribution of the location and direction of minutiae: $f(\mathbf{s}, \theta)$
3. Conditional distribution of minutiae direction given its location, and the location and direction of the nearest minutiae: $f(\theta_n | \mathbf{s}_n, \mathbf{s}_{\psi(n)}, \theta_{\psi(n)})$

It is known that minutiae tend to form clusters [20] and minutiae in different regions of the fingerprint are observed to be associated with different region-specific minutiae directions. The minutiae location is modeled by the mixture of Gaussian distribution shown in Eq. (5). The minutiae location and direction is modeled using the mixture of joint Gaussian and von-Mises distribution [6] give by Eq. (6). Given its location and the nearest minutiae, the minutiae direction has the mixture of von-Mises density given by Eq. (7).

$$f(\mathbf{s}) = \sum_{k_1=1}^{K_1} \pi_{k_1} \mathcal{N}(\mathbf{s} | \mu_{k_1}, \Sigma_{k_1}) \tag{5}$$

$$f(\mathbf{s}, \theta) = \sum_{k_2=1}^{K_2} \pi_{k_2} \mathcal{N}(\mathbf{s} | \mu_{k_2}, \Sigma_{k_2}) \mathcal{V}(\theta | \nu_{k_2}, \kappa_{k_2}) \tag{6}$$

$$f(\theta_n | \mathbf{s}_n, \mathbf{s}_{\psi(n)}, \theta_{\psi(n)}) = \sum_{k_3=1}^{K_3} \pi_{k_3} \mathcal{V}(\theta_n | \nu_{k_3}, \kappa_{k_3}) \tag{7}$$

where K_i is the number of mixture components, π_{k_i} are non-negative component weights that sum to one, $\mathcal{N}(s | \mu_k, \Sigma_k)$ is the bivariate Gaussian probability density function of minutiae with mean μ_k and covariance matrix Σ_k, and $\mathcal{V}(\theta | \nu_k, \kappa_k)$ is the von-Mises probability density function of minutiae orientation with mean angle ν_k and precision (inverse variance) κ_{k_3}. BIC is used to estimate K_i and other parameters are learned by EM algorithm.

4   Rarity Evaluation with Minutiae Confidence

The goal of the rarity study is to compute the relevant metrics from the statistic generative model. Given that model, values for the probability that in a set of n samples, a specific one with value x coincides with another sample within specified tolerance can be computed [24]. This probability is defined as specific nPRC. In the case of latent fingerprint, the specific nPRC is the probability of matching a given latent print among n 10-prints within some tolerance ϵ. Other than the specific nPRC calculation for complete fingerprints, it is important to take into account the quality of the minutiae or minutiae confidence in latent print rarity measurement due to the poor quality of friction ridge impressions.

To compute the sepecific nPRCs, we first define correspondence, or match, between two minutiae. Let $\mathbf{x}_a = (\mathbf{s}_a, \theta_a)$ and $\mathbf{x}_b = (\mathbf{s}_b, \theta_b)$ be a pair of minutiae. The minutiae are said to correspond if for tolerance $\epsilon = [\epsilon_s, \epsilon_\theta]$,

$$\| \mathbf{s}_a - \mathbf{s}_b \| \leq \epsilon_s \wedge |\theta_a - \theta_b| \leq \epsilon_\theta \tag{8}$$

where $\|\mathbf{s}_a - \mathbf{s}_b\|$ is the Euclidean distance between the minutiae locations.

The confidence of the minutiae $\mathbf{x}_n$ is defined as (d_{s_n}, d_{θ_n}), where d_{s_n} is the confidence of location and d_{θ_n} is the confidence of direction. Given the minutiae $\mathbf{x}_n = (s_n, \theta_n)$ and its confidences, the probability density functions of location s' and direction θ' can be modeled using Gaussian and von-Mises distribution given by

$$c(s'|s_n, d_{s_n}) = \mathcal{N}(s'|s_n, d_{s_n}^{-1}) \tag{9}$$

$$c(\theta'|\theta_n, d_{\theta_n}) = \mathcal{V}(\theta'|\theta_n, d_{\theta_n}) \tag{10}$$

where the variance of the location distribution (Gaussian) is the inverse of the location confidence and the concentration parameter of the direction distribution (von-Mises) is the direction confidence.

Let f be a randomly sampled fingerprint which has minutiae set $\mathbf{X}' = \{\mathbf{x}'_1, ..., \mathbf{x}'_M\}$. Let $\widetilde{\mathbf{X}}$ and $\widetilde{\mathbf{X}'}$ be the sets of $\hat{m}$ minutiae randomly picked from $\mathbf{X}$ and $\mathbf{X}'$, where $\hat{m} \leq N$ and $\hat{m} \leq M$. Using Eq. (3), the probability that there is a one-to-one correspondence between $\widetilde{\mathbf{X}}$ and $\widetilde{\mathbf{X}'}$ is given by

$$p_\epsilon(\widetilde{\mathbf{X}}) = p_\epsilon(\mathbf{s}_1, \theta_1) \prod_{n=2}^{\hat{m}} p_\epsilon(\mathbf{s}_n) p_\epsilon(\theta_n|\mathbf{s}_n, \mathbf{s}_{\psi(n)}, \theta_{\psi(n)}) \tag{11}$$

where

$$p_\epsilon(\mathbf{s}_n, \theta_n) = \int_{s'} \int_{\theta'} \iint_{|\mathbf{x}-\mathbf{x}'|\leq\epsilon} c(s'|\mathbf{s}_n, d_{s_n}) c(\theta'|\theta_n, d_{\theta_n}) f(\mathbf{s}, \theta) ds' d\theta' ds d\theta \tag{12}$$

$$p_\epsilon(\mathbf{s}_n) = \int_{s'} \int_{|\mathbf{s}-\mathbf{s}'|\leq\epsilon_{\mathbf{s}}} c(s'|\mathbf{s}_n, d_{s_n}) f(\mathbf{s}) ds' d\mathbf{s} \tag{13}$$

$$p_\epsilon(\theta_n|\mathbf{s}_n, \mathbf{s}_{\psi(n)}, \theta_{\psi(n)}) = \int_{\theta'} \int_{|\theta-\theta'|\leq\epsilon_\theta} c(\theta'|\theta_n, d_{\theta_n}) f(\theta|\mathbf{s}_n, \mathbf{s}_{\psi(n)}, \theta_{\psi(n)}) d\theta' d\theta \tag{14}$$

Finally, the specific nPRCs can be computed by

$$p_\epsilon(\mathbf{X}, \hat{m}, n) = 1 - (1 - p_\epsilon(\mathbf{X}, \hat{m}))^{n-1} \tag{15}$$

where $\mathbf{X}$ represents the minutiae set of given latent fingerprint, and $p_\epsilon(\mathbf{X}, \hat{m})$ is the probability that $\hat{m}$ pairs of minutiae are matched between the given latent fingerprint and a randomly chosen fingerprint from n fingerprints.

$$p_\epsilon(\mathbf{X}, \hat{m}) = \sum_{m'\in M} p(m') \binom{m'}{\hat{m}} \cdot \sum_{i=1}^{\binom{N}{\hat{m}}} p_\epsilon(\widetilde{\mathbf{X}}_i) \tag{16}$$

where M contains all possible numbers of minutiae in one fingerprint among n fingerprints, $p(m')$ is the probability of a random fingerprint having m' minutiae, minutiae set $\widetilde{\mathbf{X}}_i = (\mathbf{x}_{i1}, \mathbf{x}_{i2}, ..., \mathbf{x}_{i\hat{m}})$ is the subset of $\mathbf{X}$ and $p_\epsilon(\widetilde{\mathbf{X}}_i)$ is the joint probability of minutiae set $\widetilde{\mathbf{X}}_i$ given by Eq. (11).

5 Study of Madrid Bombing Case

In order to demonstrate our methodology for assessing the rarity of given specific fingerprints, we applied our approach to the Madrid bombing case. We illustrated the causes of the erroneous identification by analyzing the rarity of level 2 feature sets used by FBI during the Mayfield case. The original IAFIS encoding for LFP 17 is shown in Fig.5. Seven minutiae were marked by FBI examiners. Specific nPRC for the encoding is estimated using the approach given in section 4. The probability of existing at least one fingerprint in IAFIS databases that shares the same minutiae is 0.93. In other words, for any 470 million randomly chosen fingerprints, there's 93% possiblity that a fingerprint containing the same seven minutiae can be found. Consider that the number of fingers of global population is 63.1 billion. It's invalid to claim a indentification without considering the candidates outside the IAFIS databases.

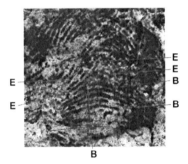

Fig. 5. Original IAFIS Encoding (LFP 17): level 2 details contain four ridge endings and three bifurcations

In the same way, we analyzed the rarity of the level 2 features given in the charted enlargement latent print in Fig.6. In order to verify whether the 15 minutia similarities marked by latent examiner can be a court room exhibit, Specific nPRC with respect to the fingers of the global population was calculated. The probability of falsely identifying the source of LFP 17 is equal to 7.8×10^{-7}. This is a fairly small probability and it provides a strong basis of FBI's identification. It implies that the cause of the erroneous identification is not the rarity degree but something else such as the minutia detection. The Office of the Inspector General (OIG) found evidence that the FBI's examiners' interpretations of some minutiae in Fig.6 were adjusted or influenced during the comparison phase by reasoning "backward" from features that are visible in the Mayfield exemplars. This bias referred to as "circular reasoning" infected the Mayfield identification.

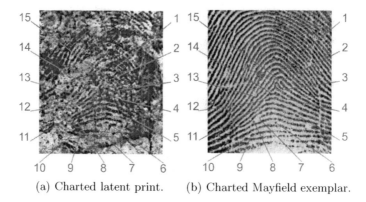

(a) Charted latent print.   (b) Charted Mayfield exemplar.

Fig. 6. Charted enlargements: (a) the charted features on LFP 17, and (b) the corresponding features on Mayfield's inked fingerprint

OIG also concluded that the unusual similarity in the pattern of level 2 details within the friction ridges on the fingers of Mayfield and Daoud was a significant factor in the misidentification. Of those 15 minutiae using to identify Mayfield, 10 were also later used to identify Daoud. These common minutiae are illustrated in Fig.7. The specific nPRC for the common minutiae is 0.014. This is a much higher probability compared to the specific nPRC for the entire 15 minutiae shown in Fig.6. It means that these 10 minutiae pattern is rather common in fingers and lacks disciminability.

The experiments on the Madrid bombing case shows our approach can be used to determine whether the latent print has sufficient exclusive details to be used to reach a decision of identification or exclusion. Instead of the inconsistent "12-point rule", proposed approaches develop and test the validity of a minimum quantitative threshold for effecting an identification on a case by case basis. The examiner can test the validity of an identification that takes into account the level 2 features and the clarity of the print.

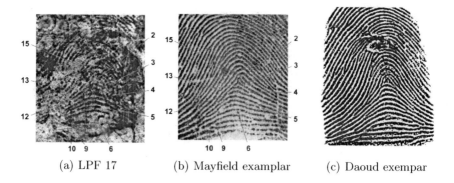

(a) LPF 17   (b) Mayfield examplar   (c) Daoud exempar

Fig. 7. Level 2 details (minutiae) used to identify Mayfield also used to identify Daoud: (a) LFP 17, (b) Mayfield examplar, and (c) Daoud examplar

6 Summary

This work is the first attempt of applying statistic methods to measure the rarity of latent prints. In order to align the latent prints, a Gaussian processes based approach is proposed to predict the core points of latent prints. It is proven that this approach can predict core points whether the latent prints contain the core points or not. Furthermore, a novel generative model is proposed to model the distribution of minutiae as well as the dependency relationship between them. Bayesian networks are used to perform inference and learning by visualizing the structures of the generative models. Finally, the probability of random correspondence is able to calculated. To further improve the accuracy, minutiae confidences are taken into account for specific nPRC calculation. Proposed method are performed on the well-known Madrid bombing case. It is shown that it is capable of estimating the rarity of real-life latent fingerprints.

References

1. US Department of Justice Office of the Inspector General: A review of the FBI's handling of the Brandon Mayfield case (March 2006),
   `http://www.justice.gov/oig/special/s0601/PDF_list.htm`
2. Wertheim, K., Maceo, A.: The critical stage of friction ridge and pattern formation. Journal of Forensic Identification 52(1), 35–85 (2002)
3. Henry, E.R.: Classification and Uses of Fingerprints, London (1900)
4. Trauring, M.: Automatic comparison of finger-ridge patterns. Nature 197, 938–940 (1963)
5. Pankanti, S., Prabhakar, S., Jain, A.K.: On the individuality of fingerprints. IEEE Trans. Pattern Anal. Mach. Intell. 24(8), 1010–1025 (2002)
6. Zhu, Y., Dass, S.C., Jain, A.K.: Statistical models for assessing the individuality of fingerprints. IEEE Transactions on Information Forensics and Security 2(3-1), 391–401 (2007)
7. Su, C., Srihari, S.N.: Generative models for fingerprint individuality using ridge models. In: ICPR 2008, pp. 1–4. IEEE, Los Alamitos (2008)
8. Chen, Y., Jain, A.K.: Beyond minutiae: A fingerprint individuality model with pattern, ridge and pore features. In: Tistarelli, M., Nixon, M.S. (eds.) ICB 2009. LNCS, vol. 5558, pp. 523–533. Springer, Heidelberg (2009)
9. Jain, A.K., Maltoni, D.: Handbook of Fingerprint Recognition. Springer-Verlag New York, Inc., Secaucus (2003)
10. Kawagoe, M., Tojo, A.: Fingerprint pattern classification. Pattern Recogn 17(3), 295–303 (1984)
11. Bazen, A.M., Gerez, S.H.: Systematic methods for the computation of the directional fields and singular points of fingerprints. IEEE Trans. Pattern Anal. Mach. Intell. 24(7), 905–919 (2002)
12. Jain, A.K., Prabhakar, S., Hong, L.: A multichannel approach to fingerprint classification. IEEE Trans. Pattern Anal. Mach. Intell. 21(4), 348–359 (1999)
13. Jain, A.K., Prabhakar, S., Hong, L., Pankanti, S.: Filterbank-based fingerprint matching. IEEE Transactions on Image Processing 9, 846–859 (2000)
14. Phillips, D.: A fingerprint orientation model based on 2d fourier expansion (fomfe) and its application to singular-point detection and fingerprint indexing. IEEE Trans. Pattern Anal. Mach. Intell. 29(4), 573–585 (2007)

15. Wang, X., Li, J., Niu, Y.: Definition and extraction of stable points from fingerprint images. Pattern Recogn. 40(6), 1804–1815 (2007)
16. Liu, M., Jiang, X., Kot, A.C.: Fingerprint reference-point detection. EURASIP J. Appl. Signal Process. 2005, 498–509 (2005)
17. Su, C., Srihari, S.N.: Latent fingerprint core point prediction based on gaussian processes. In: ICPR 2010. IEEE, Los Alamitos (2010)
18. Rasmussen, C.E., Williams, C.K.I.: Gaussian Processes for Machine Learning. The MIT Press, Cambridge (2006)
19. Garris, M.D., McCabe, R.M.: Nist special database 27: Fingerprint minutiae from latent and matching tenprint images (2000),
    http://www.nist.gov/srd/nistsd27.htm
20. Scolve, S.C.: The occurence of fingerprint characteristics as a two dimensional process. Journal of the American Statistical Association 367(74), 588–595 (1979)
21. Stoney, D.A.: Distribution of epidermal ridge minutiae. American Journal of Physical Anthropology 77, 367–376 (1988)
22. Chen, J., Moon, Y.: A statistical study on the fingerprint minutiae distribution. In: ICASSP 2006 Proceedings., vol. 2, p. II (2006)
23. Watson, C., Garris, M., Tabassi, E., Wilson, C., McCabe, R., Janet, S.: User's Guide to NIST Fingerprint Image Software 2 (NFIS2). NIST (2004)
24. Su, C., Srihari, S.N.: Probability of random correspondence for fingerprints. In: Geradts, Z.J.M.H., Franke, K.Y., Veenman, C.J. (eds.) IWCF 2009. LNCS, vol. 5718, pp. 55–66. Springer, Heidelberg (2009)

Fingerprint Directional Image Enhancement

Lukasz Wieclaw

University of Silesia in Katowice, Institute of Computer Science,
41-200 Sosnowiec, Poland

Abstract. This work presents an efficient algorithm to enhance the directional image. Orientation, as a global feature of fingerprint, is very important to image preprocessing methods used in automatic fingerprint identification system (AFIS). Proposed algorithm consists of two weighted averaging stages over a neighborhood. In the first stage the 2D gaussian kernel is used as a weight and in the second stage the differentiation mask is used. That strategy allows an effective smoothing of the orientation in the noisy areas, without information loss in the high curvatured ridges areas. Experimental results show that the proposed method improves the performance of the fingerprint identification, comparing to the results obtained by the conventional, gradient based method.

1 Introduction

Among all biometric techniques, automatic fingerprint based systems are the most popular and promising for automatic personal identification. A long history of fingerprints use as an identification tool for forensic purposes has caused its performance reach a high level [1]. Now, it is not only used by police, but also receives a wide commercial attention.

Generally, fingerprints contain two kinds of features: global features, such as a ridge pattern orientation and frequency, and local features like minutia or singular points (*core* and *delta*). As a global feature, directional image describes a local orientation of the ridge-valley structure in each point of fingerprint image (Fig.1). It has been widely used for fingerprint image enhancement[2][3], singular points detection[4][5][6] and classification[7][8]. Unfortunately there are many low quality fingerprint images caused by poor skin condition (scars), noisy acquisition devices or bad imprint techniques. Therefore, quality of the directional image relies heavily on the readability of the ridge-valley structure. Due to the fact that the orientation estimation is usually the first stage of fingerprint image analysis, directional image enhancement has become a necessary and common step before image enhancement and feature extraction in the AFIS.

There are essentially two ways to improve the estimation of the orientation: filtering-based[9][10] and model-based[11][12][13][14] enhancement methods. Filtering-based methods operate only at the local region and thus they cannot solve missing patches in the fingerprint image[13], while the model-based methods rely on the global regularity of orientation values around the singular points. However, forensic images of latent fingerprints not always contain those singular points. Therefore, proposed method is filtering-based, that contains double-stage smoothing.

H. Sako, K. Franke, and S. Saitoh (Eds.): IWCF 2010, LNCS 6540, pp. 185–192, 2011.

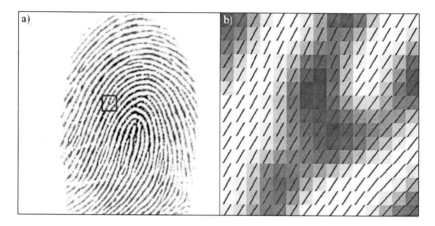

Fig. 1. a) Original fingerprint image, b) magnified area with marked dominant orientation of each pixel

2 Directional Image Estimation

Generally, there are two categories of methods to compute the directional image (also called *orientation field* or *directional field*): pixel-alignment based[7][15][16][17] and gradient based methods[2][5][10][18][19]. Typically, the pixel-alignment-based methods compute the differentiation (fluctuation) of neighboring pixels values in a fixed number of reference orientations. The orientation of smallest fluctuation of gray values is expected to be the reference orientation of central pixel. Hence, the accuracy of the estimated orientation is limited to fixed number of discrete values, but those approaches are more resistant to noise. Tasks, like tracing finger furrows lines or computing the ridge frequency, require continuous values, therefore the most frequently adopted gradient based method[2][10] is the least mean square method[18].

Since the gradients are the orientations at pixel scale, the orientation of ridge is orthogonal to average phase angle of pixels changes value, indicated by gradients. The main steps of the least mean square algorithm are as follows[2]:

1. Compute the gradients $\partial_x(i,j)$ and $\partial_y(i,j)$ at each pixel of fingerprint image $I(i,j)$. Depending on the computational requirement, the gradient operator may vary from the simple *Sobel* operator to the more complex *Marr-Hildreth* operator.
2. Estimate the local orientation in $\omega \times \omega$ blocks, centered at pixel $I(i,j)$ using the following equations:

$$\mathcal{V}x(i,j) = \sum_{u=i-\frac{\omega}{2}}^{i+\frac{\omega}{2}} \sum_{v=j-\frac{\omega}{2}}^{j+\frac{\omega}{2}} 2\partial_x(u,v)\partial_y(u,v) \tag{1}$$

$$\mathcal{V}y(i,j) = \sum_{u=i-\frac{\omega}{2}}^{i+\frac{\omega}{2}} \sum_{v=j-\frac{\omega}{2}}^{j+\frac{\omega}{2}} (\partial_x^2(u,v) - \partial_y^2(u,v)) \tag{2}$$

$$\theta(i,j) = \frac{1}{2} \tan^{-1} \left(\frac{\mathcal{V}x(i,j)}{\mathcal{V}y(i,j)} \right) \qquad (3)$$

where $\theta(i,j)$ is the least square estimate of the local ridge orientation at the $\omega \times \omega$ block (16×16 for 500dpi) centered at pixel $I(i,j)$. Mathematically, it represents the direction that is orthogonal to the dominant direction of the *Fourier spectrum* of the $\omega \times \omega$ window.

3 Orientation Smoothing

Due to the presence of some unreliable elements, resulting from heavy noise, corrupted ridge and furrow structures, minutiae and low gray value contrast, estimated local ridge orientation may not always be correct (Fig.2).

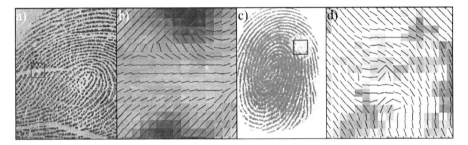

Fig. 2. a,c) Original low quality fingerprint images, b,d) magnified areas with corrupted orientation values marked

The orientation smoothing stage is expected to reduce the noise and compute a reliable directional image. The orientation smoothing method, based on averaging the unit vectors of doubled orientation over a neighborhood, is widely used because of its high resolution and simple implementation[2]. However, averaging of the doubled trigonometrically calculated values has high computational cost. Moreover, large areas of heavy corrupted data will still affect the final orientation values. Therefore, this work proposes an improved method of orientation smoothing with differentiation mask, which not only has good performance in heavy noise areas, but also preserve the orientation values of high-curvature, singular points area.

In the first step a 2-dimensional low-pass Gaussian filter is used to modify the incorrect local ridge orientation. The weighted averaging is separately computed for two ranges of orientation values respectively:

1. For $45° > \theta(u,v) > 135°$ compute the vertical weighted mean factors in 8×8 blocks:

$$M_v(i,j) = \sum_{u=i-\frac{w}{2}}^{i+\frac{w}{2}} \sum_{v=j-\frac{w}{2}}^{j+\frac{w}{2}} (\theta(u,v) - z)\, \partial(u,v) G_f(u-i,v-j) \qquad (4)$$

where:

if $\theta(i, j) < 45°$ then $z = 0$, otherwise $z = \pi$.

The vertical weight W_v is given by:

$$W_v(i, j) = \sum_{u=i-\frac{w}{2}}^{i+\frac{w}{2}} \sum_{v=j-\frac{w}{2}}^{j+\frac{w}{2}} \partial(u, v) G_f(u - i, v - j) \qquad (5)$$

2. For $45° \leq \theta(u, v) \leq 135°$ compute the horizontal weighted mean factors in 8×8 blocks:

$$M_h(i, j) = \sum_{u=i-\frac{w}{2}}^{i+\frac{w}{2}} \sum_{v=j-\frac{w}{2}}^{j+\frac{w}{2}} \theta(u, v) \partial(u, v) G_f(u - i, v - j) \qquad (6)$$

The horizontal weight W_h is given by:

$$W_h(i, j) = \sum_{u=i-\frac{w}{2}}^{i+\frac{w}{2}} \sum_{v=j-\frac{w}{2}}^{j+\frac{w}{2}} \partial(u, v) G_f(u - i, v - j) \qquad (7)$$

3. Finally filtered orientation is calculated using weighted mean by:

$$\theta_f(i, j) = \begin{cases} \frac{(M_v(i,j)W_v(i,j)) + ((M_h(i,j)+\pi)W_h(i,j))}{W_v(i,j)+W_h(i,j)} & \text{if} \quad M_d(i, j) > \frac{\pi}{2} \\ \frac{(M_v(i,j)W_v(i,j)) + (M_h(i,j)W_h(i,j))}{W_v(i,j)+W_h(i,j)} & \text{if} \quad M_d(i, j) \leq \frac{\pi}{2} \end{cases} \qquad (8)$$

where:

– $\partial(u, v)$ is gradients ratio given by:

$$\partial(u, v) = |\partial_x(u, v) \partial_y(u, v)| \qquad (9)$$

– $G_f(x, y)$ is 2-dimensional Gaussian filter:

$$G_f(x, y) = \frac{e^{-\frac{x^2+y^2}{2\sigma^2}}}{\sqrt{2\pi\sigma^2}} \qquad (10)$$

– σ is the standard deviation of the Gaussian distribution. For the purposes of this work $\sigma = 2$.

– $M_d(i, j)$ is difference of weighted mean factors:

$$M_d(i, j) = M_v(i, j) - M_h(i, j) \qquad (11)$$

In the second step, the orientation smoothing is based on the reliability of estimated orientation, which corresponds to a differentiation values of neighboring pixels. A larger neighborhood (16×16) is used to compute the differentiation values:

$$D_f(i, j) = \sum_{u=i-\frac{w}{2}}^{i+\frac{w}{2}} \sum_{v=j-\frac{w}{2}}^{j+\frac{w}{2}} |\theta_f(i, j) - \theta_f(u, v)| - z \qquad (12)$$

where:
    if $|\theta_f(i,j) - \theta_f(u,v)| > 90°$ then $z = \pi$, otherwise $z = 0$.

Finally, the entire first stage is performed once again, with the exception that the Gaussian filter $G_f(x,y)$ is replaced by multiplicative inverse of differentiation:

$$G_f(x,y) = \frac{1}{D_f(x,y)} \qquad (13)$$

4   Experimental Results

The proposed algorithm has been applied on two types of testing data. The first type is fingerprint images database, which contains 960 fingerprint images (in 500dpi resolution) from 120 fingers, with 8 images from each finger. The second type is specially synthesized orientation images (Fig. 5c-g).

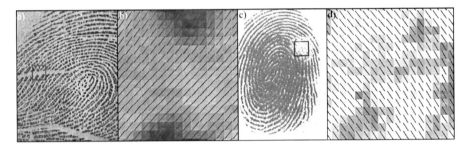

Fig. 3. a,c) Original low quality fingerprint images, b,d) magnified areas with enhancement orientation values marked

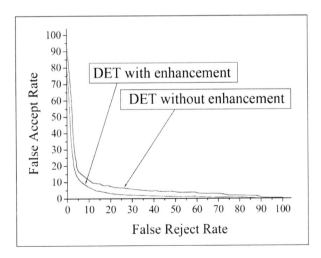

Fig. 4. DET curves (red line - recognition system without enhancement, blue line - recognition system with enhancement)

Table 1. Effect of enhancement on the final recognition accuracy

Method	Equal Error Rate
Without Enhancement	11.35%
With Enhancement	8.1%

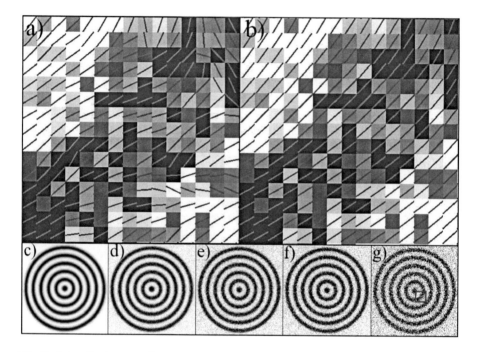

Fig. 5. Magnified areas of 200-level noise image with enhancement orientation values marked: a) corrupted orientation values, b) enhancement orientation values. Testing images: c) noiseless image, d) 50 level of noise, e) 90 level of noise, f) 150 level of noise, g) 200 level of noise.

Fingerprint images in database was selected from NIST Special Database, FVC database samples, and captured with a live-scanner. Fig. 3 for comparison, shows two examples of orientation smoothing results of fingerprint images, selected from this database.

In order to obtain the performance characteristics such as EER, on first testing data an fingerprint image enhancement algorithm[20] was evaluated. In the next step the NIST's NFIS2 open source software were used for feature extraction and matching[21]. Directional image enhancement results in a notable reduction of Equal Error Rate, as shown in Fig.4 and Table 1.

As there is no ground truth for the orientation field of fingerprints[5] and a truly objective error measurement cannot be constructed, there were special images prepared (Fig. 5c-g) in order to evaluate the effectiveness of the proposed

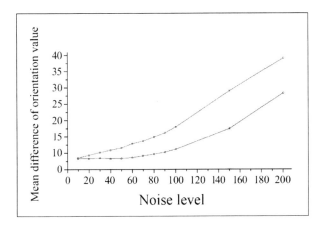

Fig. 6. Mean difference between orientation estimated from noiseless image and orientation estimated from varied noise level images. Blue line - enhancement orientation, red line - orientation without enhancement.

method. This database contains 91 images of various noisiness. One image in the set (Fig.5c) is an ideal noiseless image, and the rest are randomly noised. In proposed procedure, the mean difference between orientation estimated from noiseless image and orientation estimated from varied noise level images, has to be measured.

The results summarized in Fig.6 show that proposed directional image enhancement method leads to a notable reduction of noise influence.

5   Conclusion

In this paper a new method for the fingerprint directional image enhancement has been presented.

It can be concluded from evaluated experiments, that the estimated results are accurate and robust to noise, by using proposed algorithm.

Further work will consider the application of this method, combined with more resistant to noise pixel-alignment-based method, however still maintaining high resolution of continuous orientation values.

Experimental results show that this method has a good resistance to high level noises and has low computational cost.

Acknowledgment

This paper was supported by the grant no. N N519 574038 from Ministry of Science and Higher Education, Poland.

References

1. Hanson, M.: Fingerprint-based Forensics Identify Argentina's Desaparecidos. IEEE Comput. Graph. Appl. 20(5), 7–10 (2000)
2. Hong, L., Jain, A.K., Wan, Y.: Fingerprint Image Enhancement: Algorithm and Performance Evaluation. IEEE Trans. on Pattern Analysis and Machine Intelligence 20(8), 777–789 (1998)
3. Chikkerur, S., Cartwright, A.N., Govindaraju, V.: Fingerprint enhancement using STFT analysis. Pattern Recogn. 40(1), 198–211 (2007)
4. Liu, M., Jiang, X., Kot, A.C.: Fingerprint reference-point detection. EURASIP J. Appl. Signal Process., 498–509 (2005)
5. Bazen, A.M., Gerez, S.H.: Systematic Methods for the Computation of the Directional Fields and Singular Points of Fingerprints. IEEE Trans. Pattern Anal. Mach. Intell. 24(7), 905–919 (2002)
6. Wrobel, K., Doroz, R.: New Method For Finding a Reference Point in Fingerprint Images With the Use Of The IPAN99 Algorithm. Journal of Medical Informatics & Technologies 13, 59–64 (2009)
7. Hong, L., Jain, A.K., Prabhakar, S.: A Multichannel Approach to Fingerprint Classification. IEEE Trans. Pattern Anal. Mach. Intell. 21(4), 348–359 (1999)
8. Costa, S.M., Fernandez, F.J., Oliveira, J.M.: A New Paradigm on Fingerprint Classification using Directional Image. In: SIBGRAPI, p. 405 (2002)
9. Bolle, R., Hong, L., Jain, A.K., Pankanti, S.: An identity-authentication system using fingerprints. Proc. of the IEEE 85(9), 1365–1388 (1997)
10. Maio, D., Maltoni, D.: Direct gray-scale minutiae detection in fingerprints. IEEE Trans. Pattern Anal. Mach. Intell. 19(1), 27–40 (1997)
11. Monro, D.M., Sherlock, B.G.: A model for interpreting fingerprint topology. Pattern recognition 26(7), 1047–1055 (1993)
12. Gu, J., Zhou, J.: Modeling orientation fields of fingerprints with rational complex functions. Pattern Recognition 37(2), 389–391 (2004)
13. Li, J., Wang, H., Yau, W.: Nonlinear Phase Portrait Modeling of Fingerprint Orientation. In: IEE Proc. Control, Automation, Robotics, and Vision Conf., vol. 2, pp. 1262–1267 (2004)
14. Birchbauer, J., Bischof, H., Ram, S.: Active Fingerprint Ridge Orientation Models. In: Tistarelli, M., Nixon, M.S. (eds.) ICB 2009. LNCS, vol. 5558, pp. 534–543. Springer, Heidelberg (2009)
15. Jain, A.K., Karu, K.: Fingerprint classification. Pattern Recognition 29(3), 389–404 (1996)
16. Halici, U., Ongun, G.: Fingerprint classification through self-organizing feature maps modified to treat uncertainties. Proc. of the IEEE 84(10), 1497–1512 (1996)
17. Hong, L., Jain, A.K., Pankanti, S., Prabhakar, S.: Filterbank-based fingerprint matching. IEEE Trans. Image Processing 9(5), 846–859 (2000)
18. Kass, M., Witkin, A.: Analyzing Orientated Pattern. Computer Vision. Graphics and Image Processing 37, 362–397 (1987)
19. Hong, L., Jain, A.K.: On-line Fingerprint Verification. IEEE Trans. Pattern Anal. and Mach. Intell. 19(4), 302–314 (1997)
20. Porwik, P., Wieclaw, L.: The New Efficient Method of Fingerprint Image Enhancement. Int. Journal of Biometrics 1(1), 36–46 (2008)
21. http://fingerprint.nist.gov

What Kind of Strategies Does a Document Examiner Take in Handwriting Identification?

Yoko Seki

National Research Institute o Police Science
6-3-1, Kashiwanoha, Kashiwa-shi, Chiba, 277-0882, Japan
seki@nrips.go.jp

Abstract. A document examiner examines handwriting mainly by a qualitative method based on his/her knowledge and experiences. The qualitative examination, compared with the quantitative examination, possesses less objectivity and is believed to be less reliable. However, an examiner's opinion is, in fact, highly reliable. The knowledge and strategies that a document examiner uses is discussed in this paper. Four kinds of classification experiments where diagram-like 36 handwriting samples written by 6 writers were used as stimuli were done by visual inspection and cluster analysis. Results of the experiments suggested that the examiner utilized his knowledge on writing motion even when the classification target was a diagram drawn by the reconstruction of a handwriting sample.

Keywords: handwriting, cluster analysis, visual inspection.

1   Introduction

A document examiner examines handwriting mainly by a qualitative method based on his/her knowledge and experiences. The qualitative examination, compared with the quantitative examination, possesses less objectivity and is believed to be less reliable. However, an examiner's opinion is, in fact, highly reliable. This is because the examiner has accumulated knowledge about the handwriting and chooses the strategy and variables that are most appropriate to his/her case. The fact that people other than the examiner cannot understand his/her decision-making process decreases the reliability of the document examiner's decision. So, an analysis of the strategies and variables an examiner uses and the quantification of them will contribute to the establishment of the objectivity in the examination.

There are two main means to ensure the reliability of the strategies that a forensic document examiner takes. One is the quantification of handwriting characteristics and the application of statistical method to handwriting examination. The other is to evaluate the expertise of a document examiner. This approach is a part of cognitive science. There have been various efforts in both area of quantification and cognition [1, 2, 3, 4, 5].

H. Sako, K. Franke, and S. Saitoh (Eds.): IWCF 2010, LNCS 6540, pp. 193–199, 2011.

In Japan, there have been various attempts to establish quantitative approach in handwriting identification of Japanese characters [6, 7, 8]. There are, however, some problems arising from the complexity of character system.

There are two major character systems, Kanji characters and Hiragana characters in Japan. Hiragana characters originated in the running style of Kanji characters but the characteristics of Hiragana characters are much different from those of Kanji characters from the standpoint of handwriting identification.

Characteristics of Hiragana characters, in comparison with Kanji characters, are the simplicity in the structure and the complexity of a stroke.

Simplicity in the structure: A Hiragana character is composed of 1 through 3 strokes and a Kanji character is, on the other hand, composed of 10 strokes in average,. Some Kanji characters are composed of more than 20 strokes. The fact that there are more stroke intersections in a Kanji character than in a Hiragana character explains that Kanji characters give a document examiner more observation clues than Hiragana characters. There is, in another word, a larger degree of freedom in writing movement in Hiragana characters than in Kanji characters. There is another difference in the structure. Most Kanji characters have two components though Hiragana characters are not divided into definite parts.

Complexity in a stroke: Hiragana characters originated in the running style of Kanji characters. And average length of a stroke is longer in Hiragana characters than in Kanji characters. These explain the complexity in a stroke of Hiragana characters. A Hiragana stroke changes its direction in rounded manner and a Kanji stroke, on the other hand, in angular manner.

There have been many experiments on writer identification of Kanji characters based on the quantification of the characteristics and statistical methods and they have achieved a successful outcome.

Many Japanese document examiners find it more difficult to examine Hiragana characters than Kanji characters. They claim the difficulty in the description of the characteristics of Hiragana characters, large intra individual variance and small inter individual difference in comparison with Kanji characters. All of them are attributed to the simplicity and the complexity of Hiragana characters.

There have been, however, no attempts to evaluate the expertise of a document examiner in Japan. This is because the main route to establish objectivity in hand-writing identification has been thought to be the establishment the quantification and the application of the statistical method. But, it is necessary for the establishment of the objectivity in the handwriting identification to analyze the expertise of a document examiner because of the necessity of the human inspection in the course of the hand-writing identification even after the establishment of the computational handwriting examination.

So, evaluation of the expertise of a Japanese document examiner in the examination of Hiragana character is discussed in this paper.

2   Materials and Method

Four kinds of classification tasks were done.

2.1   Handwriting Samples Used for the Experiments

2.1.1   Collection of Handwriting Samples

Six subjects, who were adult male and right handed, wrote 2 kinds of Hiragana characters, '＜' and 'つ,' six times respectively. There were 36 handwritten samples per character, that is, there were 36 '＜' samples and 36 'つ' samples. Both characters were written in one stroke.

2.1.2   Coordinate Measurement

X-y coordinate was measured at 21 measuring points of each sample. Measuring points were defined as a stroke beginning, a stroke terminal and 19 points that divided a stroke equally. Coordinates were then standardized as to the origin and the size.

2.1.3   Reconstruction

Handwriting samples were reconstructed by connecting 21 measuring points. An example of the original and reconstructed samples was shown in fig.1.

2.2   Classification

A document examiner, who had a twenty-year experience as a forensic document examiner participated the classification task. Classification task was done on each kind of character.

Classification task was to classify 36 samples into 6 groups. The task was done on respective character. There were four kinds of classification tasks. Table 1 shows each classification condition.

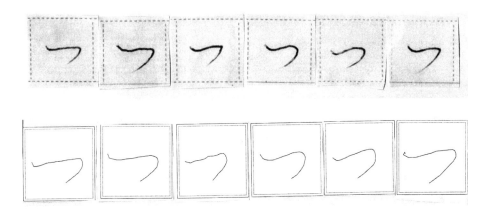

Fig. 1. Examples of original handwriting (top) and reconstructed handwriting (bottom) of the same writer

2.2.1 Classification 1

An examiner classified thirty six reconstructed samples into six groups according to the similarity of the samples by visual inspection. The classification task was done on two characters, that is, '〈' and '⊃' respectively.

The examiner was instructed to classify 36 'patterns' or 'diagrams' into 6 groups. He was not instructed as to the number of samples included in one cluster. He was interviewed as to the reasons of his classification after the task.

2.2.2 Classification 2

In classification 2, the classifier and the samples used for the classification were the same as Classification 1, but the classifier was instructed to classify 36 reconstructed 'handwriting' samples, not 'diagram' into 6 groups. He was not instructed as to the number of the samples included in one cluster, either.

He took the classification task one moth after Classification 1.

The examiner was also interviewed as to the reasons of his classification after the task.

2.2.3 Classification 3

Thirty-six reconstructed samples were classified using cluster analysis. X-y coordinate value at 21 measuring points was used as a variable. Cluster analysis finished at the stage where clusters were merged into 6.

2.2.4 Classification 4

The examiner, same as Classifications 1 and 2, classified 36 'original' handwriting samples. He was instructed to classify 36 handwriting samples into 6 groups. He was not instructed as to the number of the samples included in one cluster.

Classification task was done one month after classification 3.

The examiner was interviewed as to the reasons of his classification after the task.

Table 1. Classification condition

Classification Type	stimulus reconstruct / original	classificaion inspection / statistics
Classification 1	reconstructed & pattern	visual
Classification 2	reconstructed & character	visual
Classification 3	reconstructed	statistics
Classification 4	original	visual

3   Results and Discussion

Correct classification ratio was calculated to each classification task and character.

3.1   Correct Cluster

The writer of a cluster was defined as follows: A cluster was defined as, for example, the writer No.1's cluster if the largest number of the samples contained in the cluster was written by the writer No.1. So, if a cluster contained 6 samples and three of them were written by the writer No.1, two of which written by the writer no.4, one of which written by the writer No.6, the cluster was defined to be the writer No.1's cluster. Each cluster was assigned to one of 6 writers following the same definition.

3.2   Correct Classification Ratio

Correct classification ratio was calculated as follows: Correct classification ratio was defined as the average of correct ratio of all clusters. Correct ratio of a cluster was defined as the average percentage of correct samples contained in the cluster.

Table 2 shows the correct classification ratio.

Table 2. Percentage of correct classification

Classification Type	Percent Correct '〈' (%)	Percent Correct 'つ' (%)
Classification 1	41.7	56.2
Classification 2	67.1	64.4
Classification 3	42.9	47.6
Classification 4	100.0	77.9

3.3   Classification Results

Classification by visual inspection of original handwriting (Classification 4) showed the highest correct classification ratio in both kinds of characters. This was not surprising because the original handwriting had various kinds of information other than shape. The interview with the examiner supported that. The examiner took into account of the pen pressure and the horizontal to vertical ratio in both original handwriting '〈' and 'つ'. He also valued the angle at the point where the stroke direction changed in '〈' and the curvature and the relative length of the stroke terminal in 'つ'.

In Classifications 1 (visual inspection and pattern condition) and 2 (visual inspection and character condition), higher correct classification ratio was observed in the classification of the reconstructed 'handwriting' (Classification 2) than 'pattern' (Classification 1) in both characters. This gives us some suggestions as to what kind of information or strategies a human uses in a decision-making process. The examiner was given the same stimuli in both classification tasks but the standpoint where he recognized them was different. In the course of the interview, he answered he ignored the difference in the stroke beginning in the classification of the 'character', although he paid attention to the variation of the stroke beginning in the classification of the 'pattern'. He also pointed out that the existence of the variation at the stroke beginning in 'handwriting' even if they were written by the same person. He also pointed out that he had guessed the terminating manner of a stroke from the rough shape and had used the guess for the classification of the reconstructed 'handwriting'. These suggest that a document examiner utilizes his knowledge on the relationship between the handwritten character shape and the kinematic aspects of writing even if the observation target lacks 'line quality.'

Comparison between Classifications 1 (visual inspection and pattern condition) and 3 (cluster analysis) is also suggestive. Correct ratio was not significantly different between the two classification tasks. The difference in the condition between the two classification tasks was the classifier, that is, a man classified the samples in Classification 1 and the statistical method classified the samples in Classification 3. There is a possibility that a man's judge as to the similarity between two stimuli is similar to that of the statistical processing.

There is another possibility concerning the strategy that a document examiner takes during the course of handwriting examination. Results of Classification 1 (visual inspection and character condition) and 4 (visual inspection and original handwriting condition) suggest that an examiner much utilizes his knowledge on the writing motion when he examines Hiragana characters. A document examiner gets less information on character shape in the examination of Hiragana characters than in Kanji characters because of the characteristic feature of Hiragana. Information on the writing motion affords effective information on decision-making process to an examiner. A document examiner possibly gets the information on the writing motion from the line quality.

4 Conclusion

Four kinds of classification tasks were conducted to investigate the strategies that a document examiner takes during the examination process of handwriting.

Results of the experiments suggest that a document examiner ascertains a writer's motion from the line quality of a handwriting examined and utilizes it.

Results also suggest that an examiner changes the strategy depending on the target.

References

1. Srihari, S.N., Cha, S.H., Lee, S.: Individuality of Handwriting. J. Forensic Sci. 47, 856–872 (2002)
2. Kam, M., Webstein, J., Conn, R.: Proficiency of Professional Document Examiners in Writer Identification. J. Forensic Sci. 39, 5–14 (1994)

3. Kam, M., Fielding, G., Conn, R.: Writer Identification by Professional Document Examiners. J. Forensic Sci. 42, 778–786 (1997)
4. Kam, M., Gunmmadidala, K., Fielding, G., Conn, R.: Signature Authentification by Forensic Document Examiners. J. Forensic Sci. 46, 1117–1124 (2001)
5. Dyer, A.G., Found, B., Rogers, D.: Visual Attention and Expertise for Forensic signature Analysis. J. Forensic Sci. 51, 1397–1404 (2006)
6. Wakahara, K., Kawamura, T., Mitsui, T.: Identification of Handwriting by Personal Computer. Japanese J. Applied Psychol. 12, 13–21 (1987) (in Japanese)
7. Wakahara, K., Kawamura, T., Mitsui, T.: Identification of Handwriting by Personal Computer (2). Japanese J. Applied Psychol. 13, 19–25 (1988) (in Japanese)
8. Misaki, K., Umeda, M.: Handwriter Identification using Quantitative Features Extracted from Character Patterns. Japanese J. Sci. Technol. Identification 2, 71–77 (1997)

3LSPG: Forensic Tool Evaluation by Three Layer Stochastic Process-Based Generation of Data*

York Yannikos, Frederik Franke, Christian Winter, and Markus Schneider

Fraunhofer Institute for Secure Information Technology SIT
Rheinstr. 75, 64295 Darmstadt, Germany
`firstname.lastname@sit.fraunhofer.de`

Abstract. Since organizations cannot prevent all criminal activities of employees by security technology in practice, the application of IT forensic methods for finding traces in data is extremely important. However, new attack variants for occupational crime require new forensic tools and specific environments may require adoptions of methods and tools. Obviously, the development of tools or their adaption require testing using data containing corresponding traces of attacks. Since real-world data are often not available synthetic data are necessary to perform testing. With 3LSPG we propose a systematic method to generate synthetic test data which contain traces of selected attacks. These data can then be used to evaluate the performance of different forensic tools.

Keywords: White collar crime, synthetic data, Markov chains.

1   Introduction

In recent years, several studies have reported an enormous extent of fraud that has been committed in organizations often by their own employees misusing rights or resources (e.g., see [2], [5], [10], [11], [15], [17]). Since many business processes are implemented in software, IT forensic tools are required to detect fraudulent activities by finding traces in data. As the amount of data to be analyzed can be very large (e.g., several terabytes [18]), forensic tools should work very efficient and should be effective under conditions of different environments.

During tool development performance evaluation is necessary which may be a serious problem for developers who have no access to real-world data. When developing, adapting, or applying forensic tools it is necessary to know their properties, also to be able to interpret results of an application. In the context of mass data analysis the false positive rate is an example of such a property. However, real-world data are often not available for testing forensic tools.

These problems can be solved by creating synthetic data representing data created by normal and fraudulent usage of software systems. In this work, we propose a stochastic process-based method to generate synthetic test data in a systematic way. The data can then be used for tool testing, comparison, selection, and improvement. The proposed method is based on three layers of random

---

* This work was supported by CASED (`www.cased.de`).

H. Sako, K. Franke, and S. Saitoh (Eds.): IWCF 2010, LNCS 6540, pp. 200–211, 2011.

processes for data generation called Three Layer Stochastic Process-based Generation (3LSPG). We show how 3LSPG works and how it can be applied. We illustrate the proposed method by using a sample fraud type called *double payment*. In this work, we focus on IT forensic tools (for short: forensic tools) which are relevant for investigating occupational crime. However, the applicability of 3LSPG is not limited to this area.

This work is organized as follows. Sect. 2 deals with *fraud* in general and motivates the importance of fraud detection. We then compare real-world data to synthetic data in Sect. 3. In Sect. 4, we explain the mathematical foundations of Markov chains used for 3LSPG, the structure of which is described in Sect. 5. In Sect. 6, we give a description of the sample fraud pattern *double payment* and an application example. Then, in Sect. 7, we explain the benefit of 3LSPG and afterwards discuss related work in Sect. 8. Finally, we close with our conclusion.

2   Fraud

Fraud is an illegal activity based on a false statement where the fraud-committing person knows that the statement is false. The victim relies on the false statement and finally suffers on a damage as result [20]. When we use the term *fraud* in this work we use it in the context of occupational crime, i.e., we focus on criminal clandestine activities by employees against their organization that lead to a damage of the organization's success. By doing so, the employee violates his fiduciary duties for the purpose of direct or indirect benefit. In the context of information system misuse several fraud categories exist. Examples are credit card fraud, money laundering, telecommunications fraud, medical fraud, or scientific fraud. For more information on these categories we refer to [2], [9], [16].

Statistics of recent years show that fighting occupational crime is of high importance for the economy due to enormous losses. Germany's Federal Criminal Police Office (BKA) states organizations' losses of more than €3.4 billions through related criminal activities in the year 2008 [6]. Furthermore, the BKA assumes a high dark figure of undetected occupational crime. This underlines the need for better fraud detection methods.

In several cases it can be very difficult to detect fraudulent employees since they often do not have to circumvent any security controls at all to successfully achieve their goals, unlike attacking outsiders who try to break into systems. When committing fraud these employees mostly execute the same or very similar work steps compared to doing normal daily work. This superimposition of fraudulent and legitimate behavior often makes the detection of fraud very complicated. For the synthetic generation of data with integrated fraudulent data sets *superimposed fraud* has to be taken into account.

3   Synthetic vs. Real Data

In general, synthetic data as well as real-world data can be applied to test the performance of forensic tools. Works that propose a combination of both also exist, e.g., see [14]. In this section, we shortly justify the necessity of synthetic data. Obviously, if real-world data with desired characteristics are available they should be used for testing. However, tool developers mostly do not have real-world data. Organizations are almost never willing to provide their data, or data containing certain types of fraud simply do not exist. In this case, there is no question which type of data can be used for testing. It is also possible that certain attacks are created by tool developers before they really have been observed. Thus having tools available before such attacks occur is useful. Even if real-world data are available, it may be likely that the sheer existence or the frequency of specific fraud cases in the data sample is uncertain or unknown at all. Instead, when having an adequate methodology for the generation of synthetic data, there may be possibilities to create data covering a wide range of relevant characteristics over which forensic tools could be evaluated. Furthermore, using synthetic data allows full certainty about contained fraud patterns since it is known which data are related to attacks.

4   Basics for 3LSPG

In this section, we sketch the basic properties of discrete time Markov chains and introduce some formalisms for 3LSPG. Sect. 4.1 summarizes Markov chain basics. In Sect. 4.2, we show how to derive conditional probabilities in a Markov model given state probabilities. Later, the solution of Sect. 4.2 is applied in 3LSPG.

4.1   Markov Chains

In the following, we summarize the relevant aspects of discrete time Markov chains. For more information on the topic we refer to [1] for instance.

Definition 1. *A finite discrete time Markov chain consists of (I) a non-void finite set $S = \{1, \ldots, N\}$ as state space with elements called states and $N \geq 1$, (II) a probability vector $\Pi^{(\tau)} = (\Pi_i^{(\tau)})_{i \in S}$ with $\Pi_i^{(\tau)} \geq 0$ and $\sum_i \Pi_i^{(\tau)} = 1$ for discrete time integer $\tau \geq 0$, where component $\Pi_i^{(\tau)}$ represents the probability that state i occurs at time τ, and (III) a stochastic matrix $P = (p_{ij})_{i,j \in S}$ with $p_{ij} \geq 0$ and $\sum_j p_{ij} = 1$ for all i where p_{ij} gives the probability that j follows i.*

Obviously, we have $\Pi^{(\tau+1)} = \Pi^{(\tau)} \cdot P$ or $\Pi^{(\tau+\sigma)} = \Pi^{(\tau)} \cdot P^{\sigma}$ with $\sigma \geq 1$. In 3LSPG S contains all relevant activities to be simulated.

Definition 2. *Let $X_0, X_1, \ldots$ be an S-valued stochastic process. It is called a Markov process if for every $\tau \geq 0$ and arbitrary states $i_0, i_1, \ldots, i_{\tau-1}, i, j$ one has conditional probability $\Pr(X_{\tau+1} = j | X_0 = i_0, X_1 = i_1, \ldots, X_{\tau-1} = i_{\tau-1}, X_\tau = i) = \Pr(X_{\tau+1} = j | X_\tau = i)$. If the conditional probabilities do not depend on τ, the Markov process is called homogeneous.*

In homogeneous Markov processes $X_{\tau+1}$ only depends on X_τ. The conditional probabilities in a Markov process are related to corresponding state transition probabilities in $P^{(\tau)}$.

In the following we use homogeneous Markov processes, i.e., the stochastic matrix P is independent of τ. Furthermore, we assume Markov chains to be aperiodic and irreducible, e.g., see [1]. Then the sequence of $\Pi^{(\tau)}$ converges to a unique equilibrium distribution Π which is given by $\Pi = \Pi \cdot P$. Note that Π is a left eigenvector of P, i.e., Π can be calculated easily for given P.

4.2   Calculation of Conditional Probabilities

In 3LSPG we assume that the probability vectors of subjects to be simulated are given. The problem is to find a corresponding stochastic matrix P. This requires to solve an inverse eigenvector problem. We now describe how to solve this problem in order to obtain a stochastic matrix P. For finding a matrix P for a given Π with $\sum_i \Pi_i = 1$ we have the following requirements:

(I) For all $i, j \in S$, there holds $0 \le p_{ij} \le 1$.
(II) For each $i \in S$, we have $\sum_j p_{ij} = 1$.
(III) $\Pi = \Pi \cdot P$.
(IV) There may be some p_{ij} with given values according to the fraud case.

Requirements (I), (II) are due to the stochastic matrix, (III) is for the equilibrium distribution. In order to obtain a solution for the problem above we combine the systems in (II) and (III) to a new system $C \cdot p^T = e^T \wedge p \in [0,1]^{N^2}$ with T for vector transposition, $p = (p_{11}, ..., p_{1N}, p_{21}, ..., p_{2N}, ..., p_{N1}, ..., p_{NN})$, $e = (1, ..., 1) \in \mathbb{R}^{2N}$, and a $(2N \times N^2)$ matrix

$$
C = \begin{bmatrix}
1 \cdots & \cdots & 1 & 0 \cdots & \cdots & 0 & \cdots & 0 & \cdots & \cdots & 0 \\
0 \cdots & \cdots & 0 & 1 \cdots & \cdots & 1 & & \vdots & & & \vdots \\
\vdots & & \vdots & 0 \cdots & \cdots & 0 & & \vdots & & & \vdots \\
\vdots & & \vdots & \vdots & & \vdots & & 0 & \cdots & \cdots & 0 \\
0 \cdots & \cdots & 0 & 0 \cdots & \cdots & 0 & \cdots & 1 & \cdots & \cdots & 1 \\
1\ 0 \cdots & \cdots & 0 & \frac{\Pi_2}{\Pi_1}\ 0 \cdots & \cdots & 0 & \cdots & \frac{\Pi_N}{\Pi_1}\ 0 & \cdots & \cdots & 0 \\
0\frac{\Pi_1}{\Pi_2}\ 0 & \cdots & 0 & 0\ 1\ 0 & \cdots & 0 & & 0\ \frac{\Pi_N}{\Pi_2}\ 0 & \cdots & 0 \\
\vdots & \ddots & \vdots & \vdots & \ddots & \vdots & & \vdots & \ddots & & \vdots \\
0 \cdots 0\frac{\Pi_1}{\Pi_{N-1}} & 0 & 0 \cdots 0\frac{\Pi_2}{\Pi_{N-1}} & 0 & & 0 \cdots 0\frac{\Pi_N}{\Pi_{N-1}}0 \\
0 \cdots & \cdots & 0\frac{\Pi_1}{\Pi_N} & 0 \cdots & \cdots & 0\frac{\Pi_2}{\Pi_N} & \cdots & 0 & \cdots & \cdots & 0\ 1
\end{bmatrix}. \tag{1}
$$

In practical cases, there may exist no transition between some states i, j, i.e., $p_{ij} = 0$. Then we can reduce the system by eliminating the corresponding components from p and columns from C denoting the result as p' and C'. Thus we obtain a reduced system $C' \cdot p'^T = e'^T$ to be solved. If this system is solvable it is usually under-determined so that infinitely many solutions for p' and p exist. Note that already one concrete solution is sufficient for 3LSPG. We first produce a general solution using algebra software and afterwards we insert given values for elements of p' respecting requirement (IV). If then the system is still under-determined, we apply a numerical approach. Therefore, we select further unknown p'_{ij}, assign values to them, and calculate the remaining p'_{ij}. Currently we use an equidistant grid over $[0, 1]$ for assigning values. Then we either receive a solution or we refine the grid size and repeat until a sufficient number of solutions have been found. If assignments lead to a solution, we obtain p', and thus P.

5   3LSPG

In this section, we explain 3LSPG. 3LSPG consists of three layers as depicted in Fig. 1. The synthetic data are generated by applying successively the Markov layer, the application data layer, and the time shifting layer simulating non-fraudulent and fraudulent subjects. First, the Markov layer produces a state sequence. Higher layer processing and generation of data depends on the results produced by lower layers. The final result is a collection of synthetic data containing traces stored in a database. E.g., in case of an ERP system the synthetic data can be considered as an extract of some relevant data attributes.

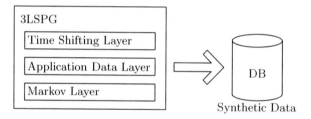

Fig. 1. The Layers in 3LSPG

5.1   Markov Layer

The Markov layer is the lowest layer in 3LSPG where we model subject activities to be simulated. Therefore, we use Markov chains based on the description in Sect. 4 on which discrete time Markov processes are then realized.

If there are different types of subjects to be simulated, we assume different state sets for each type, e.g., S_n for non-fraudulent subjects and S_f for fraudulent subjects. P has to be calculated for each type. If superimposed fraud can be assumed, then $S_n \subseteq S_f$ and corresponding state probabilities of the associated Markov chains are very close to each other since fraudsters are likely to attract no attention. To generate data at the Markov layer the following steps have to be processed for each type of subjects:

1. Definition of state sets
2. Definition of state probabilities as vector Π
3. Identification of state pairs (i, j) with existent $(p_{ij} > 0)$ and state pairs (i, j) with nonexistent $(p_{ij} = 0)$ state transitions

4. Identification of state pairs (i, j) with existent state transitions and given $p_{ij} > 0$.
5. Calculation of stochastic matrix P as described in Sect. 4.2
6. Model verification
7. Configuration of Markov processes: definition of simulation length, number of process instances, setup of state transition probabilities obtained from P
8. Generation of data

Each realization of a Markov process represents the activity of a single subject. The generated data describe these activities in an abstract way. For example, *doing a payment* is such an activity but the generated data lack relevant information, e.g., about receiver or amount. These data are necessary but not created in the Markov layer to keep the number of states as low as possible. Consequently, further processing of the generated data in a higher layer is required to add these data. Furthermore, some subsequences may always occur in the same order which may not occur in reality this way. This is due to efficiency in modeling. More diversity in subsequences is achieved through higher layer processing.

5.2 Application Data Layer

The purpose of the application data layer is the generation of application-specific data for a sequence of states that has been created by the Markov layer. The state sequence is taken as input state by state, and a state-dependent output is produced as data tuple. The output depends on the result of a (pseudo)random experiment where the probability distribution can be arbitrarily chosen. Additionally, the probability distribution may depend on the simulated subject, e.g., to allow the usage of payment limits for employees who work in accounting. When processing the state sequence to generate application data, there are three different state types to be distinguished:

- States with history-independent application data: For this type of states the application-specific data to be generated only depend on the current state.
- States with history-dependent application data: The data to be generated for this type of states depend on the current state i and on previously generated application data of preceding states. Here, the data to be generated for state i depend on the already generated data for exactly one preceding occurrence of state j.
- States without application data.

After processing in the application data layer we now have a sequence of application data for all relevant processes. So far, the simulated time is given by the discrete time of the Markov chain. For some states it may be reasonable to modify this time by adding a random time shift which is done in the time shifting layer.

5.3 Time Shifting Layer

The time shifting layer is the highest layer in 3LSPG. In the synthetic data generated so far, the simulated time at which an activity occurs is a point in discrete time associated with the corresponding state representing the activity. This point in discrete time can be considered as a time interval. As already mentioned in Sect. 5.1, there may be occurrences of state combinations and corresponding activities in the application layer which follow regular chronological patterns that may not happen in reality. Thus we use time shifting to slightly shuffle the order of activities in the application layer. Based on selectable probability distributions we create integer values as offsets that, added to the point in discrete time, result in new simulated points in discrete time. Again, each of these new time values represent a time interval in which the corresponding subject can perform an arbitrary number of activities. For the generation of time shifts we distinguish three types of states:

- States with independent time shift: For this type of states the time shift to be generated only depends on the current state, thus ignoring time shifts that were generated for preceding occurrences of states in the Markov process.
- States with dependent time shift: For this type of states the time shift to be generated depends on the state itself and on the time value including time shift assigned to another preceding state in the Markov process. Similarly to the application data layer, we restrict the history-dependency of a state i to just one occurrence of state j.
- States without time shift.

After applying the time shifting layer of 3LSPG, we have generated a collection of synthetic data in a database which describe simulated activities of the subjects over a given time. Note that the result is no Markov process anymore since it is possible that certain activities are mapped to same time intervals.

5.4   Implementation of 3LSPG

We have implemented a prototype (Java, MySQL) to model different subject activities and fraud cases. It allows the definition of Markov chains, can support the calculation of the stochastic matrices, and provides a selection of probability distributions as basis for data generation as well as a visualization of the generation result. Furthermore, an analysis interface for sample testing is available.

In the following, we give an application example of 3LSPG where we simulate activities of 50 employees including 1 fraudster in a fictional company over approx. 3 years generating synthetic accounting data. Using our prototype, the data generation for the example takes less than 25 minutes (2.8 GHz dual-core CPU, 4 GB RAM, Windows XP).

6   3LSPG Application

In this section, we outline the application of 3LSPG with an example dealing with *double payment* as fraud case which we briefly sketch first.

6.1   Sample Fraud Case: Double Payment

The fraud case *double payment* is described as follows: An employee who works in accounting and pays invoices to suppliers colludes with one supplier. From time to time the employee pays a specific invoice twice resulting in an illegal second transfer of the invoice amount to the supplier. Afterwards, both share the amount of the second payment, e.g., the employee obtains a kickback payment from the colluding supplier.

Double payment typically occurs as superimposed fraud since for the predominant part of his work the fraudulent employee behaves correctly. Since also non-fraudulent recurrent payments can exist, e.g., payments for a service contract, the identification of double payments is difficult. Given large databases with high numbers of transactions to be analyzed, forensic investigators need methods with an adequately low error rate (false positives and false negatives) due to efficiency and cost reasons.

6.2   Simulation of Double Payment with 3LSPG

We generate synthetic data by simulating activities of 49 non-fraudulent employees and a single fraudster. Afterwards, we use these data to evaluate two sample forensic tools for obtaining hints regarding double payments. In the Markov layer we use two Markov chains. One is used for the simulation of non-fraudulent employees, the other is used to simulate the activity of the fraudster. The first Markov chain has the state set $S_n = \{1, 2, 3\}$, the second has the state set $S_f = \{1', 2', 3', 4', 5'\}$ with the following interpretation:

- states 1 and $1'$: wait (including other activities relevant neither for regular payment nor double payment)
- states 2 and $2'$: payment
- states 3 and $3'$: recurring payment (same amount as preceding payment)
- state $4'$: first payment, legal (fraudster legally pays an invoice to the colluding supplier preparing the fraudulent payment)
- state $5'$: second payment, illegal (fraudster illegally pays the preceding invoice amount a second time to the colluding supplier $\rightarrow$ double payment)

Note that states 2 and 3 as well as $2'$ and $3'$ represent payments of the same amount initiated by the same employee to the same receiver that are considered to be non-fraudulent as described in Sect. 6.1. Both Markov chains differ in the previously defined state probabilities. Thus after calculating the state transition probabilities for each Markov chain, these also differ. For the Markov chains we assume the distributions $\Pi = (\Pi_1, \Pi_2, \Pi_3) = (.7, .29, .01)$ and $\Pi' = (\Pi'_1, \Pi'_2, \Pi'_3, \Pi'_4, \Pi'_5) = (.7, .28946, .00946, .00054, .00054)$. Note that we assume $\Pi_2 = \Pi'_2 + \Pi'_4$ and $\Pi_3 = \Pi'_3 + \Pi'_5$, i.e., comparable non-fraudulent and fraudulent activities occur with approximately equal probabilities. The state transitions depicted in Fig. 2 show that in each Markov chain some pairs of states without a state transition exist so that $p_{ij} = 0$ and $p'_{ij} = 0$, respectively. We assume that no additional values are given for the remaining p_{ij} and p'_{ij} which

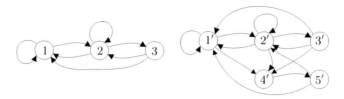

Fig. 2. Markov chain graphs for non-fraudulent (left) and fraudulent employees (right)

means that appropriate values have to be calculated. The calculation yields the following values (rounded):

$$P = \begin{bmatrix} .71 & .29 & 0 \\ .67552 & .29 & .03448 \\ .71 & .29 & .0 \end{bmatrix} \quad P' = \begin{bmatrix} .70984 & .28961 & 0 & .00054 & 0 \\ .67717 & .28961 & .03267 & .00054 & 0 \\ .70984 & .28961 & 0 & .00054 & 0 \\ 0 & 0 & 0 & 0 & 1 \\ .71039 & .28961 & 0 & 0 & 0 \end{bmatrix} \quad (2)$$

In the application data layer, there are no data generated for states 1 and 1'. For states 2, 2', and 4' history-independent data are generated, and for states 3, 3', and 5' the application data are generated with a dependency on the data of the last occurrence of the preceding states 2, 2', and 4', respectively. In the example, the receiver of occurring payments is chosen using a Gaussian distribution over a list of suppliers and payment amounts are Benford distributed. Finally, processing the data at the time shifting layer we assume that states 1

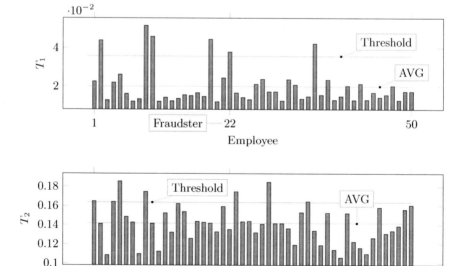

Fig. 3. Results of data analysis with sample tools T_1 and T_2

and $1'$ have no time shift, states 2, $2'$, and $4'$ have independent time shifts, and states 3, $3'$, and $5'$ are states with dependent time shift. Time shift offsets are uniformly distributed.

To illustrate testing using sample test objects, we select two simple forensic tools T_1 and T_2 for the detection of double payment. For employee E_i and supplier S_j let $\#(E_i, S_j)$ be the number of recurrent payments initiated by E_i to S_j. The fraud indicator values of T_1 and T_2 for E_k are calculated as follows:

$$T_1(E_k) = \frac{\sum_j \#(E_k, S_j)}{\sum_i \sum_j \#(E_i, S_j)} \qquad T_2(E_k) = \frac{\max_j \#(E_k, S_j)}{\sum_j \#(E_k, S_j)} \qquad (3)$$

Analyzing the generated data using T_1 and T_2 yields the charts depicted in Fig. 3 showing a calculated value for each employee. We define an appropriate threshold where all values above are considered as suspicious. T_1 shows the correct positive (employee 22) among several false positives. T_2 only shows false positives, i.e., no correct positive at all. Respecting the conditions used in this example, T_1 produces a better result than T_2 and thus is preferable.

7   Benefit of 3LSPG

When developing new forensic tools/methods, 3LSPG can be used for their improvement and comparison under different conditions. Knowledge about their properties and performance also increases the trust forensic examiners have in their results. In contrast to real-world data, which are rarely available and always representing conditions of a specific environment, 3LSPG can produce data with highly customizable characteristics. This flexibility is a significant advantage of 3LSPG. The quality of synthetic data depends on the user's ability to extract and understand the relevant characteristics of an environment. To produce synthetic data with 3LSPG for testing purposes, assumptions about the environment have to be made regarding different types of subjects, e.g., employees, fraudsters, attackers. These assumptions are used to model a real-world environment for the generation of data containing traces of these fraudsters. Another advantage is the ease of using 3LSPG. Since it is only necessary to model relevant aspects of subject activities the bootstrapping of data generation is very efficient.

8   Related Work

Markov chains have also been proposed in other works related to security and defending resources against misuse, e.g., in [3], [4]. The goal of these works was to model the behavior of attackers based on Markov chains. The proposed model can be used to assess the operational security of systems. Continuous time Markov chains are applied in order to obtain some time predictions on the security status of systems. The works exploit concepts of reliability theory for purposes of security (e.g., calculations of mean time to failure).

Models based on Markov chains for the generation of synthetic data have also been proposed for the purpose of method evaluation in completely different application areas. For instance, in [19] the authors propose Markov chain models to synthetically generate wind speed data to be used for wind energy systems.

The fraud case of *double payment* is also described in [7] where the authors propose data mining methods to detect cases of double payment. They apply data mining methods to one sample collection of data where it is *a priori* not clear whether portions of the data represent fraudulent actions. Their data mining yields some outliers, but it is not clear whether a found outlier really gives a good hint for a double payment since no analysis about false negatives or false positives can be done. As a consequence, no statement about the quality of the proposed data mining approach can be given. This confirms the necessity to work on testing forensic tools/methods as proposed in our work.

In [8], [12], the authors propose a method of generating synthetic data sets for the purpose of evaluating knowledge discovery systems. The method is based on semantic graphs and used to fill-in tables with data sets. However, this approach seems not to be efficient for our purpose of generating synthetic data by simulating sequences of subject activities since the proposed method requires dealing with joint distributions over a larger number of random variables.

Another method to generate synthetic fraud data is proposed in [13], [14]. In their work, the authors show how to generate larger collections of synthetic data from smaller collections of real-world data, where the synthetic data have the same statistical properties with respect to selected parameters as the real-world data. The method is applied for fraud in video-on-demand services. However, it still requires adequate real-world data that might not be available in many cases. Furthermore, real-world data have specific characteristics which cannot be modified in order to obtain synthetic data with other characteristics.

9   Conclusion

With 3LSPG we have proposed a systematic method to test forensic tools or methods by simulating activities of fraudulent and non-fraudulent subjects, and generating synthetic data as result of the simulated activities. The data generation based on a 3-layer concept is parameterized such that the characteristics of various relevant environments can be modeled. Synthetic data are very useful if no real-world data are available for testing. Thus 3LSPG can be used to support development of new tools or methods, or for the improvement of existing tools. It is also valuable for investigators to compare the suitability of forensic tools in different environments. As further contribution, the results of our work imply a potential to increase the trust in forensic tools, to provide examiners with better knowledge on how to interpret the results of their tools under various conditions, and to decrease resources or costs for investigations.

The application of our prototype implementation has yielded promising results. As future work we will extend our prototype (e.g, integrate further distribution types) and improve the user interface. Another aspect of interest is on the provision of a theoretical framework for the identification of relevant aspects to be modeled and for supporting users' modeling tasks.

References

1. Behrends, E.: Introduction to Markov Chains. Vieweg Verlag (2000)
2. Bolton, R., Hand, D.: Statistical Fraud Detection: A Review. Statistical Science 17(3) (2002)
3. Dacier, M., Deswarte, Y., Kaaniche, M.: Models and tools for quantitative assessment of operational security. In: IFIP SEC 1996 (1996)
4. Dacier, M., Deswarte, Y., Kaaniche, M.: Quantitative Assessment of Operational Security: Models and Tools. LAAS Research Report 96493 (May 1996)
5. Deloitte: Ten things about financial statement fraud — A review of SEC enforcement releases, 2000-2006 (June 2007), www.deloitte.com/us/forensiccenter
6. Germany's Federal Criminal Police Office (BKA): Wirtschaftskriminalität — Bundeslagebild (2008), http://www.bka.de/lageberichte/wi.html
7. Jans, M., Lybaert, N., Vanhoff, K.: Data Mining for Fraud Detection: Toward an Improvement on Internal Control Systems? In: 30rd European Accounting Association, Ann. Congr., Lisbon (2007)
8. Jeske, D., Samadi, B., Lin, P., Ye, L., Cox, S., Xiao, R., Younglove, T., Ly, M., Holt, D., Rich, R.: Generation of synthetic data sets for evaluating the accuracy of knowledge discovery systems. In: ACM KDD 2005 (2005)
9. Kou, Y., Lu, C., Sirwongwattana, S., Huang, Y.: Survey of fraud detection techniques. In: IEEE Int. Conf. on Networking, Sensing & Control (2004)
10. KPMG: Anti Fraud Management — Best Practice der Prävention gegen Wirtschaftskriminalität. White Paper (2006)
11. KPMG: Profile of a Fraudster. White Paper (2007)
12. Lin, P., Samadi, B., Cipolone, A., Jeske, D., Cox, S., Rendon, C., Holt, D., Xiao, R.: Development of a synthetic data set generator for building and testing information discovery systems. In: 3rd Int. Conf. on Inf. Techn.: New Generations (2006)
13. Lundin, E., Kvarnström, H., Jonsson, E.: A synthetic fraud data generation methodology. In: Deng, R.H., Qing, S., Bao, F., Zhou, J. (eds.) ICICS 2002. LNCS, vol. 2513, pp. 265–277. Springer, Heidelberg (2002)
14. Lundin Barse, E., Kvarnström, H., Jonsson, E.: Synthesizing test data for fraud detection systems. In: Omondi, A.R., Sedukhin, S.G. (eds.) ACSAC 2003. LNCS, vol. 2823, Springer, Heidelberg (2003)
15. Nestler, C., Salvenmoser, S., Bussmann, K., Werle, M., Krieg, O.: Wirtschaftskriminalität 2007 — Sicherheitslage der deutschen Wirtschaft (2007), http://www.pwc.de/de/crimesurvey
16. Phua, C., Lee, V., Smith, K., Gayler, R.: A comprehensive survey of data mining-based fraud detection research. Working Paper (2005) (unpublished)
17. PriceWaterhouseCoopers: Key elements of antifraud programs and controls. White Paper (2003)
18. Richard, G., Roussev, V.: Next-Generation Digital Forensics. Communications of the ACM 49(2) (2006)
19. Shamshad, A., Wan Hussin, W., Bawadi, M., Sanusi, S.: First and second order markov chain models for synthetic generation of wind speed time series. Energy 30(5) (2005)
20. Wells, J.: Corporate Fraud Handbook, 2nd edn. Wiley, Chichester (2007)

Author Index